CRISIS POLICYMAKING

CRISIS POLICYMAKING

AUSTRALIA AND THE EAST TIMOR CRISIS OF 1999

DAVID CONNERY

THE AUSTRALIAN NATIONAL UNIVERSITY

E PRESS

Published by ANU E Press
The Australian National University
Canberra ACT 0200, Australia
Email: anuepress@anu.edu.au
This title is also available online at: http://epress.anu.edu.au/policymaking_citation.html

National Library of Australia
Cataloguing-in-Publication entry

Author: Connery, David.
Title: Crisis policymaking [electronic resource] : Australia and the East Timor crisis of 1999 /
           David Connery.
ISBN: 9781921666568 (pbk.)   9781921666575 (eBook : pdf)
Series: Canberra papers on strategy and defence ; no. 176.
Notes: Includes bibliographical references.
Subjects: Australia--Politics and government.
           Australia--Foreign relations--Timor-Leste.
           Timor-Leste--Foreign relations--Australia.
Dewey Number: 320.60994

The Canberra Papers on Strategy and Defence series is a collection of publications arising
principally from research undertaken at the SDSC. Canberra Papers have been peer reviewed
since 2006. All Canberra Papers are available for sale: visit the SDSC website at <http://rspas.
anu.edu.au/sdsc/canberra_papers.php> for abstracts and prices. Electronic copies (in pdf
format) of most SDSC Working Papers published since 2002 may be downloaded for free from
the SDSC website at <http://rspas.anu.edu.au/sdsc/working_papers.php>. The entire Working
Papers series is also available on a 'print on demand' basis.

Layout by ANU E Press

Cover image: David Foote-AUSPIC

Contents

Abstract

The events in East Timor and Canberra during 1998 and 1999 provide the focus for this study of Australian Government policymaking in national security crises. The research for this study builds on a range of published government, media and academic sources, and interviews with nearly sixty Australian political leaders, public service officals and military officers. These interviews provide a deep and broad look at the Australian Government, from the top-level National Security Committee down to desk officers within the major departments of state. The subsequent examination of this evidence shows how the Australian Government operated during this crisis, as well as the broader impact of this crisis upon Australian policy.

The study uses a policy cycle as an organisational and structural heuristic to examine this inherently messy process. Five essential characteristics of Australian policymaking in national security crises provide this work's key finding. These characteristics can be summarised as a dominant executive, collegiality, a closed and secretive system, an essential role for external actors, and complex and complicated implementation.

About the Author

David Connery conducted the research for this book while completing his Doctor of Philosophy at the Australian National University's Strategic and Defence Studies Centre. Prior to this, he served in the Australian Army in regimental and staff postings including command of an air defence battery and officer training regiment, postings to Army Headquarters and Strategic Policy Division, and an appointment at the Office of National Assessments. His other published works include essays and monographs on future military capability, Australian national security planning, and Southeast Asian politics.

Acronyms and Abbreviations

AEC	Australian Electoral Commission
ADF	Australian Defence Force
AFP	Australian Federal Police
ALP	Australian Labor Party
ANAO	ustralian National Audit Office
ANZUS	Australian, New Zealand and United States Security Treaty
APEC	Asia-Pacific Economic Cooperation
ASEAN	Association of Southeast Asian Nations
ASIO	Australian Security Intelligence Organisation
ASIS	Australian Secret Intelligence Service
AusAID	Australian International Aid Agency
CDF	Chief of the Defence Force
COMAST	Commander Australian Theatre
DEP SEC S&I	Deputy Secretary Strategy and Intelligence
DFAT	Department of Foreign Affairs and Trade
DGET	Director General East Timor
DG ONA	Director General of the Office of National Assessments
DIO	Defence Intelligence Organisation
DDIO	Director of the Defence Intelligence Organisation
DOFA	Department of Finance and Administration
DPA	Department of Political Affairs (United Nations)
DPKO	Department of Peace Keeping Operations (United Nations)
DPM&C	Department of Prime Minister and Cabinet

DSD	Defence Signals Directorate
ETTF	East Timor Task Force
ETPU	East Timor Policy Unit
FADTRC	Foreign Affairs, Defence and Trade References Committee
IDC	Interdepartmental committee
IMF	International Monetary Fund
INTERFET	International Force in East Timor (UN abbreviation)
KOPASSUS	*Komando Pasukan Khusus* (Indonesian Special Forces Command)
NGO	Non-governmental organisation
NSCC	National Security Committee of Cabinet
ONA	Office of National Assessments
SCG	Strategic Command Group
SCNS	Secretaries Committee on National Security
SES	Senior Executive Service
SPCG	Strategic Policy Coordination Group
TNI	*Tentara Nasional Indonesia* (the Indonesian Army)
UNAMET	United Nations Mission in East Timor (11 June–25 October 1999)
UNTAET	United Nations Transitional Administration in East Timor (25 October 1999–20 May 2002)
USPACOM	US Pacific Command
VCDF	Vice Chief of the Defence Force

Bureaucratic Classifications

In Australia, the Secretary is a department's senior official. The Secretary is responsible for all aspects of the department's performance and provides policy advice to the responsible minister of state. The Secretary is usually a career public servant, not a political appointee in the American sense. The equivalents in the Office of National Assessments (ONA), Australian Secret Intelligence Service (ASIS) and Australian Security Intelligence Organisation (ASIO) are called 'Director General'. The Department of Defence is a 'diarchy' where the Secretary and Chief of Defence Force (a General or equivalent) have separate responsibilities, but are jointly responsible to the Minister of Defence.

The classifications below the Secretary in most departments are (compared to equivalent Australian Army officer ranks):

- Deputy Secretary (Army equivalent: Lieutenant General)

- First Assistant Secretary (Army equivalent: Major General)

- Assistant Secretary (Army equivalent: Brigadier)

- Director (Army equivalent: Colonel)

- Deputy Director/Assistant Director (Army equivalent: Lieutenant Colonel)

- Policy Officer (Army equivalent: Captain or Major)

Acknowledgements

While the responsibility for this work is mine, a number of people contributed in different ways. Firstly, I wish to acknowledge the people who brought independence to Timor-Leste: Timorese, Australian, Indonesian and others. Their sacrifice and contribution is a reminder of the human face of conflict and the imperative behind work such as this. My thanks also go to five other groups of people: my family, Jane, Georgia and Annabelle; a wonderful group of academic mentors including my PhD supervisors—Ross Babbage, Alan Stephens and Ron Huisken—and others including Hugh White, Bob Breen, Paul 't Hart, Des Ball and Rob Ayson; my wonderful friends and extended family; and my commanding officers and supervisors who encouraged me to continue studying and supported me through my studies and career.

Thanks to for the editorial support from Scott Hopkins, Meredith Thatcher and Greg at Qote!

Chapter 1
Australian Policymaking and the East Timor Crisis

An Under-Explored Topic

The East Timor Crisis of 1999 has received considerable attention in Australia. This attention has included accounts of the events and the military operations that year, especially those involving the International Force East Timor (INTERFET).[1] There have been some descriptions and analysis of how Australia's actions in this crisis affected its regional standing,[2] and one paper about how the crisis was managed between Washington and Canberra.[3] There have been numerous books about the rights and wrongs of Australian policy,[4] and a short but sharp critique by William Maley which focused on the Department of Foreign Affairs and Trade (DFAT).[5] Unusually, DFAT also produced a book outlining its involvement in this crisis after only two years had passed.[6] However, as James

---

1 A comprehensive account of the events of 1999 is presented in Don Greenless and Robert Garran, *Deliverance: The Inside Story of East Timor's Fight for Freedom*, Allen and Unwin, Crows Nest, NSW, 2002. Other major works include Alan Ryan, *Primary responsibilities and primary risks: Australian defence force participation in the International Force East Timor*, Land Warfare Studies Centre, Duntroon, Canberra, 2000; Paul Kelly, *The March of the Patriots: The Struggle for Modern Australia*, Melbourne University Press, Carlton, Vic, 2009, Chapter 35; David Dickens, 'The United Nations in East Timor: Intervention at the Military Operational Level', *Contemporary Southeast Asia*, vol. 23, no. 2, 2001; Bob Breen, *Mission Accomplished—East Timor*, Allen & Unwin, Crows Nest, NSW, 2000; Tim Fischer, *Seven Days in East Timor: Ballots and Bullets*, Allen & Unwin,

St Leonards, NSW, 2000; and Des Ball, 'Silent Witness: Australian Intelligence and East Timor', in Ball, James Dunn, Gerry van Klinken, David Bourchier, Douglas Kammen and Richard Tanter (eds), *Masters of Terror: Indonesia's Military and the Violence in East Timor in 1999*, Canberra Papers on Strategy and Defence No. 145, Strategic and Defence Studies Centre, The Australian National University, Canberra, 2002.

2 For examples, see Cavin Hogue, 'Perspectives on Australian Foreign Policy, 1999', *Australian Journal of International Affairs*, vol. 54, no. 2, 2000; Peter Chalk, *Australian Foreign and Defense Policy in the Wake of the 1999/2000 East Timor Intervention*, RAND MR 1401, Santa Monica, 2001; James Cotton, *East Timor, Australia and Regional Order: intervention and its aftermath in Southeast Asia*, Routledge, London, 2004; and Fran Kelly, 'Alexander Downer on East Timor', *The Howard Years* (website), ABC Television (Australia), 2008, available at <http://www.abc.net.au/news/howardyears/>, (see Further Resources: Episode 2 tab), accessed 27 June 2009.

3 Coral Bell, 'East Timor, Canberra and Washington: A Case Study in Crisis Management', *Australian Journal of International Affairs*, vol. 54, no. 2, 2000.

4 For examples, see Lansell Taudevin, *East Timor: Too Little Too Late*, Duffy and Snellgrove, Sydney 1999; James Cotton, 'Against the Grain: The East Timor Intervention', *Survival*, vol. 43, no. 1, 2001; and Clinton Fernandes, *Reluctant Saviour: Australia, Indonesia and the independence of East Timor*, Scribe, Melbourne, 2004.

5 William Maley, 'Australia and the East Timor Crisis: Some Critical Comments', *Australian Journal of International Affairs*, vol. 54, no. 2, 2000.

6 Department of Foreign Affairs and Trade, *East Timor in Transition 1998–2000: An Australian Policy Challenge*, Commonwealth of Australia, Canberra, 2001.

Cotton has noted, even this 'official' version of the events surrounding East Timor's transition to independence failed to pay much attention to the process of Australian policymaking itself.[7]

This study addresses the gap identified by Cotton and aims to improve our understanding of Australian policymaking during the East Timor crisis of 1999. In doing so, this study describes the crisis policymaking system as it existed in 1999, before recounting the events of late-1998 through to the military intervention by INTERFET in September 1999. After that, the study uses Peter Bridgman and Glyn Davis' Australian Policy Cycle to structure the discussion and provide the baseline for characterising Australian policymaking.[8] This examination shows how Bridgman and Davis' typical characteristics of Australian policymaking are modified during crises—which is defined here as 'a tract of time during which the conflicts within an international relationship rise sharply above normal level, threatening damaging change or transformation'.[9] From this, the characteristics of crisis policymaking are presented in the concluding chapter. This introduction continues with an outline of the research methodology, especially the Australian Policy Cycle and the sources used, and a description of Australia's crisis policymaking system as it stood in 1999.

Policymaking and the Policy Cycle

In this study, 'policymaking' refers to the process of providing advice to ministers and implementing their subsequent decisions.[10] While this sounds straightforward, Meredith Edwards captured the complexity of policymaking by articulating a number of qualifications:

Policy processes are non-linear; they can move backwards as well as forwards and stages might occur in a different order from the model.

Organisational structures are important to policy development and will influence the process.

Players and networks operating in the process influence policy outcomes.

---

7   Cotton, *East Timor, Australia and Regional Order*, p. 123. Paul Kelly's chapter on political-level decision-making makes a very useful contribution to our understanding of Australian policymaking in this crisis (Kelly, *The March of the Patriots*, Chapter 35).
8   Peter Bridgman and Glyn Davis, *The Australian Policy Handbook*, 3rd edn, Allen & Unwin, Sydney, 2004.
9   Coral Bell, *Crises and Policy-makers*, Canberra Studies in World Affairs, no. 10, Department of International Relations, The Australian National University, Canberra, 1982, p. 2.
10   I am grateful to my friend and colleague, Bob Wylie, for his lucid contribution to this definition.

Political considerations are all-pervading: 'Good policy processes can tame, but only to a degree, the political process.'[11]

With these caveats in mind, a policy cycle describes the process in separate, linked steps. These steps usually begin with efforts to identify issues and gather information so that insider experts can present options to leaders who, in turn, may make decisions. Once made, decisions are implemented—often by officials and sometimes by society at large. Other rational models include an evaluation stage, which allows for a return to the start of the cycle or process.[12] The strength of the policy cycle concept lies in its representation of sequential tasks where policy is developed, decided and then implemented. The cyclic design also highlights the process nature of government, describes how knowledge is synthesised, and provides a way to examine actual policy.[13]

This study uses the Australian Policy Cycle as an organising heuristic. When used in this way, the policy cycle structures the analysis and allows each phase to be examined discretely. The Australian Policy Cycle presents these phases as issue identification, policy analysis, policy instruments, consultation, coordination, decision, implementation, and evaluation which—since this is a cycle—returns to the issue identification phase (see Figure 1). This study groups the phases into separate chapters: the early phases from issue identification to policy instruments are grouped under the heading 'Developing policy advice'; the middle phases of coordination and consultation as 'Bringing advice together'; and the later phases of decision, implementation and evaluation as 'Decision and beyond'.

Crisis policymaking—and so this study—is overwhelmingly concerned with process rather than the merits of 'good or bad' policy. The activities involved in crisis policymaking may involve efforts to:

> prevent crises from occurring, to prepare for a better protection against the impact of a crisis agent, to make for an effective response to an actual crisis (including decision-making), or to provide plans and resources for recovery and rehabilitation in the aftermath of a crisis.[14]

---

11   Meredith Edwards, *Social Science Research and Public Policy: Narrowing the Divide*, Academy of Social Sciences in Australia Policy Paper No. 2, Canberra, 2004, pp. 6–7.

12   For an example of a rational-comprehensive approach to policy, see Yehezkel Dror, *Public Policymaking Reexamined*, Chandler Publishing Company, Scranton, 1968. Another example of a policy cycle can be found in Bill Jenkins, 'Policy analysis: Models and approaches', in Michael Hill (ed.), *The Policy Process: A Reader*, Harvester Wheatsheaf, Hemel Hampstead, 1993, pp. 34–39.

13   Bridgman and Davis, *The Australian Policy Handbook*, p. 22–23.

14   Uriel Rosenthal and Bert Pijnenburg, 'Simulation-orientation scenarios: An alternative approach to crisis decision-making and emergency management', in Uriel Rosenthal and Bert Pijnenburg (eds), *Crisis Management and Decision Making: Simulation Oriented Scenarios*, Kluwer Academic Publishers, Dordrecht, 1991, p. 3.

Crisis policymaking is therefore one mode of national security policymaking, which is marked by efforts to counter threats—real or perceived—by changing the policymaking structures and processes in ways that allow government to manage urgent and pressing challenges to its interests and objectives.[15]

Figure 1: The Australian Policy Cycle[16]

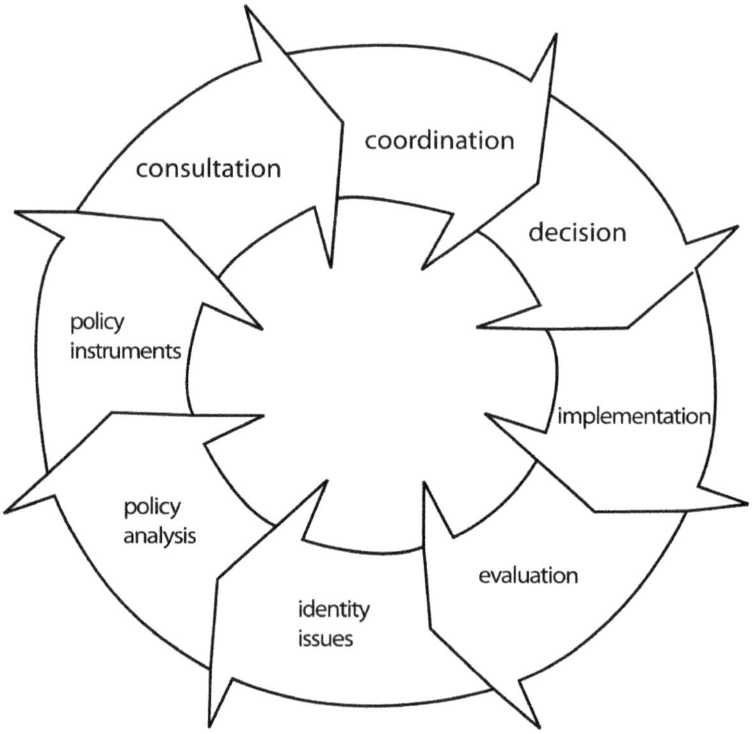

Sources

The new data for this study was a series of sixty interviews conducted by the author with those involved in national security policymaking before and during the East Timor crisis. These interviewees represented a broad cross-section of the bureaucracy—including the Department of Prime Minister and Cabinet (DPM&C), DFAT, the Department of Defence (Defence), Australian Federal Police (AFP), Australian Agency for International Development (AusAID), and the Australian Electoral Commission (AEC)—and included officials who worked

---

15   Crisis policymaking differs from Dror's 'policymaking under adversity', although crisis is one type of adverse condition. For Dror, crisis is differentiated from everyday adversity by the time available, suddenness of imposing events and need for rapid decision-making (see Yehezkel Dror, *Policymaking Under Adversity*, Transaction Books, New Brunswick, 1986, p. 181).
16   Bridgman and Davis, *The Australian Policy Handbook*, p. 26.

at different levels within these organisations. Interviews were also conducted with three ministers (all were members of the National Security Committee of Cabinet—NSCC—in 1999),[17] other political figures, ministerial staff and two officials formerly of United States Pacific Command (USPACOM).[18] Two interviewees provided work diaries from the crisis, which contained valuable information about events and meeting agendas (including notes from 1999 meetings of the NSCC, the Strategic Policy Coordination Group (SPCG), and Defence working groups).

Two main types of written sources were consulted. While the range of official sources about policymaking during the East Timor crisis is presently limited, some evidence can still be gathered from the public record. For instance, the Australian Government has produced one book on the East Timor crisis, which describes the role of the DFAT in the events of 1998–2000. While this book includes a number of important and relevant documents and news releases, it cannot be considered authoritative because official Australian documents are not cited among its sources. A number of submissions and testimonies to a Senate Enquiry on East Timor and Senate Estimates hearings in 1999–2000 also form part of the official record, although they contain little about policymaking process.

The second group of written sources included media reporting, academic articles, and published accounts including memoirs and theses. These sources include some that drew heavily on interviews with key actors,[19] or were written by the actors themselves.[20] As expected, these sources represented a wide range of viewpoints and issues, each with a unique focus and bias.

It is certain that new sources will become available as more participants speak of their experiences, or new documents are released. Such information is likely to add to, or perhaps contradict, aspects of this study. As a result, the conclusions presented are necessarily open to challenge, although the record is unlikely to be fully settled for many decades hence.

---

17   While often called 'NSC' in Australia, this case study retains NSCC to differentiate it from the US NSC.

18   While many interviewees agreed to be identified, some were reluctant because the East Timor crisis is still sensitive in Australia, particularly for those who are currently serving as government officials. These interviewees are identified by an interview number in this study.

19   Such as Ryan, *Primary responsibilities and primary risks: Australian defence force participation in the International Force East Timor*; Greenlees and Garran, *Deliverance: The Inside Story of East Timor's Fight for Freedom*; and ABC Television (Australia), *The Howard Years* (Episode 2), 24 November 2008, available at <http://www.abc.net.au/news/howardyears/content/s2422684.htm>, accessed

27 June 2009.

20   Such as Ali Alatas, *The Pebble in the Shoe: The Diplomatic Struggle for East Timor*, Aksara Karunia, Jakarta, 2006; Jamsheed Marker, *East Timor: A Memoir of the Negotiations for Independence*, McFarland and Co, Jefferson, 2003; and Fischer, *Seven Days in East Timor*.

Australia's National Security Policymaking System in 1999

Former Prime Minister John Howard came to office in 1996 with views about the failings of the previous government to manage national security, and some suspicions about the bureaucracy. Interviewee 051-06 recalled:

> He wanted to avoid a situation where the prime minister was running and determining everything. He did not think that was healthy. And second, the idea that officials should be running things and have such a strong influence, I think he was suspicious about that, especially because the people who had been working in SPCG and key areas to do with foreign and defence policy had been there for a while under Labor.[21]

Interviewee 052-06 saw another reason for Howard's views:

> I think that the prime minister, in a substantial way, felt that Treasury had been too dominant in closing down policy development in the government.[22]

Howard also had clear ideas about policymaking in his government. He wanted ministers to have authority and be responsible for implementing policy in their area. He wanted to assert a high degree of political control over policymaking, without asserting complete personal control over everything.[23] According to another interviewee, Howard was not in favour of networks of committees either within the Cabinet or the bureaucracy in most areas of policy as Interviewee 052-06 recalled:

> But national security and defence he regarded somewhat differently. Because of the structured nature of the military and because of the way they dealt with issues we looked separately at the way in which coordination was handled.[24]

What developed over the next three years was a more formalised crisis policymaking system that retained some of its previous flexibility. This section describes the policymaking system in the immediate lead-up to the East Timor

---

21 Interview with 051-06, by telephone, 31 August 2006. 051-06 was a senior government official with direct knowledge of the East Timor case. A similar view was expressed by Hugh White (Interview, Canberra, 21 December 2005). Professor White was Deputy Secretary Strategy in Defence from 1995–2000. He acted as Secretary of the Department from August–September 1999.
22 Interview with 052-06, Sydney, 27 September 2006. 052-06 is former senior government official with direct knowledge of NSCC, SCNS and the East Timor case.
23 Interview with 051-06.
24 Interview with 052-06.

crisis of 1999. This discussion is conducted by analysing the formal structures for crisis—and national security—policymaking in the political, policy and administrative domains.[25] The discussion also shows how the formal model needed adapting when the Australian Government faced a significant national security crisis.

The Political Domain under Howard

Howard created the NSCC immediately upon becoming prime minister. Like previous committees, the NSCC was small and its formal membership was limited to six ministers: the prime minister and his deputy, the treasurer, the attorney general, and the foreign and defence ministers (see Table 1).[26]

Table 1: The National Security Committee of Cabinet (NSCC) — 1999

Members	
Prime Minister	John Howard
Deputy Prime Minister	Tim Fischer (Jan–Jun) John Anderson (Jul–)
Foreign Minister	Alexander Downer
Defence Minister	John Moore
Treasurer	Peter Costello
Attorney General	Daryl Williams
Officials	
Secretary, DPM&C	Max Moore-Wilton
Chief of the Defence Force	Admiral Chris Barrie
Secretary, Dept. of Defence	Paul Barratt (Jan–Aug) Hugh White (Aug–Sep, Acting) Allan Hawke (Oct–)
Secretary, DFAT	Ashton Calvert
DG Office of National Assessments	Kim Jones

---

25 The political domain includes Cabinet, Cabinet committees and smaller grouping of ministers and their personal advisers. The policy domain is based on senior officials from 'traditional' national security departments such as Defence, DFAT, DPM&C, Treasury and the intelligence community. The administrative domain comprises a variety of interdepartmental and intra-departmental mechanisms. These domains overlap (see Glyn Davis, *A Government of Routines: Executive Coordination in an Australian State*, Centre for Australian Public Sector Management/MacMillan, South Melbourne, 1995, pp. 136–40).

26 Other ministers were co-opted as necessary. These included, at various times, ministers with responsibilities for transport, immigration, justice and customs.

The presence of these senior ministers allowed the NSCC to make important decisions without reference to Cabinet. The NSCC was therefore the 'bridge' of national security policymaking because it was the place of decision and a link between different positions within government.

Ministers would generally make attendance at the NSCC a priority;[27] it was an acknowledged decision-making body about important issues and, according to former Defence Minister John Moore, it was 'a very good way of doing business':

> It enabled you as minister to put the story in the political sense, and have the technical back-up available at the time. So there could not be any of this stuff that you get in the other portfolios, of 'well that's a great idea but let's have the officials look at it'—that's a great way to defer a decision and it all goes back to square one. ... So in these circumstances decisions could be made at the time.[28]

Consequently, the senior officials responsible for the advice—and also generally the implementation—became more important to the NSCC as time went on.[29] In the period before 1999, attendance by officials followed the Cabinet model, whereby they would be invited for specific items and leave the room while the ministers debated points.[30] This mode was changing by 1999, by all accounts due to the influence of the East Timor crisis.

By then, attendance by officials and ministerial advisers was becoming more frequent. With this increased and more diverse presence, NSCC meetings were conducted in a semi-structured way—much like a well-directed seminar.[31] The prime minister, who would always chair meetings unless he was overseas, would start by asking for an intelligence update from the Director General of the Office of National Assessments (DG ONA),[32] and he would ask the Secretary of DFAT and the Chief of the Defence Force (CDF) for their views. From there, discussion would turn to the formal agenda or issues of the day, and this would flow until (usually) the prime minister summarised the discussion and sought agreement or

---

27   Interview with the Hon. Tim Fischer, Canberra, 1 August 2006. Fischer was Deputy Prime Minister from March 1996 until July 1999. He headed the Australian Parliamentary delegation to East Timor in August 1999.
28   Interview with the Hon. John Moore, Sydney, 29 November 2006. Moore was Defence Minister, and a member of NSCC, in 1999.
29   Interview with 051-06.
30   John Moore gave one example where discussions were 'going to become political' and that a decision could not be made in front of the public servants (Interview, 29 November 2006). Interviewee 051-06 said that the prime minister often 'cleared everyone out', leaving the ministers and maybe his International Adviser in the Cabinet Room.
31   Interview with Paul Barratt, Melbourne, 23 December 2005. Barratt was Secretary of the Department of Defence from 1998 to August 1999 and attended NSCC and the Secretaries Committee on National Security (SCNS). Dr Ashton Calvert described NSCC as 'business-like' (Interview in Canberra, 19 May 2006). Dr Calvert was Secretary of DFAT in 1999 and also attended NSCC and SCNS.
32   When domestic security matters are discussed, this briefing is given by the Director General of the Australian Security Intelligence Organisation (ASIO).

made a decision. This format was generally conducive to broad discussion. As a former attendee—former Secretary of the Department of Defence Paul Barratt— noted: 'It was always a very open environment for people to have their say.'[33]

Longer and contiguous opportunities to attend the NSCC allowed the officials present to get a better understanding of NSCC deliberations than could be obtained from minutes and debriefings by their ministers. According to Admiral Chris Barrie, who was a participant in the NSCC, 'the great benefit was we all knew just what part of the jigsaw puzzle was being played with at the time'.[34] The ability to hear the entire debate, judge the mood of the meeting and see the non-verbal signals helped in this regard.

In normal circumstances, NSCC agenda items would be discussed beforehand at the Secretaries' level, or sometimes in the lower-level SPCG. Formal, written submissions would also go through a 'coordinating comments' process like other Cabinet business. This process reflected the very strong norm of 'no surprises', the desire to present agreed recommendations to the NSCC, and the need to reduce complexity so that decisions could be made by the ministers.

The frequent meetings of the NSCC also helped to make it into an effective committee. Tim Fischer explained that familiarity with communication processes, good support from the bureaucracy, the atmosphere of the Cabinet room and 'a couple of drills' all helped to ensure that, when the NSCC was called together quickly, it could function effectively.[35]

This description of Howard's NSCC presents a picture of a well-run, cohesive and focused group. However, the NSCC was still a place of politics. Ministers kept an eye on the political importance of issues, and they also played out some (apparently limited) competition among themselves. The way it operated was also dependent upon personalities and the prime minister's authority. While Howard had created this machinery so that he did not have to run everything, the NSCC put him in the position where he could be the dominant political figure in any crisis, if he so chose.

The Policy Domain: SCNS and the SPCG

Despite the wider trend of change in the public service after Howard came to power in 1996, the basic national security policymaking structure in the policy domain changed little. While those responsible looked closely at whether the

---

33   Interview with Paul Barratt. Ashton Calvert described the atmosphere of NSCC in a similar way.
34   Interview with Admiral Chris Barrie, Canberra, 5 April 2005. Admiral Barrie was Chief of the Defence Force from 1998–2002. He was an invited official at NSCC and a member of SCNS in 1999, and had previously attended the Strategic Policy Coordination Group (SPCG) when he was Vice Chief of the Defence Force.
35   Interview with Tim Fischer.

existing arrangements were desirable, the existing Secretaries-level committee was retained in the broad shape of Paul Keating's time and renamed as the Secretaries Committee on National Security (SCNS). The previous government's SPCG was also retained.[36]

The SCNS membership generally reflected the NSCC ministers, including the secretary of DPM&C, the CDF, DG ONA and the Secretaries of Defence, DFAT, Attorney General's and Treasury (see Table 2).[37]

Table 2: Secretaries Committee on National Security (SCNS) — 1999

Secretary, DPM&C	Max Moore-Wilton
Chief of the Defence Force	Admiral Chris Barrie
Secretary, Department of Defence	Paul Barratt (Jan–Aug) Hugh White (Aug–Sep) Allan Hawke (Oct–)
Secretary, DFAT	Ashton Calvert
Secretary, the Treasury	Ted Evans
Secretary, Attorney Generals Dept	Tony Blunn
DG Office of National Assessments	Kim Jones

This grouping allowed the key senior officials responsible for policy development and implementation to discuss issues in a closed environment before taking their views to the NSCC. It was also a venue where agreement could be reached on some matters, thus relieving the NSCC of some of its workload and taking some of the heat out of interdepartmental disagreements.[38] Just which decisions were taken at this level was reliant upon a keen awareness of what their respective ministers would accept, and the relationship between the prime minister and the Secretary of DPM&C.[39]

SCNS was typically a monthly meeting in 1999, but it met on an *ad hoc* basis if necessary. Its agenda varied, but generally SCNS considered important, long-term issues with broad impacts on national security and the government. These included complex issues such as security for the 2000 Summer Olympics in Sydney, discussions about defence projects, and policy considerations.[40] Thus SCNS played a major role in determining spending priorities and highlighting

---

36   Interview with 052-06.
37   Although the Secretary of the Treasury and Secretary of Attorney General's Department did not usually attend NSCC. Interviewee 052-06 thought there were clear expectations that the departmental secretary, and not a deputy, would attend. In contrast, Chris Barrie did not think there was any obligation to attend SCNS all the time.
38   Interview with 052-06. Others thought SCNS could do more. For example, Ashton Calvert described it as 'an energised and lively forum' that would 'break new ground'.
39   Interviews with Paul Barratt and Chris Barrie.
40   Interviews with Hugh White and Ashton Calvert.

the impact of policy options across portfolio areas. SCNS also became a rehearsal for the NSCC, as its members reviewed items going forward to the ministerial group. According to some former participants, including Paul Barratt, this served to 'prevent debate in NSCC and [avoided] presenting an untidy picture for ministers to try and pick through'.[41]

Despite its key position in the formal national security policymaking structure, SCNS would not be a main player in any crisis. There were good reasons for this. First, most SCNS members would be heavily committed during a crisis, particularly to the NSCC, their internal departmental processes and other essential departmental work. Second, the members themselves—similar to the political leaders—would not consider themselves experts on the details of the issues. They needed briefings and submissions from their staff to make sense of the cable traffic and intelligence reports, and time to talk to important stakeholders. Thus, using SCNS during a crisis would impose a substantial workload on already-pressed staff and risked having senior leaders spend unnecessary time in meetings.[42]

Strategic Policy Coordination Group

The SPCG was established in 1988 to 'ensure effective consultation among departments on strategic and security policy issues in peacetime, and to provide a mechanism for coordinating advice to government in times of crisis',[43] and it continued to play this role in 1999. It remained the only standing body—short of SCNS—where the senior officials from the major national security departments could come together and work through security issues. In doing so, the SPCG often reconciled positions and built consensus before proposals were submitted to SCNS or the NSCC, which meant this group often acted like a 'policy clearing house' for the more senior levels.[44]

There are different views on what the SPCG of 1998-99 could do and how effective it was. For some, the SPCG was a useful and flexible grouping of senior officials. It derived some strength from the ability to call the members together at very short notice, and for its ability to be an action-oriented—rather than

41   Interview with Paul Barratt. Interviewee 052-06 and Hugh White made similar comments.
42   Interviews with Ashton Calvert and Hugh White. SCNS limited utility in crisis was also noted by Alan Dupont, 'Taking out policy insures country against trouble', *Australian*, 7 November 2000, p. 15.
43   Eric Andrews, *The Department of Defence*, Oxford University Press, South Melbourne, 2001, p. 261.
44   Interviews with Air Vice-Marshal Kerry Clarke, Canberra, 2 August 2005; Martin Brady, Canberra, 16 August 2005; and 014-05, Canberra, 5 July 2005. Air Vice-Marshal Clarke was Director General Joint Operations and Plans in Strategic Command Division in 1998–99. Brady was Director, Defence Signals Directorate in 1999, and acting Deputy Secretary Strategy in August–September. Interviewee 014-05 was a former senior government official with direct knowledge of the SPCG.

deliberative—body. This was possible because its members were sufficiently senior to carry their departments once agreement was reached in the meeting (see Table 3).[45]

Table 3: Strategic Policy Coordination Group (SPCG)—Principal Members, 1999

Deputy Secretary, DFAT	John Dauth
Deputy Secretary Strategy and Intelligence, Defence	Hugh White (Jan–Aug)
	Martin Brady (Sep–Oct)
Vice Chief of the Defence Force	Air Marshal Doug Riding
First Assistant Secretary, International Division, DPM&C	Peter Varghese

Similarly, SPCG members sometimes deputised for their Secretaries at the NSCC and SCNS, and some played important roles in other committees, such as Defence's Strategic Command Group (SCG). The informal nature of the SPCG was considered a strength because different departments could come together as equals in terms of policy responsibility. This allowed the discussions to roam widely, without creating the angst about responsibilities that might be experienced if such a discussion occurred in more formal settings. It also allowed the agenda to change as the situation demanded.[46]

According to this view, the SPCG's ability to function was based upon strong relationships and trust between its principals. Indeed, Hugh White described the SPCG as 'more like a community than a committee'.[47] Members were expected to refrain from 'silly games' when dealing with each other and to state their positions clearly. Potentially acrimonious discussions were taken outside the meeting so that a consensus could be achieved wherever possible.[48]

This same level of familiarity, informality and norm of consensus led some to see the SPCG of this time quite differently. One interviewee implied that this familiarity could create something like 'groupthink', as some personalities and their views dominated discussions.[49] Informality had other limits as well. It was difficult to create a working agenda and deal with an increased number

---

45 Interviews with Hugh White and 032-05 (identity protected), by telephone, 29 September 2005.
46 The Australian Government carefully allocates policy responsibilities, and under normal conditions any attempt by one department to 'meddle' outside their portfolio will provoke a reaction from the custodian. The description of the informal nature of the SPCG was provided in interviews with Ashton Calvert and 032-05.
47 Interview with Hugh White.
48 Interviews with 032-05, Hugh White and Kerry Clarke. Andrews described an earlier SPCG as 'a joint team' that worked 'with great amicability' to produce a major policy document (Andrews, p. 261).
49 Interview with Major General Michael Keating, Canberra, 25 August 2005. Major General Keating became Head, Strategic Command Division in Defence in May 1999.

of attendees in times of crisis. At times, the SPCG's collegiality was tested by clashes based on differing departmental cultures.[50] Interviewee 046-06 also thought the high degree of informality made the SPCG almost meaningless:

> It was never allowed to be anything more than where a discussion took place. No policy came out of it, people presented their views and that was the end of it. There were no minutes or records of conversation. It was just an exchange of views.[51]

The lack of a clear agenda or mandate could also make the SPCG appear slightly dysfunctional, according to Michael Scrafton:

> The reason why I say it was slightly dysfunctional, and did not work as well as it could, was that the broader grouping came to be dominated by the headline issues of the day'.[52]

The implication of this focus on the news of the day was that the SPCG could have trouble planning ahead and aligning departmental efforts.

Departmental Machinery

Individual departments also developed structures to support national security policymaking. The general focus of these included internal decision-making about the allocation of resources and priorities, representing views of the different components of the department or agency, and preparing senior leaders and ministers for their committees.

DFAT method of responding to crises changed little after 1996, using a formal organisational division for this purpose (now called the International Security Division).[53] On the other hand, Defence changed its formal structure to improve operational planning. This included making the SCG more responsive and better focused, raising a subordinate Strategic Watch Group to monitor potential crises, and establishing a Strategic Command Division to support the CDF and conduct interdepartmental liaison (see Figure 2).

---

50 Interview with Michael Scrafton, Melbourne, 5 August 2005. Scrafton was Assistant Secretary Regional Engagement, Policy and Programs at the start of 1999. He became Acting First Assistant Secretary International Policy in August 1999, and attended the SPCG at times.

51 Interview with 046-06, Canberra, 6 May 2006. Interviewee 046-06 is a former senior ADF officer with direct knowledge of the SPCG.

52 Interview with Michael Scrafton.

53 Department of Foreign Affairs and Trade, *Annual Report 2006–2007*, Commonwealth of Australia, Canberra, 2007, pp. 111–13.

Figure 2: The National Crisis Management Machinery, Showing the Department of Defence's Formal Structure—1999

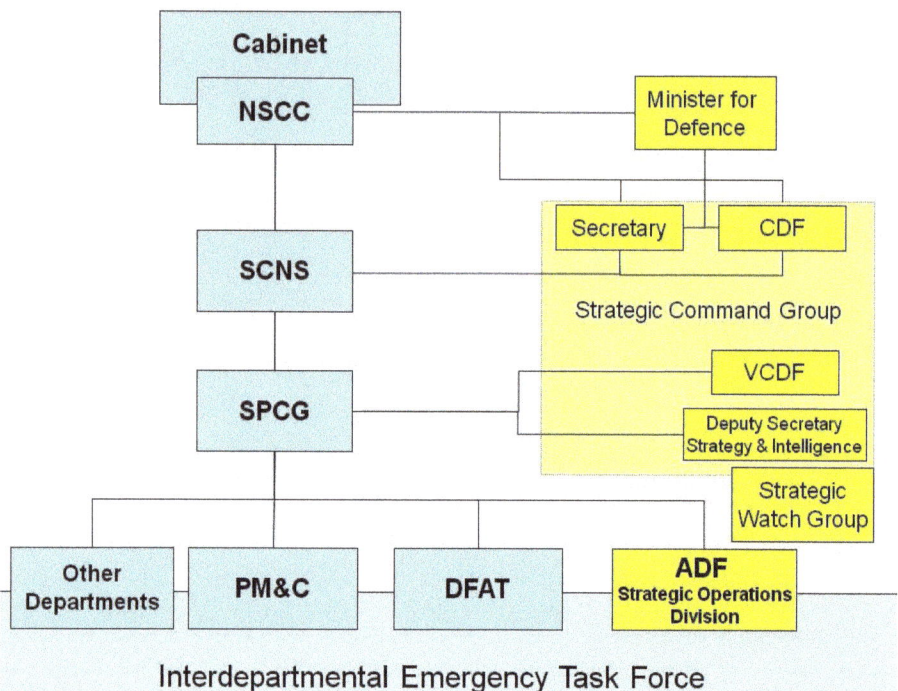

Strategic Command Group

The Strategic Command Group (SCG) was an innovation introduced by CDF Admiral Barrie to replace the 'operational' or 'augmented' Chiefs of Service Committee.[54] The group included the CDF, the Vice Chief of the Defence Force (VCDF), the Service chiefs and the head of the Strategic Command Division; and civilian officials including the departmental Secretary, Deputy Secretary Strategy and Intelligence (DEP SEC S&I), Director of the Defence Intelligence Organisation (DDIO), and First Assistant Secretary International Policy. It was also normal for the senior operational commander, known as Commander Australian Theatre (COMAST), to participate by video link from Sydney, while other officers would be invited as necessary.[55]

---

54   Interview with Chris Barrie.
55   In the Australian system, COMAST is responsible for managing operations using forces assigned from the ADF.

The SCG adopted a formal structure and role in 1998 that separated it from the more management-focused Chiefs of Service Committee and Defence Executive.[56] This role was to provide operational advice to the CDF, in his capacity as commander of the Australian Defence Force (ADF) and in his shared role as principal adviser to the Minister for Defence. The SCG could be called together quickly and would meet as the situation required. It also helped the CDF (and the Secretary) to prepare for the NSCC, and for other officials such as the DEP SEC S&I and VCDF to prepare for the SPCG.

The conduct of an SCG meeting was highly dependent upon the CDF's personal preferences and style.[57] These preferences extended from the selection of attendees to the way decisions were recorded. The SCG rarely had a formal agenda in 1999. Instead, the CDF would start with an intelligence brief from the DDIO and then go to the major issues of the day or take points from attendees.[58] The minutes were generally circulated in the form of a brief list of decisions and not subjected to a review or acceptance process, giving the CDF a high degree of control over the agenda and the final say over outcomes.

The SCG was supported by the Strategic Watch Group. This group's purpose was to identify potential crises or issues that might require SCG attention. This group included a range of policy and intelligence officials at the Colonel level who met regularly, or as needed, to consider situations that may become concerns. Once the SCG began to meet regularly about a crisis, the Strategic Watch Group generally ceased to meet on that issue, and returned to scanning the environment for signs of another crisis before convening again.

The committees mentioned here were the main bodies of the formal crisis management machinery in 1999, but they were by no means the only elements. For example, it was common to form interdepartmental committees or task forces to provide advice to the Secretaries. Other committees and working groups, such as the Heads of Intelligence Agencies Meeting, the Standing Advisory Committee-Protection Against Violence and the Heads of Commonwealth Law Enforcement Agencies, might also be considered as part of the national security and crisis policymaking machinery. However, the three government-level committees identified—the NSCC, SCNS and the SPCG—had central roles in the process and were the critical forums for decision-makers and advisers.

---

56 The Chiefs of Service Committee was a meeting of the senior uniformed officers to discuss military matters (usually, the departmental Secretary and a few other senior officials were invited to attend). The Defence Executive was an internal committee, consisting of the senior uniformed and civilian officers, which considered administrative and budgetary matters.

57 Interview with Allan Behm, Canberra, 5 May 2005. Behm was First Assistant Secretary International Policy in 1998 and First Assistant Secretary Strategic Policy in 1999–2000.

58 Interviews with Chris Barrie and Michael Keating.

This section has set the scene for the case study by describing the Australian Policy Cycle and its limitations, and outlining Australia's formal crisis policymaking system. The next chapter provides the context for the later discussion of policymaking by outlining the events that constituted the East Timor crisis, from the perspective of Australian policymakers.

Chapter 2
A Brief Outline of the East Timor Crisis: The View from Canberra

'This is big'

A number of books have been published about East Timor's history during the period 1945–99,[1] and those efforts will not be replicated here. Instead, the main focus of this study falls on the seat of Australia's Government, Canberra, during the period after December 1998 when Prime Minister John Howard wrote to Indonesia's President B.J. Habibie concerning the future of East Timor. This event represents the beginning of this case study, as more Australian Government agencies became involved in developing, and then managing, new policies concerning East Timor. The period concludes in late October 1999 when Australian Government agencies began a transition from crisis policymaking to a 'steady state' of operations in Canberra. This steady state began when *ad hoc* groups, established to manage or coordinate policy with regard to East Timor, were disbanded or incorporated into formal departmental and agency structures.

Although December 1998 has been chosen to start this case study, the East Timor issue had been a part of the Australian policy scene since 1974. Questions of legitimacy, sovereignty, human rights and moral debt had ebbed and flowed in Australian politics over the course of the intervening three decades, until the issue was renewed by a debate about East Timor policy within the Australian Labor Party (ALP) in November–December 1997.[2] While this debate was passionate and controversial, the prospect for a new Australian Government policy towards East Timor did not arise until an external event established the necessary conditions—the replacement of Indonesia's President Soeharto by his Vice President, B.J. Habibie, on

20 May 1998. The arrival of those conditions was somewhat of a surprise for Australian policymakers—as was the new policy environment in Jakarta.

---

1   For example, see John Taylor, *Indonesia's Forgotten War: The Hidden History of East Timor*, Pluto Press, Leichhardt, 1991.
2   See Anthony Burke, 'Labor Could Be Set For A Backflip on East Timor', *Canberra Times*, 22 December 1997. It is also important to note that Australia was engaged in East Timor on the official side before 1998, primarily through the Australian Agency for International Development (AusAID), which had been involved in humanitarian and development projects in East Timor.

This policy environment was defined by one of the new Indonesian president's first major policy statements, where he announced that his government would consider granting 'special autonomy' to East Timor.[3] Australian policymakers saw an opportunity to achieve three interwoven outcomes in these new conditions. The first and most important outcome desired by Australian policymakers in 1998 was a better relationship with Indonesia. Perhaps more than any other single issue, Indonesia's conduct in East Timor had been viewed negatively by many in Australia and this had implications for the entire Australia-Indonesia relationship. From the Australian perspective, healing this 'running sore' was one way to correct this problem.[4]

The second desired outcome was to see Indonesia's economy recover from the 1997 economic crisis, while maintaining a degree of stability during its transition from dictatorship to democracy.[5] At the time, Australia was concerned that instability in Indonesia would have a negative effect on Australia's own prosperity and security, and saw assistance as a way of showing Australia's value as a friend in the region.[6] The third outcome—and arguably the lowest priority—was the desire to improve the humanitarian situation in East Timor. Senior officials thought that a different political arrangement offered some chance of ending the guerrilla

---

3   Habibie vacillated over this point for a few days. Compare his position as cited in Don Greenlees, 'Habibie rules out Timor referendum', *Australian*, 4 June 1998, to the announcement reported by Jay Solomon, 'Habibie Offers East Timor Special Status', *The Wall Street Journal Europe*, 10 June 1998. Howard made his first public appeal about East Timor to Habibie over a week before this: see Rebecca Rose, 'Howard Urges Habibie To Act On East Timor', *West Australian*, 26 May 1998, p. 4

4   The difficulty caused to the bilateral Australia-Indonesia relationship by the ongoing conflict within Indonesia's East Timorese province is described in Department of Defence, *Australia's Strategic Policy, Commonwealth of Australia*, Canberra, 1997, p. 22. Contemporary analysis of the East Timor issue also stressed the irritant issue as a motive for Australian action in 1999 (see Carl Thayer, 'Australia-Indonesia Relations: The Case of East Timor', paper presented at the *International Conference on Australia and East Asian Security into the 21st Century*, Department of Diplomacy, National Cheng Chi University Taipei, Taiwan, 8 October 1999, p. 4. The logic of 'solving the running sore' is strongly criticised by William Maley, 'Australia and the East Timor Crisis: Some Critical Comments', *Australian Journal of International Affairs*, vol. 54, no. 2, 2000, p. 153 and p. 155, who finds the notion of breaking the relationship to fix it absurd; and James Cotton, *East Timor, Australia and Regional Order: intervention and its aftermath in Southeast Asia*, Routledge, London, 2004, p. 213.

5   This point is made by Foreign Minister Alexander Downer, 'CEDA Luncheon Address', 20 July 2000, available at <http://www.dfat.gov.au>, accessed 12 April 2006. It was also mentioned as being 'interwoven' with the issue of Australia's medium-term relationship with Indonesia in an interview with Ashton Calvert.

6   Speeches such as Alexander Downer, 'Indonesia's Challenges: How Australia Can Help', paper presented at the *International Conference on Indonesian Economic Stabilisation and Recovery*, Australian National University, Canberra, 23 November 1998, available at <http://www.foreignminister.gov.au/speeches/1998/981123_indonesia.html>, accessed 20 April 2009; and Alexander Downer, 'Australia—Stability in the Asia Pacific', speech to the Harvard Club, New York, 8 June 1998, available at <http://www.foreignminister.gov.au/speeches/1998/stability-asia_jun98.html>, accessed 20 April 2009, which emphasise the economic imperatives of Australia's interests at this time. Downer used another speech in July 1998 to suggest changes that could be made to East Timor's relationship with Indonesia, which shows how the Australian Government saw room to discuss Timor without being accused of interference in Indonesia. See Alexander Downer, 'A Long Term Commitment: Australia And East Asia', speech to the Indonesian Council on World Affairs and the Indonesia-Australia Business Council, Borobodur Hotel, Jakarta, 9 July 1998, available at <http://www.foreignminister.gov.au/speeches/1998/980709_icwa_iabc.html>, accessed 20 April 2009.

conflict, and perhaps the opportunity to develop the province's economy and obtain more international aid.[7] As will be discussed later, independence for East Timor was not an Australian policy preference at this time.

While the most visible discussions (in mid-1998) about East Timor's future were being conducted through the United Nations–Portugal–Indonesia 'Tripartite Talks',[8] Australian diplomats soon began consulting a number of influential Timorese about acceptable political arrangements.[9] According to the survey report by DFAT, the majority view called for a transitional autonomy arrangement that would be followed by a referendum in the future. Interestingly, the word 'independence' was not mentioned in the published survey report or covering letter.[10]

Australia's internal policymaking process also increased in tempo. Foreign Minister Alexander Downer began taking weekly briefings on East Timor from June 1998[11] and a small, informal meeting of senior Department of Foreign Affairs and Trade (DFAT), Department of Prime Minister and Cabinet (DPM&C) and Defence officials convened to discuss Australian policy options.[12]

Significant events occurred on other fronts around the same time. East Timor experienced further violence in October and November 1998, which increased international attention on the situation. At the same time, the Tripartite Talks appeared to falter as Indonesian claims about troop withdrawals were discredited in the media[13] and the parties found common ground elusive.[14] Support for 'action' was also gaining momentum in Australia as new evidence

---

7   Interview with Ashton Calvert and David Goldsworthy, 'East Timor,' in Goldsworthy and Peter Edwards (eds), *Facing north: a century of Australian engagement with Asia*, Melbourne University Press, Carlton, Vic, 2003, p. 225.

8   These talks recommenced in June 1997. See Ali Alatas, *The Pebble in the Shoe: The Diplomatic Struggle for East Timor*, Aksara Karunia, Jakarta, 2006, Chapter 9, for an account of their progress to mid-1998.

9   The major efforts included those by Nick Warner, then First Assistant Secretary Southeast Asia Division in DFAT, to consult a number of identified East Timorese leaders; and by the Australian Ambassador to Indonesia, John McCarthy, who consulted the noted East Timorese resistance leader and future President, Xanana Gusmão (Department of Foreign Affairs and Trade, *East Timor in Transition 1998–2000: An Australian Policy Challenge*, Commonwealth of Australia, Canberra, 2001, pp. 26–27).

10   Department of Foreign Affairs and Trade, *East Timor in Transition*, pp.177-79. Kelly argues that this survey identified the East Timorese preference for autonomy to be only a bridge to an independence vote in three to five years time (Paul Kelly, *The March of the Patriots: The Struggle for Modern Australia*, Melbourne University Press, Carlton, Vic, 2009, p. 485–86).

11   Interview with Ashton Calvert. See also Don Greenlees and Robert Garran, *Deliverance: The Inside Story of East Timor's Fight for Freedom*, Allen & Unwin, Crows Nest, NSW, 2002, p. 80.

12   Interview with Hugh White.

13   The 'shuffling' of Indonesian combat troops in East Timor was widely reported and described as a charade. See Don Greenlees, 'Leak shows no E Timor troop cuts', *Australian*, 30 October 1998, p. 1; and Australian Associated Press, 'Downer denies Aust intelligence wanting', *AAP Information Services Pty Lt*d, 1 November 1998.

14   While Alatas argues that the talks were proceeding 'at an encouraging pace', they were suspended for a short time in November 1998 before an agreement was reached to recommence in January 1999 (Alatas, *The Pebble in the Shoe: The Diplomatic Struggle for East Timor*, pp. 145–46). These difficulties are noted in the text

about the killings of journalists at Balibo in 1975 was uncovered in October 1998.[15] Finally, it became known to officials that the Australian Government wanted to develop an initiative to start their new term. Interviewee 052-06 recalled how 'the government recognised that, to some extent, Indonesia was falling into a dangerous vacuum and Australia needed to express some views which would help, from our point of view, to crystallize the situation', although there was no agreed way forward among the major national security departments.[16] These conditions presented an opportunity for a policy initiative.[17]

The exact form of the initiative came to be known as the 'Howard Letter' (see Appendix). This letter revised important elements of Australia's position on East Timor's future and provided something of a catalyst for the events of 1999.[18] Importantly, the letter contained support for Habibie's decision to offer autonomy to East Timor and reaffirmed Australia's support for East Timor remaining a part of Indonesia.[19] But Howard also encouraged Habibie to see East Timor as a political—that is, domestic—problem rather than a foreign policy matter. This letter also recommended building a review mechanism into an autonomy

---

of the 'Howard Letter' (see Appendix) and the analysis contained in Department of Foreign Affairs and Trade, *East Timor in Transition*, p. 29 and p. 31. See also Nicholas Wheeler and Tim Dunne, 'East Timor and the New Humanitarian Intervention', *International Affairs*, vol. 77, no. 4, 2001, p. 812.

15   See Jonathon Holmes, 'East Timor—Balibo: A Special Report', *Foreign Correspondent*, ABC Television (Australia), 20 October 1998, available at <http://www.abc.net.au/foreign/stories/s401582.htm>, accessed 20 April 2009). This report led to a re-opening of the Sherman Enquiry into the Balibo killings of 16 October 1975. This atrocity involved the murder of five Australian-based newsmen by Indonesian forces and some Timorese militia.

16   Hugh White recalls a discussion in June 1998 where the prospect of changing Australian policy to calling for an act of self-determination was discussed, but 'no clear conclusion was reached ... in that discussion' and the proposal was not raised again with Defence (Hugh White, 'The Road to INTERFET: East Timor—1999', unpublished paper, copy in author's possession, 2007, p. 2).

17   Greenlees and Garran, *Deliverance: The Inside Story of East Timor's Fight for Freedom*, pp. 84–85. The idea of 'opportunity' was expressed in interviews with Ashton Calvert and 064-07, Canberra, 5 July 2007. Interviewee 064-07 is a former ministerial staffer and government official.

18   A DFAT submission described the policy suggestions contained in the letter as a 'major shift' (see Department of Foreign Affairs and Trade and AusAID, *Submission to the Senate Foreign Affairs, Defence and Trade References Committee Inquiry into East Timor*, Senate Foreign Affairs, Defence and Trade References Committee, Additional Information, vol. 5, Commonwealth of Australia, Canberra, 1999, p. 046). Ali Alatas agreed with that assessment, describing the letter as an 'unmistakable shift in [Australian] policy' (Alatas, *The Pebble in the Shoe: The Diplomatic Struggle for East Timor*, p. 144).

19   Paul Kelly describes the letter as a 'trap' for Indonesia, claiming that Downer and Calvert recognised that any proposed ballot was 'opening the door for independence'—no matter how far off (Kelly, *The March of the Patriots*, p. 487). Kelly subsequently portrays independence as Australia's policy objective with regard to East Timor when he claims that 'Howard and Downer did not seek East Timor's independence by accident or mistake' (p. 514). While this claim may be accurate, no interview conducted for this research (including an interview with one key protagonist who had an opportunity to make it) identified independence as Australia's preferred policy outcome in December 1998. As a result, Kelly's claim that Australia intended to see East Timor become independent inside ten years or so (and without a period of autonomy) is likely to represent post-facto justification. Further, to see independence as the real objective in December 1998 overstates the actual power that Australia had to achieve that objective, and the very real downside risk that an independent East Timor would present to Australia. As the discussion of objectives in Chapter 3 shows, it more accurate to see that the Australian Government saw independence as a possible outcome in December 1998, and as an emergent objective as the events on the ground unfolded in 1999.

package, similar to the 1988 Matignon Accords in New Caledonia, retaining Indonesian sovereignty over East Timor before a vote for independence in ten years' time.[20]

The Australian Government delivered the letter directly and quietly to Habibie via the Ambassador in Jakarta, intending to give the Indonesian President time and space to consider its proposals.[21] However the letter's contents, particularly the reference it contained to the Matignon Accords, angered Habibie and were misconstrued as a suggestion that Indonesia was acting like a colonial power.[22] This inference was unwelcome and probably spurred a new desire by the Indonesian President (or reinforced an existing one) to bring about a quick resolution to the question of East Timor's sovereignty.[23]

It is almost certain, based on interviews with Hugh White, 051-06 and 032-05 (the latter being a senior officer in a key department in 1999), that the letter was developed by then Prime Minister John Howard's international adviser, Michael Thawley; Peter Varghese, then First Assistant Secretary in DPM&C; and Deputy Secretary of DFAT, John Dauth. The draft of the letter was discussed with then Secretary of DFAT Dr Ashton Calvert, a senior analyst from the Office of National Assessments (ONA), and the Australian Ambassador in Jakarta, John McCarthy. The letter was then cleared through Howard and Downer.[24]

Further knowledge of the letter probably extended only as far as the Secretary of DPM&C, Max Moore-Wilton, High Commissioner Philip Flood in London,

---

20 The 1988 Matignon Accords between France and the people of New Caledonia included provisions on the legal status of citizens, customary law, land, devolution of powers, economic development and political representation. Most importantly, these accords allowed for a poll to determine whether the people of New Caledonia would convert 'citizenry into nationality' in 1998 (Embassy of France in Australia, 'The Noumea Accord', 5 May 1998, available at <http://www.austlii.edu.au/au/journals/AILR/2002/17.html>, accessed 20 April 2009).

21 Interview with 051-06, who is a former senior government official with direct knowledge of the East Timor crisis.

22 This reaction was reported by Australia's Ambassador, John McCarthy (Department of Foreign Affairs and Trade, *East Timor in Transition*, p. 32) and recounted in Goldsworthy, 'East Timor', pp. 228–29. This is also how Tim Fischer, then Australia's Deputy Prime Minister and a member of the NSCC, understood Habibie's reaction. See also Karen Polgaze, 'PM's Timor letter "angered Habibie"', *Canberra Times*, 3 November 1999, who quotes an interview with Indonesian Foreign Minister Ali Alatas. Noting Indonesia's deep sensitivity toward colonialism, Alatas (*The Pebble in the Shoe: The Diplomatic Struggle for East Timor*, pp. 149–50) described Habibie's reaction as a 'burst' after the Matignon reference was explained to him.

23 Alatas, *The Pebble in the Shoe: The Diplomatic Struggle for East Timor*, pp. 149–50; and Greenlees and Garran, *Deliverance: The Inside Story of East Timor's Fight for Freedom*, pp. 88–95. Goldsworthy notes other forces on Habibie's decision-making at the time, including pressure from the European Union, the US Congress and influential Indonesians (Goldsworthy, 'East Timor', p. 230).

24 Howard acknowledged the roles of Calvert, Thawley, Downer and himself in the letter's preparation (see Fran Kelly, 'John Howard on East Timor', *The Howard Years* (website), ABC Television (Australia), 2008, available at <http://www.abc.net.au/news/howardyears/>, (see Further Resources: Episode 2), accessed 27 June 2009.

and DFAT's Nick Warner.[25] Many claim that the letter was discussed at the 1 December 1998 meeting of the National Security Committee of Cabinet (NSCC);[26] indeed, Howard is said to have grabbed Downer by the arm or shoulder after the meeting and said, "This is big, this is very big."[27] However, the Minister of Defence and key officials within Defence said they knew nothing about it and denied the letter was discussed openly in the NSCC.[28] Given the limited circle of senior politicians and officials involved, it is not surprising that this initiative caught sections of the Australian national security policy community by surprise.

The situation became difficult to control once the existence of the letter was leaked sometime in late December 1998,[29] even before the story of Howard's letter broke in the Australian press on 12 January 1999. This news story was followed quickly by an official statement that confirmed Australia's preference for 'an act of self-determination at some future time, following a substantial period of autonomy'.[30] On 27 January 1999, Habibie consulted his Cabinet and decided to offer East Timor 'regional autonomy plus' in a referendum. If that offer was rejected, his government would recommend that the Indonesian

---

25   Goldsworthy claims this letter was instigated by DFAT (implying the letter was entirely their idea), through a ministerial submission on 30 November 1999 (NAA, A9737, 92/051651 part 17, Department of Foreign Affairs and Trade, 'Ministerial Submission', 30 November 1999, cited in Goldsworthy, 'East Timor', p. 227). It is more likely the text was drafted as stated above and presented formally to the foreign minister through this submission, so he could present it 'below the line' to the NSCC on 1 December 1999. Kelly states that Howard consulted Flood, who was formerly Director-General ONA (Kelly, *The March of the Patriots*, p. 488).

26   Interview with 052-06, a former senior government official with direct knowledge of the East Timor crisis. See also Greenlees and Garran, *Deliverance: The Inside Story of East Timor's Fight for Freedom,* pp. 85–86; Goldsworthy, 'East Timor', p. 221; James Cotton, 'East Timor and Australia—Twenty-five years of the policy debate', in James Cotton (ed.), *East Timor and Australia*, Australian Defence Studies Centre/Australian Institute of International Affairs, Canberra, 2000, p. 13; and Kelly, *March of the Patriots*, p. 489.

27   Greenlees and Garran, *Deliverance: The Inside Story of East Timor's Fight for Freedom,* p. 86. Howard and Downer confirmed this in a television interview series, *The Howard Years* (Episode 2), ABC Television (Australia), 24 November 2008, available at <http://www.abc.net.au/news/howardyears/content/s2422684.htm> accessed 27 June 2009.

28   Interviews with John Moore (Defence Minister in 1999), Paul Barratt (Secretary of the Department of Defence until August 1999), Chris Barrie (Chief of the Defence Force in 1999), and Hugh White. Other well-placed interviewees who also claimed that the letter caught Defence by surprise included Aldo Borgu (an adviser to Defence Minister John Moore in 1999) and Allan Behm (Canberra, 5 May 2005). Behm was First Assistant Secretary International Policy in 1998 and First Assistant Secretary Strategic Policy and Plans in 1999–2000.

29   Interview with 051-06. Another interviewee (identity protected) confirmed the period of the leak, recalling that a journalist called to ask for background on the letter. While Goldsworthy implies Indonesian officials were responsible for the leak (Goldsworthy, 'East Timor', p. 229), Clinton Fernandes claims a source that attributes the leak to a 'senior Australian diplomat' in the Jakarta embassy ('The Road to INTERFET: Bringing the Politics Back In', *Security Challenges*, vol. 4, no. 3, 2008, p. 87).

30   The story was reported in Don Greenlees, 'Howard reverse on Timor', *Australian*, 12 January 1999; and Alexander Downer, 'Australian Government Historic Policy Shift On East Timor', Media Release, 12 January 1999, available at <http://www.foreignminister.gov.au/releases/1999/fa002_99.html>, accessed 20 April 2009.

Parliament 'release East Timor from Indonesia'.[31] So despite uncertainties about its genesis, the Howard Letter ultimately helped to change Habibie's thinking on East Timor in a substantive way.

A Developing Situation

The events and decisions of January 1999 sent the Australian national security policy community into overdrive. The meeting of the Strategic Policy Coordination Group (SPCG) on 15 January highlighted Defence's disappointment with the lack of internal consultation, and provided a negative prognosis for what might happen next. Rear Admiral Peter Briggs, a participant at that meeting, recalled:

> Hugh White was very forthright, and questioned the DFAT representatives on the process and intentions of the letter. Hugh said something like 'Do you know what the f … is going to happen?'—they were taken aback at Hugh's language and expression— 'Habibie is going to accept the offer, there will be a process of self-determination which the Indonesian military will resist, and the local militias will be the tool they will resist it with, and we will end up with the ADF [Australian Defence Force] on the ground between the Indonesians and the East Timorese. We could well end up with body bags coming back to Australia.' It was an extremely strong event.[32]

Other agencies in Canberra were also working to prepare information on Australia's options by late January. Defence intelligence provided analysis of the situation in East Timor and Indonesia, including reports that pointed to Indonesian military support for militia violence.[33] Defence's Strategic Command Division produced a paper that explained what forces might be needed to conduct different types of missions, ranging from small observer missions to larger, combat-capable forces.[34] Other work was undertaken within Defence to examine the state of ADF readiness and the costs involved in preparing air and naval assets and another brigade group (of around 3500 people) for possible contingencies. While the potential for strife in East Timor was a factor, this planning seemed especially prudent given the increased potential for the ADF

---

31 Jonathon Head, 'East Timor Breakthrough', *BBC News* (United Kingdom), 28 January 1999, available at <http://news.bbc.co.uk/1/hi/events/indonesia/latest_news/263828.stm>, accessed 20 April 2009, quoting Information Minister Yunus Yosfiah's announcement on 27 January.

32 Interview with Rear Admiral Peter Briggs, who was Head Strategic Command Division in Defence from early 1997 to May 1999.

33 Des Ball, 'Silent Witness: Australian Intelligence and East Timor', in Desmond Ball, James Dunn, Gerry van Klinken, David Bourchier, Douglas Kammen and Richard Tanter (eds), *Masters of Terror: Indonesia's Military and the Violence in East Timor in 1999*, Canberra Papers on Strategy and Defence No. 145, Strategic and Defence Studies Centre, The Australian National University, Canberra, 2002, pp. 246–47.

34 Interviews with John Moore, Allan Behm and 035-05 (Canberra, 14 October 2005, identity protected).

to be called to evacuate Australian citizens from the region, given the increase in strife-prone areas including the Solomon Islands, Papua New Guinea, Bougainville and Indonesia, after sporadic violence occurred there in 1997 and 1998.[35] The proposal for increased readiness was made at the February 1999 meeting of the NSCC, and subsequently announced on 11 March.[36]

DFAT was also busy. Aside from increased consultation with both Indonesian leaders and East Timorese groups by McCarthy,[37] meetings with other countries included specific discussions about East Timor. In one example, Ashton Calvert visited Washington, DC, to consult the US Assistant Secretary of State, Stanley Roth about America's views on events. DFAT also established its own policy unit, headed by Nick Warner and managed by Chris Moraitis, to coordinate the diplomatic aspects of national policy.

DPM&C also began to look more closely at the issue. Having taken a leading role in drafting the Howard Letter, it left most of the subsequent policy development work to 'implementation departments' like DFAT and Defence. Its focus remained on keeping the prime minister informed of developments and ensuring coordination of agency activity.[38]

There was, however, a significant divergence of opinion between DFAT and Defence about any Australian response. DFAT argued that the Indonesians were responsible for security in East Timor; they were keen to use diplomacy to avoid the need to deploy a peacekeeping force to East Timor, or to have a perception arise that Australia was preparing to intervene in East Timor.[39] To this way of thinking, such a perception could create tension with Indonesia, or allow others to assume that Australia would take the lead and 'bankroll' the process.[40] Australian officials also feared this perception might discourage the Indonesians

---

35   Interview with Chris Barrie. It is important to underscore the thinking of the time, which put a priority upon evacuation contingencies and not an intervention into East Timor.
36   Interviews with John Moore, Chris Barrie, 051-06 and Aldo Borgu. It is interesting to note that the increased readiness was attributed to savings from the Defence Reform Program—see Defence Public Affairs, 'The Hon J Moore, Progress on the Implementation of the Defence Reform Program', Media Release 067/99, Canberra, 11 March 1999.
37   Department of Foreign Affairs and Trade and AusAID, *Submission to the Senate Foreign Affairs, Defence and Trade References Committee Inquiry into East Timor*, p. 047.
38   Interview with 052-06.
39   This position was expressed in the leaked cable from Calvert to Roth, and was supported by interviews with Hugh White and 012-05 (Canberra, 30 June 2005), who is an official with direct knowledge of the East Timor ballot. The desire to use diplomacy was mentioned by Alexander Downer in Andrew Fowler, 'Ties that Bind' *4 Corners*, ABC Television (Australia), 14 February 2000. Another note of DFAT's adherence to this position was made in Maley, 'Australia and the East Timor Crisis', pp. 155–58.
40   According to Carl Thayer, this view was expressed by Peter Varghese, then-FAS International Division in DPM&C. Thayer does not state his source or the remarks' context. See Thayer, 'Australia-Indonesia Relations', p. 9.

and Timorese from coming to their own compromises about the process.[41] Others, such as then Deputy Prime Minister Tim Fischer, also saw danger in being proactive. He thought overt pressure on the Indonesians or clearly visible defence preparations may force Habibie to renege on the consultation plan.[42]

On the other hand, Defence visualised multiple scenarios that could occur in the region (and East Timor in particular), ranging from new monitoring missions up to evacuations protected by ADF troops.[43] As mentioned earlier, the NSCC identified a need to increase force readiness to ensure that the ADF would be in a position to respond to any major crisis, while being prepared for a separate, additional contingency should one occur. These preparations required the overt movement of troops and equipment, increased training and additional spending on logistic support—activities that are hard to hide and difficult to attribute to anything other than preparations for East Timor in the prevailing climate. There would also be a need to engage potential coalition contributors and the United States to ensure that Australia had international support and appropriate capabilities to conduct an operation offshore.[44] Minister of Defence John Moore decided (after consultation with the Prime Minister) to ignore DFAT's concern and agree to Chief of Defence Force (CDF) Admiral Chris Barrie's recommendation to proceed with readiness planning and consultation with US Pacific Command (USPACOM). This was fortunate because it took nearly five months to prepare a second brigade group for peacekeeping operations.[45]

Defence also took the step of appointing Brigadier Mike Smith to manage part of its input to the East Timor policy process. Given the title 'Director General East Timor' (DGET), he reported directly to the CDF through the Deputy Secretary Strategy and Intelligence, Hugh White. While the initial plan was for the DGET to focus on the relationship with Indonesia, it was eventually decided to use Smith to develop an understanding of the United Nations and its processes. Smith would also be made available to command a UN peacekeeping force if one was required in East Timor, even though the idea of an intervention force (what became the International Force in East Timor, INTERFET) was still not

---

41 This reason was attributed to a DPM&C official, and is criticised by William Maley ('Australia and the East Timor Crisis', p. 157). It is not inconceivable to think that a 'Machiavellian' East Timorese element may see advantage in acting so to inflame tensions and encourage foreign intervention.

42 Interview with Tim Fischer.

43 Interviews with Chris Barrie and Air Vice-Marshal Bob Treloar, by telephone, 4 November 2005. Treloar was appointed Commander Australian Theatre in May 1999.

44 Interview with 052-06.

45 Interview with John Moore and Allan Behm. The second brigade group was declared ready by the end of June (see Robert Garran, 'The military masses for its biggest march in 30 years', *Australian*, 3 July 1999, p. 7).

under consideration.[46] Positioning Smith in this way proved to be a worthwhile foresight when the time came to work with the United Nations on the eventual peacekeeping operation.[47]

Smith established himself in a key position linking, in part, Defence, DFAT and the Department of Peacekeeping Operations at the United Nations. This 'small office' approach was selected by Defence because there was an imperative to protect information about Australia's intentions. There was also a need to avoid agitating the Indonesians, and probably DFAT, by creating a new, large policy and planning organisation. The small office also allowed Smith to move nimbly between different organisations and ensure a single ADF view was presented to key stakeholders.[48]

Other agencies were involved in planning. In addition to its mission of organising aid, the Australian International Aid Agency (AusAID) was tasked by the foreign minister to conduct an assessment of the humanitarian situation in East Timor and investigate claims that Indonesian officials were preventing food from moving around the province.[49] The Australian Electoral Commission (AEC) was asked to provide advice on electoral methods, draft an election manual and materials, and advise on whether Australia could provide further support to the popular consultation process.[50]

Activities by the United Nations also involved the Australian Government. In late March, a UN assessment mission visited Jakarta, East Timor and Canberra to scope the requirements for the proposed referendum. The Australian Government

46   Interview with 007-05, Canberra 17 June 2005. Interviewee 007-05 is a former senior ADF officer who was closely involved with Defence planning for East Timor, including knowledge of liaison activities with the United Nations.

47   After the post-ballot violence, Smith was promoted to Major General and deployed to New York (for four months) where he and his small team assisted the Military Planning Staff in DPKO in preparing for the transition from INTERFET to a UN peacekeeping force. This team subsequently deployed to Dili in late 1999 as the advance party for the Peacekeeping Force, and Smith was appointed as the Deputy Force Commander of the Peacekeeping Force in December.

48   Interviews with Chris Barrie; Kerry Clarke, Canberra, 2 August 2005; 007-05 and Matthew Skoien, by telephone, 22 December 2005. Clarke was Director General Joint Operations in Strategic Command Division in 1998–99, and Skoien was Director Indonesia Section in International Policy Division in Defence from December 1998 to September 1999.

49   Interview with Steve Darvill (Canberra, 5 July 2005) who said that the April 1999 assessment eventually blamed the delays on routine logistic problems, rather than on deliberate action by any party. Darvill was involved in operational planning as part of AusAID's Humanitarian Emergencies section in 1999. For the text of the fact-finding mission's report, see AusAID, *Report of the AusAID Fact-Finding Mission to East Timor, 10–20 March 1999*, Commonwealth of Australia, Canberra, 1999.

50   Interview with 012-05 and Australian Electoral Commission, *Submission to the Senate Foreign Affairs, Defence and Trade References Committee: Australian Electoral Commission Support for the East Timor Consultation Ballot*, Canberra, 1999, pp. 2–3.

saw this visit as an opportunity to influence the UN team's thinking on East Timor.[51] This meeting was soon followed by a delegation to UN Headquarters in New York, led by DFAT, which included Defence representatives.[52]

Other diplomatic initiatives were underway. Closer to home, Howard requested a summit with Habibie to discuss the security situation after violence occurred in Liquiçá on 6 April and Dili on 17 April 1999.[53] At this meeting, Howard sought—'as strongly as I could', albeit described as gently by others—to obtain Indonesian acquiescence for an international peacekeeping force before the ballot.[54] He had to settle for an increased number of police advisors within what was to become the United Nations Mission in East Timor (UNAMET), and for permission to open an Australian consulate in Dili.[55]

A new committee was added to the interdepartmental policymaking structure in mid-April 1999. Led by Bill Paterson, an assistant secretary in DPM&C, this semi-formal grouping met fortnightly from 16 April to discuss issues of day-to-day importance between the departments and to discuss 'options and implications'.[56] This meeting included relatively senior representatives (assistant-secretary level) from DFAT, Defence, AusAID, the Australian Federal Police (AFP), AEC, and ONA. The main agenda items at each meeting included updates on the situation in East Timor and overseas, and briefings on each agency's activities. Representatives also had the opportunity to discuss issues such as funding, Australian capabilities and interaction with the United Nations. The topics broadened later, as these meetings began to focus on Australian support for the popular consultation. The group never considered issues concerning military operations, such as the evacuation.[57]

Much of the Paterson Committee's work was, therefore, process oriented: it provided a chance for representatives to identify issues that would be discussed at forthcoming meetings by more senior committees such as the SPCG and the

---

51 Interviews with Hugh White and 012-05.
52 Interviews with Hugh White and 007-05.
53 Interviewee 052-06 described the relationship between the Australian Government and Habibie as 'quite testy' during this time, which meant the timing of the meeting was up to Habibie.
54 Fran Kelly, 'John Howard on East Timor'.
55 Department of Foreign Affairs and Trade, *East Timor in Transition*, pp. 78–81. By the time of the summit, Australian policymakers had come to the conclusion that Habibie could not agree to peacekeepers (interviews with Ashton Calvert and Hugh White). Howard acknowledged the significant political constraints upon Habibie to Fran Kelly, ('John Howard on East Timor'), so he is not likely to have pushed too hard for peacekeepers in the 90-minute private meeting with Habibie at Bali. Further, Interviewee 052-06 did not think Habibie's ability to carry agreements with the Army and his ministers was assured either. Interviewee 051-06 also expressed the concern that the military might throw Habibie out if he gave way on military peacekeepers in April. See also Alatas, *The Pebble in the Shoe: The Diplomatic Struggle for East Timor*, p. 173, who said Habibie rejected the proposal 'with great indignation'.
56 Interviews with 052-05, Matt Skoien and 012-05.
57 Interviews with 012-05, Kerry Clarke, 020-05 (by telephone, 11 August 2005) and 035-05. Interviewee 020-05 is a former senior member of DPM&C with direct knowledge of the East Timor case.

NSCC, and to coordinate the timing and content of submissions. Interestingly, the early meetings seemed to be a way of bringing DPM&C into the picture, as their officers had played little part in the detailed planning thus far.[58] It also provided another channel—in addition to contacts between departments and the existing working groups—to improve coordination at lower levels.[59]

By the end of April, in terms of establishing the mechanisms for handling the emerging crisis in East Timor, Australian policymakers had moved from being concerned observers to active participants. First, Australia had undertaken a range of significant meetings with US, UN, Indonesian, Portuguese and East Timorese representatives either to shape those groups or to seek their support. Second, a range of government agencies—including the ADF, AEC, AusAID and the intelligence community[60]—began preparations to provide services or options to government. DFAT had also been in contact with the Indonesian Government to, among other things, lobby for permission to open a consulate in Dili.[61] Third, interdepartmental interaction became more formalised at lower levels, with Paterson's Committee being established to improve information sharing between different agencies. Interaction was also facilitated by standing invitations to meetings (such as Defence's East Timor Working Group), joint delegations and individual consultations between officials.

However, there was also 'a sense [among policymakers] that events were getting out of control'.[62] The Indonesian Army (in Indonesian, *Tentara Nasional Indonesia*, or TNI) was being identified as supporting militia violence in East Timor by the media and witnesses who had been in East Timor.[63] Given the TNI's importance to securing the next phase of the crisis, this development was disconcerting for many of those watching the unfolding events.

---

58 Interviewee 035-05.
59 Interviews with 012-05, Kerry Clarke, 020-05 and 035-05.
60 On intelligence activities, see Paul Daley, 'Spy effort stepped up in Timor', *Age*, 20 March 1999, p. 5; and Ball, 'Silent Witness: Australian Intelligence and East Timor', pp. 248–52.
61 As noted earlier, AusAID already had an ongoing assistance program to East Timor. AusAID planned to deliver A$6 million in aid in Financial Year 1998–99—see Senate Foreign Affairs, Defence and Trade Committee, *Consideration of Additional Estimates (Department of Foreign Affairs and Trade)*, 11 February 1999, p. 240; and Foreign Affairs, Defence and Trade References Committee, *Economic, social and political conditions in East Timor*, 13 August 1999, p. 219.
62 Interview with Hugh White.
63 Ball, 'Silent Witness: Australian Intelligence and East Timor', pp. 251–52. Taudevin also provides his interpretation of what he told DFAT about the violence in East Timor (Lansell Taudevin, *East Timor: Too Little Too Late*, Duffy and Snellgrove, Sydney, 1999, pp. 230–34).

Organising for the Consultation

The period of the UNAMET mission, starting with the May 5 Agreement and ending with the declaration of the consultation results on 4 September 1999, marked the next phase of the crisis.

Table 4: Selected Key Events for December 1998-April 1999

19 December 1998	Howard's letter is delivered to Habibie.
12 January 1999	Details of a new policy towards East Timor are announced by the Australian Government.
12 January 1999	Details of a new policy towards East Timor are announced by the Australian Government.
27 January	The Indonesian Government announces its intention to allow the East Timorese people to vote in a popular consultation on their future status
9 February	The NSCC meets and decides its initial approach to the East Timor situation.
11 February	Xanana Gusmão is transferred from prison to house arrest.
Late February	US Assistant Secretary of State Stanley Roth meets Ashton Calvert, Secretary of DFAT.
9–11 March	Agreement-in-principle is reached in the UN–Indonesia–Portugal Tripartite Talks, with the main feature being a popular consultation for East Timor.
11 March	Agreement-in-principle is reached in the UN–Indonesia–Portugal Tripartite Talks, with the main feature being a popular consultation for East Timor.
29–30 March	The UN Assessment Mission, led by Francesc Vendrell, visits Canberra.
6 April	Liquiçá massacre.
17 April	Rampage in Dili
21–23 April	Completion of negotiations by Indonesia, Portugal and the United Nations.
27 April	Howard and Habibie meet in Bali.

Once the May 5 Agreement was announced, more agencies, notably the AFP, became involved in the Australian response. AusAID began to fund Australian agencies to prepare for, and then participate in, UNAMET activities. Australia also agreed to provide A\$20 million in cash and 'in kind' support so that the operation could commence quickly.[64]

---

64 Testimony by John Dauth of DFAT in Foreign Affairs, Defence and Trade References Committee, *Economic, social and political conditions in East Timor*, 13 August 1999, p. 220.

Events started to move at pace once the UN Security Council (UNSC) approved Resolution 1246 to establish UNAMET on 11 June 1999.[65] Just prior to the resolution, the first group of UNAMET staff and a small number of AFP officers arrived in Dili. Within a week the Australian contingent to UNAMET had grown to nearly fifty police and six military liaison officers, and voter registration started within four weeks. However, this process was marred by violence and intimidation within East Timor, to the point where some already doubted that a 'free and fair election' was possible.[66]

Activity at the AFP was intense during this period, with the main work—outside the normal anti-crime operations[67]—revolving around monitoring the operation and preparing the next rotation. This was a major issue, as Federal Agent Tim Dahlstrom recalled:

> There were a range of other issues—whether the security situation was getting better, and secondly, our capacity to actually rotate people through. The three month deployment meant we were advertising for the next group while we were still training a group to go. ... We had to move to bringing state and territory police in then as AFP secondees to build our capacity.[68]

The AFP was also involved in frequent meetings with other departments, and regularly attended DFAT meetings (and eventually, the task force formed to manage consular matters) to provide advice on operational matters during the deployment.

Defence managed a particularly sensitive diplomatic issue in this period, when Vice Chief of the Defence Force (VCDF) Air Marshal Doug Riding and First Assistant Secretary Strategic Policy Allan Behm were dispatched to Jakarta

---

65   This resolution provided a mandate to 'organize and conduct a popular consultation on the basis of a direct, secret and universal ballot, in order to ascertain whether the East Timorese people accept the proposed constitutional framework providing for a special autonomy for East Timor within the unitary Republic of Indonesia or reject the proposed special autonomy for East Timor, leading to East Timor's separation from Indonesia, in accordance with the General Agreement and to enable the Secretary-General to discharge his responsibility under paragraph 3 of the Security Agreement'. (United Nations, 'UNAMET Fact Sheet', 1999, available at <http://www.un.org/peace/etimor99/fact_bottom.htm>, accessed 20 April 2009).

66   See Charles Scheiner, 'Grassroots in the Field—Observing the East Timor Consultation', in Richard Tanter, Mark Selden and Stephen Shalom (eds), *Bitter Flowers, Sweet Flowers: East Timor, Indonesia and the World Community*, Rowman and Littlefield, Lanham, MD. 2001, pp. 115–18.

67   Interviews with Assistant Commission Adrien Whiddett, Canberra, 29 June 2005; and Assistant Commissioner Andrew Hughes, Suva, 9 September 2005. They both noted their involvement in a range of normal policing issues, which meant that the East Timor operation was a major additional task for them. Whiddett was responsible for AFP Operations in 1999, and Hughes was Director International and Operations for the AFP in 1999.

68   Interview with Federal Agent Tim Dahlstrom, Canberra, 16 August 2005. Dahlstrom was a member of the UN and Other Overseas Commitments Coordination team for the AFP in 1999. As part of this team, he was responsible for the detailed planning of the AFP's involvement (especially contingent preparation) in East Timor.

on 21 June 1999. This delegation was instigated by a Cabinet decision,[69] and a tightly-worded script was developed by ONA and DFAT that was written to protect the sources used. Riding's task was to inform senior TNI officers—including General Sugiono and General Susilo Bambang Yudhoyono—that Australia had detected evidence of the Indonesian Army's involvement in equipping and directing a number of existing civil defence units and newly-formed militias to intimidate the East Timorese people.[70] It was a blunt, but diplomatically-conducted conversation between 'close military partner[s]'.[71] Despite this, the visit had little substantive influence.[72] The Indonesian view of the security situation was far different, and Yudhoyono represented strongly for TNI's neutrality.[73] Further meetings were conducted with the Indonesian Government and with key East Timorese to convince them to maintain their promises about security before and after the ballot.[74]

By August, activity levels in other parts of Canberra appeared to decline from the levels of March and April. With UNAMET now in its implementation phase, some of the policy attention began to turn to encouraging Southeast Asian nations to be more active in the process, and to maintaining a close liaison with the United States.[75] Defence also attempted to solve a number of important logistic issues and prepared contingencies for an evacuation.

This focus on Canberra is not intended to neglect the bravery and skill of UNAMET and the East Timorese people themselves. UNAMET's overall success in fulfilling its mandate is a testimony to the qualities of all involved and the determination of the East Timorese voters. That the consultation delivered a fair reflection of the East Timorese peoples' will served to reinforce the shock felt by many—but expected by others—when serious violence erupted in Dili and other parts of East Timor on 4 September 1999.

---

69   Goldsworthy, 'East Timor', p. 241.

70   Interviews with Allan Behm, Kerry Clarke and 046-06, a senior ADF officer with direct knowledge of the East Timor crisis. See also John Lyons, 'The Secret East Timor Dossier', *Bulletin*, 12 October 1999, p. 25; Paul Daley, 'Gunning for the General', *Bulletin*, 30 June 2004; and Ball, 'Silent Witness: Australian Intelligence and East Timor'. Greenlees and Garran reproduced some of Riding's script in their book (see *Deliverance: The Inside Story of East Timor's Fight for Freedom*, pp. 167–68). Interviewee 046-06 is a former senior ADF officer with direct knowledge of the East Timor crisis. General Sugiono was TNI's Chief of Staff for General Affairs and General Yudhoyono was Chief of Staff for Territorial Affairs in 1999.

71   Greenlees and Garran, *Deliverance: The Inside Story of East Timor's Fight for Freedom*, p. 167–68.

72   Interviewee 046-06.

73   Interview with Allan Behm, and Greenlees and Garran, *Deliverance: The Inside Story of East Timor's Fight for Freedom*, p. 168.

74   See Goldsworthy, 'East Timor', p. 242–43; and Mark Riley, 'UN Backs Downer Plan to Beef Up Timor Force', *Sydney Morning Herald*, 6 August 1999, p. 1.

75   Matt Skoien and Interviewee 062-07 (Canberra, 29 June 2007) described a number of meetings with US military officials from USPACOM. Interviewee 062-07 is an ADF officer with knowledge of the East Timor case, including knowledge of planning for UNAMET, INTERFET and UNTAET.

Acute Crisis and Response

Once the extent and severity of violence became known, the plan to evacuate UNAMET personnel from East Timor (Operation *Spitfire*) commenced,[76] contingency planning for a peace operation began, and intense lobbying was conducted to muster support for an international coalition. It was also clear that UN Secretary-General Kofi Annan did not believe that the Indonesian military could maintain control of the situation. This concern resulted in a phone call to Howard on 6 September, where Annan asked whether Australia would contribute to an international force for East Timor if this was authorised by the Indonesians and the UNSC. According to Howard, he told Annan that Australia would make a significant contribution and insisted that Australia be asked to lead.[77]

Table 5: Selected Key Events for May August 1999

5 May	Tripartite agreement to establish UNAMET is signed (5 May Agreement).
3 June	Headquarters UNAMET opens in Dili.
11 June	The UNSC passes Resolution 1246 authorising UNAMET.
Late June	1st Australian Brigade is declared 'ready' for operations
29 June–4 July	Violence erupts in Maliana, Viqueque and Liquiçá.
29 June–4 July	Violence erupts in Maliana, Viqueque and Liquiçá.
16 July	Voter registration starts in East Timor.
20 July	The Age reports ADF evacuation plans for Australian and UN personnel from East Timor.
6 August	A Code of Conduct Agreement is signed between Timorese factions.
9 August	A Code of Conduct Agreement is signed between Timorese factions.
Mid-late August	Violence erupts in Viqueque (10 August), Maliana (18 August) and Dili (26 August).
12 August	FALINTIL (pro-independence militia) cantonment is complete.
24–27 August	Election campaign period.
28–30 August	Downer visits Jakarta and Dili.
30 August	Popular consultation is held; 98.6 per cent of registered voters cast ballots

---

76   1500 UN and other personnel were evacuated in the period 3–14 September 1999 (Defence Public Affairs, Hon. John Moore, 'East Timor Update', MIN 271/99, 14 September 1999, available at <http://www.minister. defence.gov.au/1999/27199.html>, accessed 20 April 2009).

77   Fran Kelly, 'John Howard on East Timor'. Howard said he insisted upon Australian leadership because the ADF was likely to represent the international force's major combat capability. Ashton Calvert said that Australia made a 'realistic assumption' about who was both best placed and willing to lead a collation prior to this. See also Department of Foreign Affairs and Trade, *East Timor in Transition*, p. 133; Greenlees and Garran, *Deliverance: The Inside Story of East Timor's Fight for Freedom*, p. 238; and Goldsworthy, 'East Timor', p. 248.

These events led to activities at many levels within the Australian Government. Crucially, the prime minister and foreign minister lobbied their counterparts in the region for support—a task helped by having many regional leaders meeting together at the Asia-Pacific Economic Cooperation (APEC) meeting in Auckland during 9–12 September 1999.[78] Howard also spoke frequently with Annan around this time.[79] At the diplomatic level, DFAT—often with direct assistance from Defence—worked to gather support for the mandate at the United Nations and among Southeast Asian states. Getting the appropriate mandate for the mission was an essential task, as the Australian Government wanted to conduct this operation under Chapter VII of the UN Charter so that it would not be a 'helpless bystander when violence broke out between factions on the ground'.[80]

Yet getting authorisation for the intervention was not complete, as the Indonesian Government still needed to acquiesce before the United Nations would consider a mandate. Once again, pressure was applied to Habibie and other Indonesian leaders from a variety of sources, including Annan, ambassadors representing the UNSC, US President Bill Clinton and, indirectly, from the World Bank.[81] Despite this effort, Habibie did not change his mind until 12 September.

At this stage, international military preparations became overt, but the size, leadership and role of such a force was still to be finalised. It was, however, certain that the United Nations would be unable to raise and deploy a force quickly—it would need at least five months to do so.[82] Australia formally confirmed its willingness to lead the force, to be known as INTERFET, soon after UN Resolution 1264 was passed on 15 September.[83]

---

78   Interview with 024-05 (Canberra, 18 August 2005), and Department of Foreign Affairs and Trade, *East Timor in Transition*, pp. 132–39. Interviewee 024-05 is a DFAT official with direct knowledge of the East Timor case.

79   Interview with 051-06. Greenlees and Garran said Howard and Annan talked five times on 5 and 6 September alone (*Deliverance: The Inside Story of East Timor's Fight for Freedom*, p. 235).

80   Interview with Kerry Clarke. Interviewee 051-06 recalled that the Australian Government was not united on the need for a Chapter VII mandate, but Howard was eventually convinced by US advice. Chapter VII of the UN Charter authorises the use of force, sanctions or other means to 'maintain or restore international peace and security' (Article 42). In circumstances where the United Nations acts to help parties maintain an agreement, Chapter VI is used and the peacekeeping force is only allowed to use force in self defence. See United Nations, *Charter of the United Nations*, New York, 1945, available at <http://www.un.org/aboutun/charter/>, accessed 20 April 2009.

81   See Kofi Annan, 'Secretary-General urges Indonesia to accept international help to restore order in East Timor at a moment of "great crisis"', *United Nations News*, New York, 10 September 1999, available at <http://www.ess.uwe.ac.uk/Timor/News14.htm>, accessed 20 April 2009; AAP, 'Clinton calls on Indonesia to let UN restore peace in East Timor', *St Louis Post-Dispatch*, 12 September 1999, p. A7; and Steven Mufson, 'World Bank Chief Warns Indonesia On Militias', *Washington Post*, 12 September 1999. See also Greenlees and Garran, *Deliverance: The Inside Story of East Timor's Fight for Freedom*, pp. 251–54.

82   Interview with Kerry Clarke.

83   As frequently occurs in international negotiations, Howard and Anan had already reached an in-principle agreement for Australian leadership that was subject to specific conditions.

Significant planning for operations in East Timor had been conducted by USPACOM in 1999, but this assumed US leadership of the peacekeeping force.[84] This assumption was out of step with Washington's political and military leadership, and so of limited utility when the crisis broke. The ADF had also conducted its own planning, but this was for a protected evacuation (Operation *Spitfire*). The evacuation task was quantitatively different in terms of size, logistic needs and probable duration from that required for a large-scale intervention. This meant rapid planning was needed to design, prepare and deploy INTERFET.

Any one of the three main tasks presented to Defence and the ADF in early September—the evacuation, deploying Australian troops overseas, and developing a coalition—would have been demanding on its own. When the three came together under conditions of tight political and media scrutiny, Defence soon found its normal working structures to be both overwhelmed and insufficient to manage the crisis.[85]

Defence responded to the increased demands for policy advice and coordination in three ways. The first was to make the SCG more responsive to the CDF's needs by increasing the frequency of its meetings and expanding its membership. This meant that the SCG began meeting daily (and sometimes twice daily) in September, at a time that allowed CDF Admiral Chris Barrie and Acting Secretary Hugh White to brief the Minister of Defence before the now-daily NSCC meeting.

An expanded membership also helped to make the SCG more effective. By September, the Canberra-based group was complemented by COMAST Air Vice-Marshal Bob Treloar and his four component commanders by video-link from Sydney. This link allowed the most senior operational commanders to hear what the strategic leadership was saying about events and intentions. In addition, representatives from the Defence Minister's office and DFAT were sometimes

---

84   Interviews with Lieutenant General Earl Hailston, USMC, by telephone, 28 March 2006; and Lieutenant General John Castellaw, USMC, by telephone, 14 February 2006. Hailston was the lead planner (J5) for USPACOM until 31 May 1999. He moved to Command III Marine Expeditionary Force in June and became responsible for deploying III Marine Expeditionary Brigade to East Timor in September 1999. Castellaw was the commander of III Marine Expeditionary Brigade in 1999 and deployed to East Timor. In his interview, Hailston recalled being directed to prepare a contingency for East Timor by the Commander USPACOM, Admiral Denis Blair, in June 1999. The resulting plan included options for a US-only task force, and a coalition task force. This recollection of US planning is consistent with another well-placed interviewee and some press reporting of the time: see Paul Daley, 'Timor: We Snub Offer To Send In The Marines', *Sunday Age*, 1 August 1999, p. 1. However, this planning has been downplayed by some interviewees and described as the normal activities of military forces.

85   The conduct of Operation *Spitfire* (the evacuation) and Operation *Stabilise* (the deployment of INTERFET) is described in Bob Breen, *Mission Accomplished—East Timor*, Allen & Unwin, Crows Nest, NSW, 2000); and Alan Ryan, *Primary responsibilities and primary risks: Australian Defence Force participation in the International Force East Timor*, Land Warfare Studies Centre, Duntroon, Canberra, 2000, pp. 68–76.

present. This went some way in ensuring that information could be passed first-hand, and that different views were available at the meeting. Such representation was also important, according to ministerial adviser Aldo Borgu:

> So they could get a sense of what the minister was thinking on different issues, and I could report back to the minister in terms of the particular things and the logic behind the things they were looking at.[86]

Table 6: Selected Key Events for September October 1999

4 September	Polls return showing that 78.5 per cent reject 'autonomy' and so vote for independence. Violence intensifies and some evacuation flights begin.
5 September	Integrationists (pro-Jakarta militia) violently reject the ballot result; the Indonesian Government begins evacuation from East Timor.
6 September	ADF evacuation starts (called Operation Spitfire). UN Secretary-General Kofi Annan asks whether Australia would be willing to lead a multinational force to restore stability in East Timor, if invited by Indonesia.
7 September	Pro-Jakarta forces begin forced evacuations of East Timorese people to West Timor and nearby Indonesian islands.
9–12 September	The APEC meeting in Auckland is used to canvass international support for, and Indonesian acceptance of, an intervention into East Timor.
12 September	President B.J. Habibie agrees to the international force.
15 September	UNSC Resolution 1264 provides Chapter VII mandate for INTERFET.
20–27 September	INTERFET arrives in East Timor with an advance group of 2000 Australian, British and New Zealand troops. Onset of severe humanitarian crisis in East Timor.
21 September	The 'Taylor Committee' is established in Australia.
12 October	INTERFET deployment is complete
25 October	The United Nations establishes a mandate for United Nations Transition Administration in East Timor (UNTAET).

Defence's second response was to create two new policy groups to deal with the crisis. The first, known as the 'East Timor Policy Unit' (ETPU), was created to focus Defence's policy work into a dedicated organisation. Under the

---

86 Interview with Aldo Borgu.

circumstances, it made sense to pool expertise to deal with the increased volume of work. Centralisation near the senior decision-makers would also cut down on the time taken to deliver that advice and make the group more responsive:

> Basically, we needed our own mini-SPCG. We needed someone to pull all of this disparate stuff together, to ask some hard questions about things that had not been thought of, and provide a bit of focus. Asking desk people to do that on top of the day-to-day [is a little much]. So there comes a time when you have to say, 'hang on, this is not going to do it and I need someone full time on this'.[87]

Others pointed to the need to create a stronger basis for coordinating policy advice than could be achieved through the normal structure.[88] Not coincidentally, ETPU also provided a way of reducing the number of people in Defence who needed to know about the operation, and so helped to control leaks.[89]

It was also clear that such a group would need to sustain a high work tempo for a considerable period of time. In anticipation of this, Mike Scrafton was appointed to lead ETPU and Peter Jennings was appointed as his deputy on 7 September 1999. Both were promoted to First Assistant Secretary so the unit could operate on a 24 hour-a-day basis. Having an official of this rank available also meant there would be 'someone senior enough to be there to talk to senior people around the place at any point in time, and to make the right judgement calls'.[90] At its height, ETPU was a group of about 12 policy officers from various parts of the department, including the Defence Intelligence Organisation, International Policy, Strategic Policy, Defence Public Affairs and the uniformed services. ETPU's role was unclear at first, but it soon began to provide a new link between senior Defence management, other departments and the ministers' offices. Its role became clearer as the intervention approached and other whole-of-government mechanisms were established to manage the crisis, such as the 'Taylor Committee' (described below).[91]

---

87   Interview with Chris Barrie.
88   Interviews with Martin Brady; Canberra, 16 August 2005; 009-05, Canberra, 20 June 2005; and Michael Scrafton, Melbourne, 5 August 2005. Brady was Director, Defence Signals Directorate in 1999, and was acting Deputy Secretary Strategy in August–September 1999. Interviewee 009-05 is a former ministerial adviser and senior Defence official. Scrafton was Assistant Secretary Regional Engagement, Policy and Programs at the start of 1999. He became Acting Head International Policy in August 1999, and was appointed to head ETPU in September 1999. He was also Defence's representative on the Taylor Committee.
89   Interview with Chris Barrie.
90   Interview with Michael Scrafton.
91   Interviews with Michael Scrafton and Matthew Skoien.

The task of assembling a multinational military coalition was complex, sensitive and—given the pressing operational tasks that needed to be monitored—beyond the capacity of Defence's Strategic Command Division to manage according to Air Vice-Marshal Kerry Clarke:[92]

> The big thing that got our attention was having to form a coalition. We hadn't put anything into that and … [we] did not have the brain space to be able to do that … it was probably one of the biggest learning curves we had.[93]

As a result of this new need, the CDF created a second organisation within Strategic Command Division called INTERFET Branch to act as a 'strategic coalition manager'. Once again, the full range of tasks for INTERFET Branch were not immediately clear, nor was there established doctrine for how to manage this delicate process—but these shortfalls were quickly addressed in discussions between Defence and DFAT.[94]

The process to get a contribution actually deployed in East Timor was sometimes lengthy. At the start, INTERFET Branch provided advice about the forces needed so that DFAT and the ETPU could canvass possible contributors. Once interest was signalled by a government (or their embassy), INTERFET Branch provided operational information to military attachés through daily briefings.[95] If the relationship progressed to an in-principle agreement to contribute, the next step involved the branch and DFAT negotiating the role, size and deployment timings for the contingent. INTERFET Branch also conducted extensive liaison on behalf of contributing nations with other Strategic Command Division planners on logistic issues like personnel and health policy. Once a commitment was made, INTERFET Branch assumed management responsibility for the contribution from DFAT, and maintained a link with the representatives of troop-contributing nations in Australia throughout the operation. This also included working with Headquarters Australian Theatre to manage contingents during their pre-deployment training in Australia prior to their actual deployment to East Timor.

Defence's third response involved obtaining support for INTERFET through direct and indirect representations to regional governments.[96] One aspect of

---

92 The normal staff of Strategic Command Division was about 30–35 ADF officers (interview with Major General Michael Keating, who headed Strategic Command Division in Defence from May 1999).
93 Interview with Kerry Clarke.
94 Interviews with Brigadier Steve Ayling, Canberra, 14 April 2005; and Kerry Clarke. Ayling was Director General INTERFET Branch in 1999.
95 Ryan, *Primary responsibilities and primary risks: Australian Defence Force participation in the International Force East Timor*, pp. 60–61.
96 Interviewee 046-06 was also keen to point out DFAT's important contribution, especially that by Australia's regional ambassadors and their staff.

this effort involved sending the VCDF, Air Marshal Doug Riding, on a rapid tour of the region to solicit troop contributions for INTERFET. Building upon the discussions between Howard and regional leaders at the Auckland APEC Meeting, Riding and a team of three staff officers set out to conduct detailed discussions in Malaysia, Singapore, Thailand, the Philippines and Brunei. The visit started poorly when the Malaysian Government changed its mind about contributing to INTERFET and Singapore offered a much smaller group than anticipated.[97] The mission was not looking promising at that stage: as Matthew Skoien, then a policy officer in Defence recalled: 'We were batting 0 from 2, and we did not think the Thais were going to make a big contribution.'[98] However, an early promise from the Philippines Government and a positive decision by the Thai Government demonstrated regional support for INTERFET, and secured important military capabilities.[99]

Another aspect of supporting INTERFET involved the very practical issue of financial management. UN operations are often characterised by their torturous financial process, arguments over funding responsibilities and long waits for reimbursement.[100] Australia sought to short-circuit similar problems by agreeing to reimburse the costs of some contingents before the formal UN trust fund was in place, and underwrote death and disability compensation for some contingents. The use of Australian funds, and the capacity to absorb some costs in the short term, played an important role in reducing the risk to a few contributing nations and increasing their willingness to participate.[101]

---

97   Having just promised to increase the number of police and observers for UNAMET, Malaysian Defence Minister Abang Abu Bakar Mustapha was quoted as saying that Malaysia was ready to contribute forces to a peacekeeping force in East Timor (see Associated Press newswires, 'Report: Malaysia ready to send peacekeeping troops to East Timor', 6 September 1999). Some in Riding's party thought that Malaysia might make a sizable contribution (perhaps an infantry battalion and a command element) and were surprised when the decision to make only a token contribution was relayed to them by Malaysian officials—Interviews with 046-06 and Matthew Skoien (who accompanied Riding on the tour); and Ryan, *Primary responsibilities and primary risks: Australian Defence Force participation in the International Force East Timor*, p. 47.

98   Interview with Matthew Skoien.

99   Interviews with 046-06 and Matthew Skoien. The team cancelled the visit to Brunei because the Bruneian Government sent word of their decision not to commit troops beforehand. The Chief of Army, Lieutenant General Frank Hickling, also used a conference of Pacific Army commanders in Singapore on 5–8 September 1999 to develop a better understanding of regional perceptions of the issue and present Australia's views on East Timor.

100   For a summary of the main financial issues concerning UN peace operations, see J. Daudelin and L.J.M Seymour, 'Peace Operations Finance and the Political Economy of a Way Out', *International Peacekeeping*, vol. 9, no. 2, 2002, pp. 100–101.

101   Brigadier Steve Ayling and Sarah Guise, 'UNTAC and INTERFET—A Comparative Analysis', *Australian Defence Force Journal*, no. 150, 2001, p. 51; and Ryan, *Primary responsibilities and primary risks: Australian Defence Force participation in the International Force East Timor*, pp. 43–45. The issue of finance will be discussed in more detail during the 'Policy Instruments' phase.

The rapid increase in workload experienced at Defence was mirrored at the national level. The NSCC began meeting almost every day, with a sole focus on the crisis and emerging response. The effect of the frequency and high-level composition of these meetings will be discussed later in this study.

Despite the increased interaction with officials, the prime minister—probably on the recommendation of Max Moore-Wilton or Michael Thawley—directed Allan Taylor (a former deputy secretary in DPM&C and then Director-General of the Australian Secret Intelligence Service, ASIS) to form a new body to help coordinate national policy and report on policy development to the NSCC. This *ad hoc* body consisted of two components. The first comprised a small secretariat of middle-ranking (Executive Level 1 and 2 or their military equivalent) officials seconded from DFAT, Defence, Immigration, AusAID and DPM&C.[102] The second group contained more senior officials representing their departments and agencies at daily committee meetings.[103]

The decision to establish the Taylor Committee reflected the prime minister's desire to streamline policy advice and a level of concern about interdepartmental coordination. However, when interviewees were asked for explanations for the new committee, they offered a variety of responses. Some thought the NSCC wanted to ensure that neither Defence nor DFAT became the lead agency, fearing this would skew Australia's responses towards these department's favoured instruments. Others thought a new body was needed because DFAT lacked the authority to coordinate the other departments, and Defence lacked the capability to do so. Another thought the Taylor Committee was a way to refocus the government on the Indonesia relationship, and improve coordination between the Australian Government and the range of UN agencies now involved in East Timor. Others saw bureaucratic motives, and thought that Moore-Wilton recommended the new structure as a way of asserting DPM&C's leadership.[104] The Committee's secretariat assembled on 21 September 1999, the day after INTERFET began to deploy, and the full committee met for the first time on 27 September.[105]

---

102   The secretariat was also referred to as a 'task group', so the Taylor Committee was also known as the 'East Timor Task Group' by some.

103   Attendees at the interdepartmental meetings were generally at the First Assistant Secretary or Deputy Secretary level. This varied according to the department's role, size, and the level of interest shown by departments—Interviews with Michael Scrafton; 028-05, Canberra, 1 September 2005; and 033-05, Canberra, 29 September 2005—identity protected. Interviewee 028-05 is a DFAT official with direct knowledge of the East Timor case.

104   This range of opinions was discussed during interviews with Chris Barrie, Hugh White, Ashton Calvert, Allan Behm, Kerry Clarke, 020-05, Michael Keating, 028-05, 051-06, 052-06 and 014-05, Canberra, 5 July 2005. Interviewee 014-05 is a former senior government official with first-hand knowledge of the Taylor Committee.

105   The creation of the Taylor Committee was flamboyantly announced by Tim Wright and Paul Daley, 'PM sets up secret unit on Timor', *Age*, 22 October 1999, pp. A1–2.

The Taylor Committee had three important functions: reporting, policy analysis and coordination. In the first function, Taylor would attend NSCC meetings and provide reports about issues his committee had been working through. In the second function, members of the committee secretariat drafted answers or policy submissions from a 'whole-of-government' perspective based on the questions and issues raised by the NSCC. While some of these briefs related to national security, many concerned Australia's views on the basic structures and modes of East Timor's future government and institutions. Taylor was firmly of the view that the work produced by the group was his responsibility (that is, the recommendations were not necessarily a consensus view from the broader committee), and this gave the secretariat an ability to produce work that did not have to reflect departmental positions.[106] Lastly, the coordination function involved deconflicting, prioritising, monitoring and convincing departments to take the lead on specific issues. This function was performed in daily meetings where the departmental representatives would discuss the issues of the day and any papers being drafted by the secretariat.

The first four to six weeks after its establishment were hectic for the Taylor Committee—an experience reflected in the DFAT Crisis Centre,[107] INTERFET Branch, ETPU and among the wide range of officials involved from other departments and agencies. By late October, some of these people went back to their normal work, while others migrated to become the 'East Timor Desk' within their respective departments and agencies. These changes returned the government to a steady state for policymaking, and so represented the end of the crisis for Australia.

This chapter outlined the events of 1998–99 from the Australian Government's point of view and described how the policymaking system changed during this crisis. The next three chapters use the Australian Policy Cycle to structure an in-depth examination of how the system worked in 1999, and the degree to which this activity reflected the typical characteristics of Australian policymaking.

---

106 Interviews with 014-05, 028-05 and 033-05.
107 As the DFAT Crisis Centre was responsible for consular issues, it has not been examined in this case study.

Chapter 3
Initiating the Policy Cycle

Previous chapters introduced the concept of crisis policymaking, Australia's system for crisis policymaking and briefly outlined the East Timor crisis from the perspective of Australian policymakers. This chapter examines policymaking during this crisis through the first three phases of the policy cycle, where policy is initiated. Each section examines one phase—starting with issue identification, then moving to policy analysis and policy instruments. The subsequent discussion is organised by using the characteristics of policymaking identified in the Australian Policy Cycle to compare crisis policymaking with the 'typical' characteristics described by Peter Bridgman and Glyn Davis. Each section concludes with observations about that phase of the cycle, and how this phase's characteristics differed from the typical.

Issue Identification

The Issue Identification phase represents the nominal start of the Australian Policy Cycle. In this phase, 'issues are selected for attention from the myriad of matters pressed on government'[1] and the problem is defined for the later stages. This phase is therefore about determining which issues the government pays attention to, and how those issues are framed as they enter the latter phases of the policymaking process. Bridgman and Davis identify four characteristics of this phase:

- Issues come to political attention based on competitive agitation from domestic actors, such as political parties, donors, interest groups, parliament and media;

- Issues might be identified to the administrative level by other domestic agents, such as government policy specialists or the courts;[2]

---

1   Peter Bridgman and Glyn Davis, *The Australian Policy Handbook*, 3rd edn, Allen and Unwin, Sydney, 2004, p. 34.
2   Bridgman and Davis would hold that competitive agitation could also influence the administrative level, while other domestic sources (especially the courts) would have an influence on the political level. The two characteristics have been made exclusive and applied to the different levels in this paper because competitive agitation seemed to have little influence on the administrative level, and a number of important domestic sources—such as the courts—played no role in this case.

- Issues can be created by the influence of external sources, such as economic change, foreign state or non-state actors, technology, demographic shifts, or legal change; and

- Issues enter the political agenda once there is sufficient 'mass appeal' to demand political attention.[3]

These characteristics do not map directly to national security crises. The most important distinction is that between the dominant role of the national leadership, and the marginal role played by other domestic actors. Also, external actors become essential in national security crises where they become protagonists with significant resources or interests. Mass appeal plays a more ambiguous role in the Issue Identification phase, as political leaders can—and do—act in advance of public opinion.

Dominant core

The core of the Australian Government, represented by the prime minister, his national security ministers and their senior officials, were the dominant domestic actors involved in issue identification in this crisis. In most cases, this group—more so than other domestic actors such as Parliament, interest groups or the media—categorised events and determined their significance for the national interest. In one important instance, the action taken by part of this group to develop the 'Howard Letter' provided a catalyst for the eventual acute crisis in September 1999. This letter also (unintentionally) shaped the problem into one of rapid political change, and ultimately into a situation with significant potential for instability and violence.

East Timor was not, however, a new issue in 1998–99 and this led the dominant core to consider East Timor through the prism of the Australia-Indonesia relationship. The Department of Foreign Affairs and Trade (DFAT) noted the fundamental importance of this relationship in their white paper of mid-1997, and expressed the influence of East Timor in this way:

> Developments in East Timor will remain important in shaping Australian public attitudes towards Indonesia and Indonesia's standing internationally. ... While the overall administration of the Province is primarily a matter for the Indonesian Government to determine, the Australian Government considers that an improved human rights situation and a greater role in the administration of the Province for indigenous East Timorese would contribute to an overall resolution of the issue.[4]

---

3 Bridgman and Davis, *The Australian Policy Handbook*, pp. 34-39.
4 Department of Foreign Affairs and Trade, *In the National Interest—Australia's Foreign and Trade Policy White Paper*, Commonwealth of Australia, Canberra, 1997, p. 62.

As a primary policy document, this statement was a high-level call by Australia for the Indonesian Government to do something—for the good of the bilateral relationship—about the situation in East Timor. It is therefore unsurprising that the Australian Government would be very interested in developments that might lead to a resolution of what was described as a 'running sore' by some.[5]

The developments of mid-1998 were therefore viewed by DFAT as a chance to advance Australia's regional relationships, particularly that with Indonesia. In Ashton Calvert's words, the new space to discuss Timor that opened after Soeharto fell in May 1998 was a chance 'to put the [Australia-Indonesia] relationship on a more stable and business-like relationship than we had through those 23 years [since 1975]'.[6] In this sense, the events of mid-1998 were an opportunity and a risk for Australia.

Consequently, the National Security Committee of Cabinet (NSCC)'s interest increased during 1998, and Foreign Minister Alexander Downer took regular briefings from his senior officials and made several visits to Indonesia throughout 1998 and 1999.[7] This involvement, which James Cotton described as 'activism' and included a visit to Jakarta to promote dialogue with East Timorese leaders,[8] shaped the issue for Australian policymakers. More broadly, the desire of the newly re-elected Coalition government (as of October 1998) to start their second term with a positive initiative was also probably another important aspect of issue identification.[9]

Other departments and agencies were not as well prepared as DFAT to identify this issue. Some had a practical involvement in Timor—for example, the Australian Electoral Commission (AEC) had been preparing for involvement in East Timor as part of the support for the forthcoming (1999) Indonesian elections, while the Australian International Aid Agency (AusAID) had provided support to Red Cross activities in the province for some time. The Indonesia Section of AusAID was also busy gathering information about development indicators in East Timor

---

5   Perhaps the earliest description of East Timor as a 'running sore' was noted by Hamish McDonald, 'Timor: Fear of 'running sore', *Age*, 29 September 1975, p. 6.

6   Interview with Ashton Calvert.

7   The Prime Minister also called the Secretary of DFAT on a number of occasions to receive briefings on the situation in Indonesia (Interview with Ashton Calvert); and Don Greenlees and Robert Garran, *Deliverance: The Inside Story of East Timor's Fight for Freedom*, Allen and Unwin, Crows Nest, NSW, 2002, p. 83.

8   James Cotton, 'East Timor and Australia—Twenty-five years of the policy debate', in James Cotton (ed.), *East Timor and Australia*, Australian Defence Studies Centre/Australian Institute of International Affairs, Canberra, 2000, p. 12. Alexander Downer's efforts were described in an interview with Ashton Calvert; and in Department of Foreign Affairs and Trade, *East Timor in Transition 1998–2000: An Australian Policy Challenge*, Commonwealth of Australia, Canberra, 2001, pp. 44–51.

9   Greenlees and Garran, *Deliverance: The Inside Story of East Timor's Fight for Freedom*, pp. 84–85. Others, such as Interviewee 064-07, saw greater continuity in government policy throughout 1998 and suggest that opportunity, rather than the election, was the impetus behind the Howard Letter.

throughout 1999, which put the agency in a strong position to respond later.[10] In contrast, Defence and the Australian Federal Police (AFP) had not given much consideration to East Timor in terms of potential operations until early 1999.[11] Indeed, the East Timor issue did not become prominent for the AFP until the Bali summit of 27 April 1999 and the actual 5 May Agreement.[12]

New issues were often identified to the administrative level by policy statements and ministerial announcements, the actions of other departments, and the media. Policy statements are usually crafted within departments, either at the behest of the minister or as a departmental initiative (best described as 'policy-in-development'). When issues are raised in this way, departments are better able to manage the issues as they have the initiative and frequently have time to prepare their position. But when issues are raised unexpectedly, such as when media stories gain political significance, departments will be reactive. It will take time for them to work through the implications and align their policy messages.

The 'Howard Letter' was the most dramatic example of how challenging reactive policymaking can be. While starting as an initiative, Australia clearly lacked a fully-developed policy on how it would approach East Timor in mid-January 1999. As a result, departments such as Defence did not have any understanding of what the government might want from it when the surprise announcement about the letter was made. This gap gave other actors—such as the media and lobby groups—time to provide advice to government and launch criticism in an effort to shape the agenda.[13] The problems with this reactive posture continued to mar the government's preparations well into March 1999, which was shown in the way Defence's need for planning lead-time continued to run at cross purposes to DFAT's view of how to manage the relationship with Indonesia.[14]

Intelligence agencies also played a role in identifying issues, particularly when they provided information not available in the public domain. In this case, Australian intelligence agencies correctly identified Indonesian military support for pro-integration militias and provided 'detailed, accurate, relevant

---

10   Interviews with Steve Darvill and Scott Dawson, Canberra, 4 April 2006. Dawson was Assistant Director General East Asia Branch in AusAID from June 1999, with responsibility for East Timor. In the post-ballot period, he headed the AusAID Task Force that dealt with the immediate emergency response and then worked on the longer-term program for East Timor.

11   While Defence's policy paper of 1997 noted the difficulty created by the Indonesian military's role in internal security, and specifically mentioned East Timor as an example of the difficulty, the reference to East Timor was made in the broader context of defence cooperation, rather than potential future operations. See Department of Defence, *Australia's Strategic Policy*, Commonwealth of Australia, Canberra, 1997, p. 22.

12   Interview with Adrien Whiddett. The Bali Summit was a meeting between Prime Minister John Howard and President B.J. Habibie that discussed the situation in East Timor (see Chapter 4).

13   For example, see James Dunn, 'Righting our Past Wrongs', *Sydney Morning Herald*, 13 January 1999, p. 11; Paul Cleary, 'A policy that's a bit light on detail', *Sydney Morning Herald*, 13 January 1999, p. 7; and Australian Associated Press, 'East Timor committee asks Howard to take stronger stance', 26 January 1999.

14   The later section on policy instruments returns to this issue.

and timely reporting to policymakers'.[15] The influence of such reporting is demonstrated in the way intelligence about military activities and sponsorship of the pro-integration militia led directly to the government's decision to send the Doug Riding/Allan Behm delegation to Jakarta in June 1999.[16] But the possession of intelligence does compel the Australian Government to act. Indeed, this case shows a clear example where the government knew about the emergence of a disturbing factor, namely the increasing involvement of sections of the Indonesian Army (TNI) with militias after January 1999, but judged that overtly confronting this fact would place the entire consultation process in jeopardy, risked a direct confrontation with Indonesia's foreign minister, and risked compromising sensitive intelligence assets.[17]

Actors close to the dominant core, such as officials or ministerial staff, can identify issues in indirect ways when they release, or 'leak', sensitive information without authorisation to agents such as the media. A number of leaks were recorded throughout 1999, including disclosures about US policy views and military intentions, and TNI involvement in violence by pro-integration militia.[18] Some of the leaks involved classified reports from the Defence Intelligence Organisation (DIO) and cables from DFAT, which were subsequently circulated in media and academic circles. These reports lead to Opposition pressure on the government and a number of critical press reports about Australian policy throughout 1999 and into the next year.[19]

---

15   This opinion was expressed by a critic of the overall use of intelligence in policymaking. See Desmond Ball, 'Silent Witness: Australian Intelligence and East Timor', in Desmond Ball, James Dunn, Gerry van Klinken, David Bourchier, D. Kammen and Richard Tanter (eds), *Masters of Terror: Indonesia's Military and the Violence in East Timor in 1999*, Canberra Papers on Strategy and Defence no. 145, Strategic and Defence Studies Centre, The Australian National University, Canberra, 2002, p. 179. Interviews with the Hon. Daryl Williams, Canberra, 17 March 2007; and 048-06, Canberra, 5 June 2006, also mentioned the importance ministers placed upon intelligence. Williams was Attorney-General (a ministerial position in Australia) and a member for the NSCC from 1996–2003. Interviewee 048-06 is a former ministerial adviser.

16   Interviews with 046-06 and Allan Behm. See also Ball, 'Silent Witness: Australian Intelligence and East Timor', p. 252.

17   Ball, 'Silent Witness: Australian Intelligence and East Timor', pp. 246–49 cites three Defence Intelligence Organisation reports identifying TNI involvement with militias from January 1999 and predicting the consequences for security in East Timor. DFAT says Australia was concerned about the deteriorating security situation after late-1998, and it 'applied consistent pressure on Indonesia' (Department of Foreign Affairs and Trade, *East Timor in Transition 1998–2000: An Australian Policy Challenge*, pp. 61–62). According to Allan Behm, the Office of National Assessments (ONA) was against a direct approach to the TNI because it could compromise intelligence sources and methods (Behm interview).

18   Jason Brown, Assistant Secretary Security for the Department of Defence, advised Senate Estimates that 28 cases of unauthorised disclosure of information about the East Timor operation were being investigated as at 10 February 2000. See Senate Foreign Affairs, Defence and Trade Committee, *Consideration of Additional Estimates (Department of Foreign Affairs and Trade)*, 9 February 2000, p. 165.

19   A few examples include Paul Daley, 'Armed with information, now what?', *Age*, 29 May 1999, p. 4; John Lyons, 'The Secret East Timor Dossier', *Bulletin*, 12 October 1999; John Lyons, 'The Timor Truth Gap', *Bulletin*, 30 November 1999, pp. 24–32; and Laurie Brereton, MP, 'East Timor: Revelations on Four Corners', News Release, 15 February 2000.

When leaks occur, senior officials generally try to pre-empt further compromises by 'compartmentalising' information so that even fewer people know the complete details of a planned policy or operation. In this way, leaks make information gathering and consultation harder, as governments limit the search for data and question the integrity of sources or agencies considered close to the leak.

While the motivations of 'leakers' probably varied in 1999,[20] the unauthorised release of official information had important effects on policymaking during this crisis. For one, leaked information that contradicted government policy embarrassed the Government, and so undermined their position on different occasions.[21] Leaks also allowed critics to direct the agenda. In one example, Opposition foreign affairs spokesman Laurie Brereton used leaks published in the media to ask detailed questions of the Government which, in this case, caused Minister Downer to make a 'clarification' on 9 August concerning Australian contact with USPACOM.[22] The leaking of sensitive military, diplomatic and intelligence material during 1999 also placed pressure upon the Australian Government to answer questions about evolving situation, which may have increased the difficultly with developing plans or negotiating with the Indonesian and US Governments.[23] While there is no direct evidence that these leaks compromised intelligence sources and methods, it is possible that the potential targets of intelligence gathering took more precautions to protect themselves from Australian (and by implication, US) agencies.

Leaks also have a corrosive effect on relationships by causing investigations (with their attendant additional work) and reducing trust between and within

---

20   On the motivations of 'leakers' or 'truth tellers', see Lance Collins and Warren Reed, *Plunging Point: Intelligence Failures, Cover-ups and Consequences*, 4th Estate/Harper Collins, Sydney, 2005, Chapter 10; Greg Terrill, *Secrecy and Openness*, Melbourne University Press, South Carlton, 2000, pp. 222–227. Rodney Tiffen describes a variety of reasons for leaking, and mentions the matter of Merv Jenkins, a DIO official who tragically took his life after being questioned about releasing information to the American government about East Timor in 1999 ('Why Political Plumbers Fail – Hypocrisy and Hyperbole in Leak Control', 2005, available at <http://soc.kuleuven.be/io/ethics/paper/Paper%20WS2_pdf/Rodney%20Tiffen.pdf>, accessed 16 June 2009). For a practical angle on leak motivation, see Bruce Marcus, 'There's a leak in my firm', *The Marcus Letter*, (no date) available <http://www.marcusletter.com>, accessed 16 June 2009.

21   For instance, the impending publication of Paul Daley's story concerning US planning forced Foreign Minister Downer to make a late night clarification about his earlier denial of any knowledge about US intentions, See Hon. Alexander Downer, MP, 'Answers to Questions Without Notice – East Timor: Peacekeeping', *House of Representatives Official Hansard*, 9 August 1999, p. 8174.

22   Laurie Brereton, MP, 'East Timor: Peacekeeping', *House of Representatives Official Hansard*, 9 August 1999, p. 8098.

23   Some of the major stories of the period that relied upon sensitive information included Don Greenlees, 'Leak shows no E Timor troop cuts', *Australian*, 30 October 1998, p. 1; Paul Daley, 'Spy effort stepped up in Timor', *Age* (Melbourne), 20 March 1999; Mark Dodd, Peter Coleman-Adams and Hamish McDonald, 'Defence report warning of violence', *Sydney Morning Herald*, 24 April 1999, p. 1 and p. 9; Paul Daley, 'Timor: We snub offer to send in the Marines', *Sunday Age* (Melbourne), 31 August 1999; and Lyons, 'The Secret East Timor Dossier'.

different agencies.[24] Then Director DIO Frank Lewincamp noted: 'There were the times when we had huge debates about [an intelligence agency] passing us information that they got from the Americans—[it became a question of] whether we could be trusted or not'.[25] This view is critical to the effective operation of intelligence agencies, for it shows how leaks can have broader implications for cooperation and ultimately policymaking.

An examination of other domestic actors is needed before the claim for dominance of the core actors in government is supported. This point will be reviewed after the important role of external actors is considered.

Essential external actors

The available evidence points to the prominence of external actors and influences in both creating and then promoting East Timor as an issue for Australian policymakers in 1998–99. Some were macro-forces such as the Asian economic crisis and the emergence of humanitarian intervention as a factor in international relations. Other influences, such as the notion that Australia was now living within an 'arc of instability' and thoughts that the United States wanted its allies to do more in the wake of the Kosovo conflict, added to the broad range of reinforcing external drivers.[26] However, it remains difficult to identify the exact influence or importance of influences such as these for identifying issues for Australian policymaking, except insofar as they establish the context for events of the time.

It is much easier to establish the importance of proximate external actors and influences such as the attitudes and actions of the Indonesian Government, and the location of East Timor and its long history as an issue in Australia and internationally. One change had an unmistakable impact on what was to occur—the resignation of President Soeharto in May 1998 and the subsequent

---

24 Investigations over leaks continued for some time after the crisis. For example, the Defence Signals Directorate (DSD) was investigated after accusations they had organised foreign agencies to intercept conversations by Opposition MP Laurie Brereton—see Australian Associated Press, 'DSD boss denies spying on Brereton', *Sydney Morning Herald*, 1 May 2003, available at <http://www.smh.com.au/articles/2003/05/01/1051382039622.html>, accessed 27 June 2009; and Robert Hill, 'Blick Report into DSD and East Timor leak investigations', Minister of Defence Media Release 88/03, 10 July 2003, available at <http://www.minister.defence.gov.au/Hilltpl.cfm?CurrentId=2938>, accessed 28 April 2009.

25 Interview with Frank Lewincamp, Canberra, 4 July 2005. Lewincamp was Director DIO from 1998–2005.

26 On US attitudes towards alliances post-Kosovo, see Linda Kozaryn, 'US, NATO Allies Plan New, Improved Alliance', *American Forces Information Service*, 21 September 1999; Richard Haas, 'Kosovo: U.S. Policy at Crossroads', 10 December 1998, Brookings Institute, Washington, DC, available at <http://www.brookings.edu>, accessed 25 January 2006; and Strobe Talbot, who was quoted as saying 'Many Americans are saying: Never again should the United States have to fly the lion's share of the risky missions in a NATO operation and foot by far the biggest bill …' in Michaela Hertkorn, 'The relevance of perceptions in foreign policy: a German-U.S. perspective', *World Affairs*, vol. 162, no. 2, 2001, p. 62. The 'arc of instability' was an expression coined to describe Australia's fractious neighbourhood as it appeared in 1999. Its genesis is discussed in Robert Ayson, 'The "Arc of Instability" and Australia's Strategic Policy', *Australian Journal of International Affairs*, vol. 61, no. 2, 2007, pp. 217–21.

statements by President-designate B.J. Habibie about his willingness to reconsider East Timor's status within Indonesia.[27] While Howard began to shift ground on Australian support for Soeharto during the lead-up to the latter's resignation on 20 May, the Prime Minister had not made any public statements calling for a reconsideration of the East Timor issue to that point; indeed, calls by others to do so were explicitly rejected by government leaders.[28] It was not until 24 May that Downer broached the issue of change in East Timor, and Howard repeated that call a day later.[29] Further, it was not until after President Habibie made public comments about re-thinking the issue on 9 June 1998 that the Australian Government took active measures to support the policy change, including offering DFAT to facilitate intra-Timorese dialogue and survey East Timorese opinion about their future status.[30]

The main stumbling point to a better understanding of East Timor was the Indonesian Government's identification of this as a diplomatic issue. This perspective meant that it was more concerned about dealing with its problems through international negotiations and measuring its success in terms of foreign reactions, rather than focusing on the domestic aspects of the problem such as discontent among the East Timorese. Indonesia's acknowledgement of this point led to its acceptance of Australia's offer to canvass East Timorese opinion on the situation, although the differing perspective continued well into early 1999.[31] As such, external factors based around the political changes in Jakarta were instrumental to bringing this issue from 'watching brief' status to the fore of the Australian Government's agenda.

Australia was, however, still a long way from committing to a military operation in mid-1998. But once again, issues generated overseas—and particularly in East Timor—influenced the policy agenda throughout late-1998 and 1999. For example, the violence in Alas (a town in East Timor) and Jakarta in November 1998, and the stalling of the Tripartite Talks described above, were almost certainly on the government's mind as the Howard Letter was sent. Continuing

---

27   Howard also made use of the changed situation in Jakarta to call for 'movement by the Indonesians in relation to East Timor', in Rebecca Rose, 'Howard Urges Habibie To Act On East Timor', *West Australian*, 26 May 1998, p. 4.

28   Geoffrey Barker, 'Australia Bends To People Power', *Financial Review*, 16 May 1998, p. 25. However, Howard remained firm that the 'problem of East Timor' was best solved by using Australia's good standing to promote 'gradual change'. See Jeremy Cordeaux, 'Transcript of the Prime Minister, The Hon John Howard MP', Radio 5DN (Adelaide), 18 May 1998, available at <http://www.pm.gov.au>, accessed 12 February 2006.

29   See Department of Foreign Affairs and Trade, *East Timor in Transition 1998–2000: An Australian Policy Challenge*, p. 24; and Agence France-Presse, 'Australia urges Indonesia to tackle irritant of East Timor', 25 May 1998.

30   See Department of Foreign Affairs and Trade, *East Timor in Transition 1998–2000: An Australian Policy Challenge*, pp. 24–26.

31   A problem recognised by DFAT in an un-referenced cable mentioned in David Goldsworthy, 'East Timor,' in Goldsworthy and Peter Edwards (eds), *Facing north: a century of Australian engagement with Asia*, Melbourne University Press, Carlton, 2003, p. 225 and p. 232.

violence early in 1999, especially in Liquiçá and Dili was central to the Australian request for the Bali Summit in April. Even the 5 May Agreement itself, which had such a dramatic influence on Australian policy and action for the following few months, was only indirectly influenced by Australia. This influence was exercised by visits to the United Nations by the combined DFAT and Defence delegation, and by impressing the importance of issues such as security to UN interlocutors.[32]

The pattern whereby external actors were important for agenda setting continued right up to the deployment of the International Force in East Timor (INTERFET). While domestic actors exerted some pressure,[33] the Australian Government was more concerned about the Indonesian Government's views because its agreement was needed before action could be taken in East Timor. This agreement was essential because the Australian Government wanted to avoid provoking conflict with Indonesia, and for pragmatic reasons such as an inability to forcibly enter East Timor without undue risk. The Australian Government also identified the need to influence other UN members to support the consequent action, and was very mindful of US attitudes. However, once the external conditions were set by Indonesia's acquiescence, the UN mandate and US support for the mission, the Australian Government was able to harness the considerable domestic support for intervention.

Marginal domestic actors

Australian interest in East Timor's future was clearly driven by a number of sources, and competitive agitation from domestic actors featured among them. However, these sources were not the most important for determining Government policy in this case.

The issue had been given energy once again after agitation by the Opposition ALP's spokesperson, Laurie Brereton, in late 1997. This led to a consequent shift in the ALP's policy toward recognising the right of self-determination for the East Timorese in early 1998.[34] The impact of the ALP intervention

---

32 Interviews with 007-05 and Hugh White; and Department of Foreign Affairs and Trade, *East Timor in Transition 1998–2000: An Australian Policy Challenge*, pp. 72–75.

33 For examples of this pressure, see Alan Dupont and Anthony Bergin, 'UN Force Critical to Peace in East Timor', *Australian Financial Review*, 29 March 1999; Paul Robinson, 'Unions Plan Action On Timor Violence', *Age*, 3 May 1999, p. 6; Brian Toohey, 'PM's Dilemma on Timor Peace Force', *Sun Herald*, 1 August 1999, p. 49; and Sean Aylmer, 'Timor: Downer Says There's No Rift With US', *Australian Financial Review*, 2 August 1999, p. 7, which mentions the parliamentary pressure being applied by opposition spokesperson Laurie Brereton.

34 Scott McKenzie, 'Tough Line on Timor', *Herald-Sun*, 22 November 1997, p. 4; and Anthony Burke, 'Labor Could Be Set For A Backflip on East Timor', *Canberra Times*, 22 December 1997.

on government thinking is difficult to judge from the public record, but it is unlikely that government ministers would acknowledge this agitation as a factor in their ultimate actions.[35]

A number of groups in Australia were vociferous in their support for East Timorese independence throughout 1998 and 1999, including the Catholic Church, some ex-service groups, academics, students and non-governmental organisations (NGOs).[36] Their attempts to raise East Timor as a policy issue included representations to the Senate (see below), and even some protests involving low-level violence against the Australian prime minister and foreign minister during February–May 1998. These efforts were supported by strident calls from East Timorese emissary José Ramos Horta for greater Australian attention and aid, who'd campaigned frequently in Australia during the preceding decade.[37]

Local interest in East Timor increased after Habibie's June announcement on special autonomy, and again after the 'Balibo Five' issue re-surfaced in October 1998 (leading the government to re-open the Sherman Inquiry in November of that year).[38] In addition, the Australian Senate ran a public enquiry throughout 1998 and 1999 in an attempt to examine the social and political conditions in East Timor. As the crisis developed, this committee—along with meetings conducted as part of the Senate Estimates process—often quizzed officials about events and positions and heard testimony from a variety of (private) witnesses that contradicted government policy.[39]

---

35   Greenlees and Garran think Brereton's pressure—and the pressure of Gareth Evan's legacy—was felt by Downer, although they do not identify whether this was a direct influence (*Deliverance: The Inside Story of East Timor's Fight for Freedom*, pp. 80–81). Fernandes cites the ALP policy change as being 'a critical factor in the independence of East Timor' (Clinton Fernandes, *Reluctant Saviour: Australia, Indonesia and the independence of East Timor*, Scribe, Melbourne, 2004, p. 31). But given the centrality of Habibie's decisions to Australian action, and the complete surprise that accompanied the Howard letter, these attributions seem to overstate the influence of Australia's Opposition in this case.

36   Howard commented on the diversity of this coalition of interests that supported East Timor in Fran Kelly, 'John Howard on East Timor', *The Howard Years* (website), ABC Television (Australia), 2008, available at <http://www.abc.net.au/news/howardyears/>, (see Further Resources: Episode 2), accessed 27 June 2009. A good summary showing the variety of groups and individuals which agitated for East Timor's independence in 1998–99 can be found in Foreign Affairs Defence and Trade References Committee, *Final Report into the Inquiry into East Timor*, Senator John Hogg (Chair), Commonwealth of Australia, Canberra, 2000.

37   *Australian*, 'Timorese demand better effort', 2 April 1998, p. 7.

38   Alexander Downer, 'A Long Term Commitment: Australia And East Asia', Speech to the Indonesian Council on World Affairs and the Indonesia-Australia Business Council, Borobudur Hotel, Jakarta, 9 July 1998, available at <http://www.dfat.gov.au>, accessed 12 April 2006. This enquiry—the second conducted into the 1975 Balibo murders by Sherman—was sparked by a media report that interviewed a reported eyewitness to the atrocity. For that report, see Jonathon Holmes, 'East Timor—Balibo: A Special Report', *Foreign Correspondent*, ABC Television (Australia), 20 October 1998, available at <http://www.abc.net.au>, accessed 21 January 2006.

39   For example, transcripts of Senate Estimates from 2 December 1999 record departmental officials being questioned extensively about the effect of Barratt's sacking from the position of Defence Department Secretary, just prior to the East Timor operation (see Senate Foreign Affairs, Defence and Trade Committee, *Consideration of Budget Estimates: Supplementary Hearings (Defence Portfolio)*, 2 December 1999, available at <http://www.

These domestic groups had some influence on political leaders and public opinion about Indonesia, particularly in the way some disclosures forced the Government to respond to matters that it probably did not wish to address at the time. For instance, the revelation of Indonesian deceit about troop rotation, which was presented in documentary form by activist Andrew McNaughton, came around the same time as the Government was looking for a new initiative on East Timor, and as the Tripartite Talks were facing difficulties (see Chapter 2).[40]

But this agitation did not have a major impact on the Australian Government's policies towards East Timor in 1998. While Howard acknowledged the existence of Australian advocates for East Timor in one interview about this period, he seems to consider them more as a curiosity than a strong force that the Government needed to reckon with.[41] The lack of progress towards the objectives of some of these domestic actors—specifically those advocating for an end to Indonesian rule in East Timor or an end to Australian recognition of Indonesian sovereignty—also shows how the Australian Government put a higher priority upon supporting Soeharto and the crisis-affected Indonesian economy in early 1998 than for meeting the demands of domestic actors. Indeed, the Australian Government's record of political and practical support made it difficult for it to accede to any demand for a rethink on East Timor until the situation changed dramatically in May that year. Advocacy later in that year had some impact upon keeping the East Timor issue in the media, but on balance it was electoral timing, an appreciation of the new political circumstances in Indonesia and the evolving external situation (in regards to the Tripartite Talks) that seems most likely to have drawn the Government to take the major policy step of sending the 'Howard Letter'.

It is possible, however, to identify how an emerging consensus made it easier for the government to change policy toward East Timor and then act after the acute crisis occurred. Howard himself described this coalition of interests as 'fertile ground' to allow a new policy direction in late 1998.[42] Richard Woolcott also made an interesting point that a range of different groups—including

aph.gov.au>, accessed 2 December 2007, pp. 4–10). For an example of a private witness testimony, see William Fisher in Foreign Affairs, Defence and Trade References Committee, *Economic, social and political conditions in East Timor*, Hearing of 9 September 1999, available at <http://www.aph.gov.au>, accessed 6 December 2006, pp. 464–73.

40   As reported in Don Greenlees, 'Leak shows no E Timor troop cuts', Australian, 30 October 1998, p. 1. See also Sonny Inbaraj, 'East Timor: Disclosure on Troops Mocks Jakarta's Credibility', 3 November 1998, available at <http://www.etan.org/et/1998/november/1-7/03disclos.htm>, accessed 27 June 2009.

41   Howard mentions this coalition of interests twice in an edited interview for the ABC Television documentary, *The Howard Years*, noting that there 'always had been' a 'lively constituency' for change in Australia's policy regarding East Timor. Given Howard's renowned 'nose' for public opinion, it would be remarkable if he did not know about these groups and their concerns and opinions (Fran Kelly, 'John Howard on East Timor').

42   Fran Kelly, 'John Howard on East Timor'.

the Labor left, Catholic groups and the One Nation party—who generally opposed the government's foreign policy were supportive of the Government's emerging populist-nationalist line on East Timor.[43] When this support was added to mainstream (and sometimes nationalistic) opinion that favoured action to halt the post-ballot violence, a strongly supportive media and bipartisan parliamentary support, competitive agitation largely disappeared as a factor in issue identification. As a result, the government found itself with fewer constraints and some room for manoeuvre when the decision was made by the international community to intervene towards the end of September 1999.

Mass appeal

Just as most domestic actors had only a marginal influence on issue identification, the mass appeal of the Timor issue in both the domestic and international spheres was patchy until September 1999. But when the public (and the various interest groups described above) came to be fully behind intervention, mass appeal supported and enabled the Australian Government's policy preferences.

While Indonesia's actions in East Timor after 1975 had been debated and condemned by some sections of the Australian community, East Timor's status remained an obscure issue for the Australian public until the Santa Cruz massacre of November 1991.[44] One explanation for its lack of prominence was that successive Australian Governments tried to separate East Timor from the broader Indonesia relationship.[45] While violence and other acute events resuscitated the issue from time to time, the ensuing protest or discussion occurred without East Timor becoming a mainstream political issue in Australia.[46]

Pressure mounted on the Australian Government throughout 1999, and there were times when it had to act, despite its preferences. For example, the decision

---

43   Richard Woolcott, 'The consequences of the crisis over East Timor', in Bruce Brown (ed.), *East Timor— The Consequences*, New Zealand Institute of International Affairs, Wellington, 2000, p. 28. Woolcott was a former Secretary of DFAT and Ambassador to Indonesia. Interviewee 048-06 described this convergence of opinion as 'incredibly ironic' given the usual 'left wing' opposition to the use of military force.

44   It is difficult to register the place of East Timor in Australian public consciousness. Moreen Dee, for instance, thinks the East Timor issue was 'generally unregarded' until 1991 and the Santa Cruz (or Dili) massacre, where the TNI killed at least 250 people. Further, it is difficult to judge whether this incident had a lasting impact on popular consciousness—see Moreen Dee, '"Coalitions of the Willing" and Humanitarian Intervention: Australia's Involvement with INTERFET', *International Peacekeeping*, vol. 8, no. 3, 2001, p. 3. One indicator may be the way perceptions of the 'Indonesian threat' among Australians changed after major events in East Timor. As McAllister showed, the perception of Indonesia as a threat rose after its 1975 invasion of East Timor and again after Santa Cruz (to around three in ten). In both instances, the threat had been relatively low for the period before the event. See Ian McAllister, *Attitude Matters: Public opinion in Australia towards defence and security*, Australian Strategic Policy Institute, Canberra, 2004, Figure 5, p. 20.

45   Nancy Viviani, 'Australia Indonesia Relations—Past, Present and Future', *Senate Foreign Affairs, Defence and Trade References Committee, Additional Information, vol. 2*, Commonwealth of Australia, Canberra, 1999, p. 3.

46   McAllister, *Attitude Matters: Public opinion in Australia towards defence and security*, p. 10.

to break military ties with the TNI, largely because of suspected KOPASSUS[47] involvement with the militias, was not supported by the Department of Defence according to Aldo Borgu:

> But it was literally a government-directed edict. I can remember ... others [in Defence] trying to argue that we should not go down that path, but [John] Moore's office, the Prime Minister's Office and to an extent [Foreign Minister] Downer realised that we had to go along with it because the wider Australian public just would not stand for maintaining that relationship—and there was also a need to send a message to the Indonesians as well.[48]

While other calls were made to intervene, the government resisted these until its conditions for military action were satisfied.[49] Interviewee 052-06 said this was a close-run thing:

> It appeared as if Indonesia was becoming unacceptable to the Australian people as a governing force in East Timor, so I think politically the pressure was on the government to ensure that the government was registering its concerns with the Indonesians, showing that it had a plan to deal with the issue, and I think that when one sees violence on the streets then that has a negative impact on the government.[50]

In this case, the public's 'sense of collective morality, justice or responsibility'[51] saw a great number of people take interest in the issue after the September violence, and around 90 per cent of Australians eventually either supported or strongly supported the intervention.[52] This high level of support meant that the government was not constrained in pursuing its preferences, and was able to point to significant public backing to justify its actions. This was important later, when the government floated the 'Timor Tax' to raise money to pay for the intervention force.[53]

---

47 KOPASSUS—*Komando Pasukan Khusus* (Indonesian Special Forces Command).
48 Interview with Aldo Borgu. See also Australian Associated Press, 'Moore defends joint military ops with Indonesia', 28 March 1999.
49 For a sample of the pressure from international NGO, see Sidney Jones, 'East Timor: Stop the Violence', *Human Rights News*, 6 July 1999.
50 Interview with 052-06.
51 One Roy Morgan poll described the East Timor situation as the 'dominant issue' of September 1999 (Roy Morgan Research, *L-NP Draws Closer On Primary Vote As ALP Support Eases*, Finding No 3228, 28 September 1999, available at <http://www.roymorgan.com>, accessed 26 August 2006). See also Allan Gyngell and Michael Wesley, *Making Australian Foreign Policy*, Cambridge University Press, Cambridge, 2003, p. 193.
52 This data was taken from a poll of 1164 people in 2000 (see McAllister, *Attitude Matters: Public opinion in Australia towards defence and security*, Table 6, p. 24).
53 Under this proposal, Australians earning over A$50 000 would pay an additional 0.5 per cent levy to help fund the intervention. See Reuters News, 'Howard would consider one-off tax for Timor troops', 28 October 1999; and Agence France-Presse, 'Affluent Aussies to fund peacekeeping in East Timor',

It is difficult to attribute the government's policy actions solely to public opinion. As Interviewee 064-06 remarked:

> Sure public opinion was significant in that made it a big political issue, but that was not what was driving them [the Cabinet] … they all thought, this is an outrage, particularly since Australia had invested the amount of money and diplomatic capital and personnel in this process. To see these thugs go in there, and to see the military stand aside and let it happen, I think people [in the Cabinet] were genuinely really disgusted … [so] how do you separate public opinion from the outrage of people in Cabinet?[54]

While domestic public opinion might be important, there is also a case to be made for the effect of international opinion and its influence on events and government options. When asked about this, Ashton Calvert thought that the 'lack of an appetite' for earlier action among the international community was another important influence on events:

> And why was it possible to have INTERFET after the vote and after the violence and why it wasn't possible to have it before? … Simply because international opinion was so appalled at the spectacle of what was unfolding after there had been a vote. … The mood in Australia would not have been sufficient by itself. It was the broader international focus, the media and in the bigger countries like the United Sates and the bigger countries of Europe, demanding that something had to be done.[55]

Regardless of the actual effect or where the weight of opinion is generated, at least one political leader acknowledged that informed public opinion is difficult to ignore in a crisis:

> Nowadays there can be mass sentiment about human rights abuses anywhere in the world because of information technology. And you know the communities of the world demand that action be taken against cruelty, against human abuse. And governments have to work out ways of doing that and my point is that in the case of East Timor we did find a way of doing so.[56]

---

23 November 1999. Although there was little if any public disagreement with the measure, the Government never implemented it.

54 Interview with 064-07. Ashton Calvert also noted public pressure in September 1999, but said the Australian Government remained focused on getting policy 'on a better basis'.

55 Interview with Ashton Calvert.

56 Alexander Downer, 'International Crisis Resolution: The Example of East Timor', Oxford, 26 January 2000, available at <http://www.dfat.gov.au>, accessed 23 January 2006.

So while political leaders might promote an issue when popular support is ambivalent or divided, or bury an issue when it runs against their preferred course of action, it is difficult to ignore mass appeal if it arises. That the mass appeal of the East Timor issue suited the government's preferred course of action was undoubtedly a factor that gave the government significant room to move in September 1999.

Observations about Issue Identification

The Issue Identification phase in national security crises had some very different characteristics from those proposed by Bridgman and Davis. In this case, the Prime Minister, his NSCC ministers, and a few very senior officials—including the Secretary of the Department of Prime Minister and Cabinet (DPM&C), the Prime Minister's International Adviser Michael Thawley, Allan Taylor and some senior DPM&C, Defence, ONA and DFAT officials—played dominant roles by channelling information and identifying policy issues for the government. As a consequence, domestic lobby or interest groups had little real influence on the government despite their efforts through the media, parliamentary inquiries and individual approaches.

External actors were more important than these marginal domestic actors for identifying issues in this case: whether foreign governments, international institutions or (to some extent) nebulous international opinion, these actors created numerous issues for Australian policymakers throughout the year. In one sense, international actors have some similarities with domestic lobby groups: they can change their minds quickly, get caught in their own internal politics and influence some people. Unlike domestic lobby groups, external actors may have significantly more military, diplomatic and financial resources available to them. Some of them also have the potential to deploy these resources quickly to protect or advance their interests. This highlights national security policy as a multi-actor international phenomenon, where the actions of one have consequent effects on others.

The general public's influence upon the Issue Identification phase is more difficult to place. On one hand, the East Timor issue failed, over a long period, to gain 'mass appeal'; it was not even an issue in the Australian federal election of October 1998.[57] While mass appeal grew in September 1999, it is likely that the government would have acted in much the same way without that massive level of support—except perhaps in the way they announced the 'Timor Tax'. While the government's course was no means unalterable, the planning and discussions underway with the United Nations and the United States since

---

57 For example, East Timor was not mentioned in an analysis of voter issues by Roy Morgan Research, 'The Mood of the People & the Election—Listen Carefully', Finding No 1001, 1 September 1998, available at <http://www.roymorgan.com>, accessed 14 February 2006.

February (and especially March) 1999, and official statements about East Timor that year, allow one to infer that the Australian Government was committed to some kind of intervention before the public demanded it. As a result, this situation would have been very interesting had 'mass appeal' run against the government's preferred policy line, or if the Indonesian Government had not acceded to the intervention force in September 1999.

This evidence allows the 'typical' characteristics of the Issue Identification phase to be modified for crisis policymaking:

- The prime minister, his national security ministers and their senior officials are the dominant domestic actors in issue identification and, by extension, problem definition;

- Foreign actors and events (especially governments) have the ability to place issues on the crisis policy agenda when they intend to harm Australian interests, when the interests of Australia's allies and friends are threatened, and when high levels of interdependence mean that threats to others' interests are viewed as threats to Australia;

- Other domestic actors have a limited ability to identify issues in a crisis; and

- Mass appeal plays a limited role in issue identification.

Policy Analysis

The second phase of the policy cycle involves analysis of the policy issue, which is defined by Bridgman and Davis as using research and logic to develop options for decision-makers.[58] The Policy Analysis phase has five main characteristics in their model:

- A 'rational comprehensive' analytical method is sought, but it may be accompanied by the 'extrarational factors' of judgement, experience and intuition;

- While policy experts (including bureaucrats and ministerial staff) may still dominate, ministers use an increasing range of non-government sources for analysis;

- The process is iterative because information is incomplete, people disagree over objectives and parameters shift;

---

58   Bridgman and Davis, *The Australian Policy Handbook*, p. 47.

- Policy is analysed according to the dominant 'framework' of the policy area; and

- Policy is presented as options for decision-makers.[59]

This phase is about the way policymakers define, evaluate and then present alternative courses of action to the decision-makers in Cabinet. While crisis policymaking shows certain similarities with the model, there are some differences, including a greater role for extrarational factors in crises and little to support any significant role for 'outside experts'.

Anything but a rational-comprehensive method

Policy departments are generally structured and organised to perform policy analysis in a rational and comprehensive manner. This is particularly evident in Defence, where a structured policymaking process starts from top-level policy documents such as white papers, and ends with decisions to buy equipment, develop different kinds of combat units or execute military operations.[60] Despite acknowledging this 'ideal', Bridgman and Davis believe strictly rational policy analysis is rare because it is difficult to achieve agreement on the aims and to develop a clear understanding of the means available.[61] The East Timor case confirms the tenuous position of the rational-comprehensive method, and shows how analysis is influenced by a range of extra-rational means when policymakers are dealing with a crisis and are hampered by shifting national objectives.

Most of the major policy analysis in the East Timor case was conducted by small groups of very senior officials and a few working groups or task forces that formed just for this crisis. The influence of small groups of senior officials was clearly seen in the production of the Howard Letter. In this instance, only about 10 people had knowledge of the letter or input into its contents.[62] While this policy was developed and implemented with speed and secrecy, the full

---

59   Bridgman and Davis, *The Australian Policy Handbook*, pp. 47–57.

60   Defence produced a new white paper immediately after the East Timor crisis, published as Department of Defence, *Defence 2000—Our Future Defence Force*, Commonwealth of Australia, Canberra, 2000. The most recent white paper is Department of Defence, *Defending Australia in the Asia-Pacific Century: Force 2030*, Commonwealth of Australia, Canberra, 2009. In between these documents, the Australian Government frequently reviewed defence policy though documents such as Department of Defence, *Australia's National Security: A Defence Update 2007*, Commonwealth of Australia, Canberra, 2007. Defence's contemporary, structured policymaking process is described in Department of Defence, *Strategy Planning Framework Handbook*, Defence Publishing Service, Canberra, 2006.

61   Bridgman and Davis, *The Australian Policy Handbook*, pp. 48–49.

62   See above in Chapter 2, pp. 18–19. It is important to note that the overall policy direction toward East Timor was canvassed among a wider group of officials in mid-1998. However, the entire group was not directly consulted on the actual detail of the subsequent letter to President B.J. Habibie (Interview with Hugh White), and Defence was not permitted to produce papers on East Timor around this time without the express permission of its minister (Interview with Paul Barratt).

range of consequences was not anticipated. As a result, the implications for the full range of policy instruments—particularly for the Australian Defence Force (ADF)—were not canvassed before the letter was sent.[63]

Other small groups of more junior officials had important roles in managing the crisis (as outlined in Chapters 1 and 2), and most of these were formed and structured to promote rational-comprehensive consideration. Thus Defence's East Timor Working Group and the Department of Prime Minister and Cabinet's (DPM&C) Paterson Committee were designed to ensure that expertise and information could be pooled from all the major stakeholders, and work could be conducted under the auspices of different authorities. For example, Defence's working group met frequently up until the 30 August ballot (noticeably, with shorter meeting durations as time went on), and these helped to work through different opinions among agencies.[64] However, these meetings were also mainly information exchanges and tasking opportunities rather than policy discussions.[65]

Despite these structural attempts to unify analysis, policymaking could scarcely be described as comprehensive or rational in that it followed known or repeatable processes toward agreed objectives. Hugh White described policy analysis during the crisis in this way:

> I think you would have to say that it was not a rational process that started with a clear set of objectives and then took an orderly set of steps towards achieving those objectives. It was a process that aimed to manage the consequences of events as they broke over us, with a very broad sense of a few long-term preferences ... so I don't think it was a structured or formal policy process, nor was it a tightly documented process either. There is no doubt about that..[66]

More junior officials working within Defence and DFAT confirmed this view:

> My sense was the decision-making and reaction to the announcement was made between individuals at high levels, and that a lot of us in policy development and planning were pretty much playing catch-up. We were pretty much in the dark. In the first few weeks after the

---

63 Interviews with John Moore, Chris Barrie, Paul Barratt, Hugh White and Allan Behm.
64 Interview with 035-05.
65 Interview with Andrew Hughes, who had direct involvement in AFP planning for UNAMET. Hughes described how some operational issues were discussed openly and forcefully in interdepartmental meetings around September 1999.
66 Interview with Hugh White.

[Howard] Letter, we provided advice on some of the planning issues and implications, but the actual policy decisions that lay behind were made hurriedly, in corridors and by telephone calls among key people.[67]

... but I got this sense throughout, certainly over at DFAT, that we were never working to a grand strategic plan or meeting grand strategic objectives, other than general stability in the region—which is an overriding objective—and facilitating the process with least cost to Australia.[68]

A major main reason why policy analysis unfolded in this way was the continued change in Australia's strategic objectives throughout the crisis. As Table 7 shows, Australia's strategic objectives around this crisis went through numerous iterations in 1998 and 1999, to the point where none of the four main objectives from December 1998 and March 1999 had been achieved by September 1999. While most interviewees referred to the relationship with Indonesia, including Australia's overriding interest in avoiding conflict and ensuring Indonesia's stability and transition to a democracy as priority objectives throughout the year, other objectives changed throughout.[69] Those changes were not peripheral. They included, for example, a change in the desired future status of East Timor from autonomy within Indonesia (held until at least June 1999) to 'painless divorce' by September. They also changed from not wanting to involve the ADF in operations in Indonesian territory, to leadership of an international coalition. In other words, the objectives for policy analysis—the bedrock of the rational-comprehensive approach—evolved until the Australian Government adopted the emerging reality of an independent East Timor as its policy objective.

Policymakers were also under significant time pressure at different points during the crisis. For example, issues would sometimes be raised in the NSCC for decision that day. There was simply no time to go through formal processes or to seek other opinions. NSCC members and officials applied what they knew of their objectives in a largely intuitive way to the new situation to produce a decision.[70]

In some instances, the range of inputs for policy analysis might have been deliberately restricted for tactical reasons. White noted that warning of the Howard Letter might have jeopardised the process, either by giving Indonesia

---

67   Interview with Matt Skoien.
68   Interview with 062-07.
69   This view of Australia's interests was supported in interviews with Hugh White; Interviewee 024-05; Aldo Borgu; and Interviewee 032-05, by telephone, 29 September 2005, identity protected. Another who supported this view was Woolcott, p. 29. A number of other interests were also mentioned during interviews, including the desire to avoid refugee flows from East Timor and Indonesia, and the importance of perceptions of Australian leadership credentials in the region.
70   Interviews with Hugh White and Paul Barratt.

time to refuse the initiative or by giving critics enough time to rally potential opposition. William Maley and Lansell Taudevin also point to this issue, but they ascribe it to a view that the officials involved in policy analysis do not want to listen to dissenting views.[71] The desire to maintain secrecy by using a compartmentalised planning process also restricts the number of people involved in policy analysis. This control became more pronounced after policy and intelligence information leaked in mid-1999.

Table 7: Australia's Strategic Objectives — March to September 1999

Date	Objectives	Sources
December 1998	'It might be worth considering, therefore, a means of addressing the East Timorese desire for an act of self-determination in a manner which avoids an early and final decision on the future status of the province. One way of doing this would be to build into the autonomy package a review mechanism along the lines of the Matignon Accords in New Caledonia ... The successful implementation of an autonomy package with a built-in review mechanism would allow time to convince the East Timorese of the benefits of autonomy within the Indonesian Republic.'	'Howard Letter' (see Appendix 1)
March 1999	• East Timor would remain a part of Indonesia. • East Timor does not disrupt Australian-Indonesian relations. • East Timor does not disrupt ADF-TNI relations. • Australia does not have large parts of the ADF deployed in East Timor.	Interview with Hugh White
March 1999	• Seek engagement with Indonesia to develop a sense of shared strategic interest. • Enhance Indonesia's self-defence capabilities and interoperability between the ADF and TNI in key areas. In relation to an 'independent' Timor: • For East Timor not to develop close military ties with a country hostile to Australia. • For East Timor not to disrupt the territorial integrity of Indonesia	Department of Defence (a)

---

71   See William Maley, 'Australia and the East Timor Crisis: Some Critical Comments', *Australian Journal of International Affairs*, vol. 54, no. 2, 2000, p. 159; and Lansell Taudevin, *East Timor: Too Little Too Late*, Duffy and Snellgrove, Sydney, 1999, pp. 247–50.

March 1999	• Continued recognition of Indonesian sovereignty over East Timor. • Support for close involvement of the people of East Timor in decisions about their future. • Support for an act of self-determination ... preferably following a long period of autonomy, while accepting the possibility of independence. • Reconciliation among East Timorese. • Support for a peaceful and orderly transition. • Support for the long-term development of East Timor.	DFAT (b)
1 August 1999	'It makes sense for us to be neutral and let the people of East Timor make up their own minds without us influencing them.'	Interview with Alexander Downer (c)
20 September 1999	• Restore peace and security • Protect the United Nations mission and enable it to carry out its functions • Facilitate the delivery of humanitarian assistance	Deputy Prime Minister John Anderson (d)
September 1999	'The military had to get in, deliver the Security Council Resolution, get out and get a UN blue helmet operation in ... The other objective was to minimise the regional damage from leading a regional coalition [into East Timor].'	Interview with Michael Scrafton
September 1999	• 'Don't go to war with Indonesia.' • 'Try to undertake this in a way that keeps relations with Jakarta on an even keel.' • '[Lead] the operation, at least in the early phases, but not in a high profile or public way [and] not get people killed.'	Interview with 009-05
August–September 1999	'Ensure a painless divorce.'	Interview with 032-05

Sources: (a) Department of Defence, 'Department of Defence Submission', *Senate Foreign Affairs, Defence and Trade References Committee, Additional Information, Volume 5*, Commonwealth of Australia, Canberra, 1999, p. 111; (b) Department of Foreign Affairs and Trade, *Submission*, p. 046; (c) L. Murdoch, 'We're Neutral On Timor: Downer', *Sun Herald* (Melbourne), 1 August 1999, p. 35.); and (d) Mr John Anderson MP, 'East Timor: Peacekeeping', *House of Representatives Official Hansard*, 20 September 1999, p. 9925.

Judgement, or having a sense of the issues, was mentioned by a number of interviewees:

> In these situations you just have to make a judgement about what the appropriate way is ...[72]

---

72   Interview with 048-06.

> There was a sense in which to some people, I think Habibie himself and some of his advisers, they were sort of weary of East Timor ...[73]

> The first is that very early on, they had a sense this was getting out of control.[74]

While these quotes are given in different contexts about different aspects of the case, they demonstrate the importance of *coup d'oeil*—the 'inward eye' or intuition[75]—that senior leaders reputedly use to come to quick judgements about complex situations. White described the approach to analysis in a slightly different way:

> It [analysis] was much less formalised that the equivalent military deliberate planning process, where someone writes down the aim, situation and the constraints and the rest of it. There is a bit of a cultural point there. That's not the way a civilian policy culture tends to work.[76]

While decision-making will be discussed in Chapter 5, these examples show the importance of the extra-rational factors of experience, intuition and individual critical skills in policy analysis.

While forgoing a rational-comprehensive analytical process may have advantages in terms of speed and security, less-thorough analytical processes can have less than satisfactory consequences. For instance, the process for developing the Howard Letter shows how implications can be overlooked; while the ability to influence the 5 May Agreement was criticised as a missed opportunity to shape policy in Australia's favour. White recalled:

> We also failed to recognise—which we would have if we had run through a more formal policy process—that the critical pressure point ... [was] the negotiations in New York that led to the Tripartite Agreement. The fact that we failed to make any significant attempt to make an impact on those negotiations beyond the conversations we had with Vendrell when he was here in March meant that the opportunity to press for a full-scale military peacekeeping operation in the pre-popular consultation was lost, and it was lost by the lack of an appreciation that such a force was strongly in Australia's interests. That was a position we ended up pushing, but we failed to recognise that soon enough or recognise what to do to bring it about soon enough.[77]

---

73   Interview with Ashton Calvert.
74   Interview with Hugh White.
75   This concept is drawn from Clausewitz's writings about military genius (Carl von Clausewitz, *On War*, trans Michael Howard and Peter Paret, Princeton University Press, Princeton, 1976, pp. 102–103).
76   Interview with Hugh White.
77   Interview with Hugh White. Others would disagree and argue that Australia was formally excluded from the Tripartite process and had been asking the Indonesians to accept international help to maintain security

An iterative process

Policymaking in this crisis tended to follow an iterative process. In this case, the main issues for iteration included the government's position on the future status of East Timor and the ADF's prospective roles in the event of a military commitment.

As Table 7 shows (above), the government's preferred position on the future status of East Timor started as 'an act of self-determination in a manner which avoids an early and final decision on the future status of the province' in December 1998.[78] By March 1999 this preferred status had been modified to 'support for an act of self-determination ... preferably following a long period of autonomy, while accepting the possibility of independence'.[79] By late September 1999, the preferred outcome had become a highly pragmatic 'painless divorce'.[80]

The changes in national objectives had a significant impact on Defence and the ADF. In January, when the mission was still unclear, the ADF produced a discussion paper covering a broad range of military options to explain the types of forces that could be assembled, their broad military capabilities (from peace monitoring to combat operations), and the indicative cost of each option. Political direction soon settled on a mid-range option, where the intervention would take the form of a services-assisted evacuation—a mission of short duration that involves only a minimum level of offensive combat capability. With this tasking, Defence increased the readiness of 1st Australian Brigade for peace operations and leased a fast catamaran (named the HMAS *Jervis Bay* once in service) to provide additional troop-lift and cover the planned maintenance for HMAS *Tobruk*.[81] However, after the violence of early September and firming of the US position against taking a leadership role, the assumed commitment of providing 2000 troops to an international mission or even fewer to an evacuation grew to over 5000 troops, and included the new and unexpected role of leading that coalition.[82]

These two instances show that the ability of strategic objectives to change and the importance of external factors in national security policymaking make an

---

during the ballot since January (Interview with Ashton Calvert). Francesc Vendrell was the Director, Asia and the Pacific Division, UN Department of Political Affairs.

78   See the Howard Letter in Department of Foreign Affairs and Trade, *East Timor in Transition 1998–2000: An Australian Policy Challenge*, p. 182 (reproduced as an appendix below).

79   Department of Foreign Affairs and Trade and AusAID, 'Submission to the Senate Foreign Affairs, Defence and Trade References Committee Inquiry into East Timor', *Senate Foreign Affairs, Defence and Trade References Committee, Additional Information, vol.* 5, Commonwealth of Australia, Canberra, 1999, p. 046.

80   Interview with 032-05.

81   Interviews with 035-05 and Bob Treloar, who led ADF operational planning in 1999.

82   Greenless and Garran, *Deliverance: The Inside Story of East Timor's Fight for Freedom*, p. 239. The figure of 2000 troops was given by Defence Minister John Moore, and quoted in Jane Nelson, 'Australia ready to go to Timor without US', *Reuters News*, 9 September 1999.

iterative process almost mandatory. Events that create surprise, such as Habibie's offer of a referendum, introduce new dimensions that make a review of previous decisions necessary. On the military side, the continuing deterioration of the security situation and the changing nature of the task meant that Defence had to create new planning organisations, and the ADF had to bring additional units to operational readiness. The broader international interest in events (especially in September 1999) meant that DFAT and Defence had to conduct more careful consultation with potential coalition partners in a very short period.

Policy insiders dominate ... period

This case shows how crisis policymaking is dominated by internal policy experts—with expertise being largely defined by one's official role. As the preceding section noted, only a small number of people were closely involved in policymaking: namely ministers and their advisers, appointed career officials drawn from the main national security policy departments, senior officials of agencies with immediate involvement as policy instruments (such as the AFP and AEC), and the intelligence community. Although external parties attempted to influence decisions (as noted in the section on Issue Identification), this had minimal impact. One such example was noted by Maley, who lamented his failed attempt to convince DFAT officials about the need for preparations for the 'worst case'.[83] Another example was an attempt by the Centre for Democratic Institutions to identify the main issues concerning the forthcoming ballot. This workshop had official involvement, but it seems little emphasis was placed on getting information from it.[84] These examples show how domestic groups or individuals outside government have difficulty when trying to influence the Policy Analysis phase in crises.

Nor does every department and agency get to play equally in the Policy Analysis phase for national security issues. It is possible to identify four groups in this case, although there was some flexibility in this taxonomy. The first was the policy-driving group consisting of DFAT and Defence, where the former was first among equals. These departments used key committees such as the NSCC and the Strategic Policy Coordination Group (SPCG), and their authority over policy submissions, to control the major bureaucratic initiatives in 1999.

The second group consisted of advice agencies such as AFP, AEC and AusAID. Each group was widely consulted on the details of its involvement, but generally

---

83   Maley, 'Australia and the East Timor Crisis', p. 160, note 167.

84   While this workshop was a 'second track diplomacy' (officials-to-officials) meeting, it helped officials within the Australian Government to identify potential problems with the ballot process. While two Australian Government officials spoke at the workshop, there were no others listed among the participants despite the wide range of East Timorese participants. See Centre for Democratic Institutions, *Managing Transition in East Timor Workshop*, Australian National University, 26–29 April 1999; and Interview with 012-05.

the advice agencies would only provide information on their specialist area or comments on submissions drafted by the lead agency.[85] Andrew Hughes' response was typical of those from advice agencies: I wasn't expected to advise much on issues of national policy. Mine was more a technical role. ... I'd also give updates on how we were tracking, training our people, and the logistics of that.[86]

Advice agencies might also undertake their own analysis, but this was often in response to a request by others. For instance, AusAID conducted an assessment of the humanitarian situation in East Timor in March 1999 at the request of the foreign minister.[87] Intelligence agencies play a different role, primarily due to the strict doctrinal separation between policy and intelligence. As a result, one may expect to find that the Australian intelligence agencies played no role in policy analysis—but that would underestimate the individuals who represented their agencies and their ability to present information in a way that shaped policy discussion.

DPM&C falls into its own category. This department played a central role in setting the broad direction of policy, and also a coordinating role. Thus DPM&C was a key player on the main committees, and individuals within it could be—and reportedly were—influential in discussions. The department could also exercise an informal veto over policy proposals.[88] But the small size of DPM&C and vast range of issues to be covered in 1999 meant that its officers tended to play a background role, speaking up when they needed to, but leaving the main analytical work to the other departments.

Lastly, some groups could have played a role in this crisis but did not. Foremost among these were the Treasury and the Department of Finance and Administration (DOFA). In the Australian system, the Treasury provides economic policy advice to government and DOFA manages the Commonwealth's budget (among other responsibilities). Aside from DOFA's routine advice on budgets, neither department appeared to play a significant role.[89] The implications of their absence will be discussed in the next section on policy instruments.

Dominant frameworks

Discussions of 'dominant frameworks' or 'paradigms' in policymaking are often loaded and vitriolic—loaded in the sense that dominant paradigms are considered inherently bad and a limit on creative thought, and vitriolic in that

---

85 Interviews with Steve Darvill and Andrew Hughes.
86 Interview with Andrew Hughes.
87 Department of Foreign Affairs and Trade and AusAID, 'Submission', pp. 076–085.
88 Interview with Michael Keating.
89 No person interviewed for this study could remember a significant instance of involvement by either Treasury or the Department of Finance and Administration.

policymakers who follow the dominant framework are often accused of being narrow-minded and inflexible.[90] The discussion of frameworks also touches on the structure/agency debate, for it implies people are unable to think or act beyond the structurally mandated assumptions of their organisation. This discussion tries to avoid a judgemental position, noting instead that both DFAT and Defence made different assumptions about what Australia should be preparing for in 1999, and these assumptions took the character of separate dominant frameworks.

Based on the evidence gathered during the interviews, DFAT's actions concerning East Timor in 1999 could be characterised as adopting a 'best case' position. This view contributed to a policy preference of pressuring the Indonesian Government to keep its word and maintain security which, in turn, made it essential to minimise activity that might betray that position.

The reasons for taking such a position may not be related to a dominant framework. Avoiding situations that would antagonise Indonesia, and perhaps lead to a disruption of ties before the popular consultation, made policy sense to many. Viewed another way, this focus on the best case may have also been necessary because DFAT has relatively few resources to assign to problems. DFAT probably only had around 15–20 policy officers assigned to the East Timor issue before mid-September 1999.[91] It is reasonable to expect that, with so few resources available, effort would be focused on limited, most likely options.

However, a number of interviewees (notably from outside DFAT) felt this tendency to plan for the best case represented DFAT's preferred way of thinking:

> DFAT is inclined to think optimistically (so their) focus was therefore on avoiding conflict …[92]

> DFAT has a kind of 'beautiful idealism' that is its main operational paradigm. That is, you can negotiate your way out of everything and that diplomacy will always solve the problem.[93]

> … it was you [Defence] take a dim view, we'll [DFAT] take the rose-tinted view and never the twain shall meet.[94]

---

90   For example, see Maley, 'Australia and the East Timor Crisis', pp. 158–60.

91   This figure should be compared to the resources devoted by Defence to this crisis at the strategic level. In addition to the nearly 30 people involved in the East Timor Policy Unit, many of Strategic Command Division's 30 staff were working on crisis issues. The author observed at least 15 policy officers working on this crisis within Army Headquarters—a number probably replicated in Air Force and Navy Headquarters as well. The Defence Intelligence Organisation also had a small, 24-hour crisis action team.

92   Interview with Hugh White.

93   Interview with Allan Behm.

94   Interview with 046-06.

While empirical work by Allan Gyngell and Michael Wesley would dispute the presence of an idealistic streak in DFAT's culture,[95] Defence's approach was noticeably different because it revolved around planning for a broad range of contingencies before focusing on the worst case, which is often defined in terms of levels of violence or resources.[96] But even Defence was not planning for the worst case before September 1999, because—as mentioned earlier—it has been directed to prepare for a Services-assisted evacuation only.

Defence's own difficulty with seeing problems through its dominant framework of operations was demonstrated by the way little planning was conducted for the nation-building aspects of the intervention. According to one interviewee:

> My area ... started to see some of the operational planning coming out of Defence, and we saw what we thought were some gaps in that—in terms of aid to the civil power when there was no civil power. And we started asking questions about how the 'civilian' side was going to be managed. Who was going to be doing the electricity supply, water and administrative tasks? We had a strong sense that Defence's planning up to that stage had not considered those questions. Very good [operational] planning to get troops on the ground and to get control and establish order, but the next step did not seem to us to have been well-considered.[97]

This view of events was supported by other interviewees, who acknowledged little had been done to prepare for the post-intervention phase of the crisis.[98] Then-Chief of the Defence Force Chris Barrie acknowledged that the intervention was always going to involve more than just stabilising the situation, but stressed that Defence's priority was to restore law and order:

> Our mandate was to provide security. The actual nation-building and stuff belonged to the UN, but blind Freddie could have seen that was going to come out of Australia. It had to. And the sooner we can hand the whole thing off to the UN the better.[99]

The curious issue here is that Australia led INTERFET because the United Nations could not have organised its own force in time to prevent more destruction in Timor.[100] Why would anyone have thought that the United Nations could organise a nation-building operation any faster? A related issue concerned the

---

95   Gyngell and Wesley, *Making Australian Foreign Policy*, pp. 73–77.
96   This view was also expressed by John Castellaw. His comments show that the 'worst-case' view is a trait held by more than one nation's military.
97   Interview with 028-05.
98   Interviews with Chris Barrie and Michael Scrafton.
99   Interview with Chris Barrie.
100   Department of Foreign Affairs and Trade, *East Timor*, p. 133. Geoffrey Robinson wrote that he was told it would take three months to deploy a UN peacekeeping force ('With UNAMET in East Timor—An Historian's

idea that operations and nation-building would occur sequentially—that is, the force would restore order, then others would come in to restore services and ultimately develop national institutions. As the experience of Timor and elsewhere shows, this is faulty thinking because people will become impatient while the follow-on organisations prepare themselves—some will try to seize political power themselves, while others may resort to new forms of violence to assert their position. This type of thinking shows the difficulties of working within dominant paradigms and provides some evidence for the benefits of adopting a more integrated, 'whole-of-government' approach to national security policymaking.

Despite this, there were a number of instances where the dominant paradigm was sidelined, including the way DFAT allocated some diplomatic tasks to Defence officials, and the way officials cooperated in a range of committees. This shows a significant pragmatic (and often cooperative) streak in crisis policymaking, and also shows that dominant frameworks may be shaped or resisted by individuals. One interviewee also argued that, at the very top level, the NSCC proved successful at bringing convergence in thinking which made dominant frameworks unimportant.[101] This convergence was assisted by the presence of a very influential prime minister and strong ministers, and also the situation itself. The presence of ministerial advisers in the Policy Analysis phase adds another element that can break the dominant framework down.

Observations about policy analysis

The East Timor case study shows the need for modifications to Bridgman and Davis' characteristics during crisis policymaking. The first change is the need to empathise extra-rational factors, such as judgement, in crisis. The way key policy advice appears to have been generated—in this case—by the top layer of officials, and the limited attention paid to formal analysis of the options through methods such as cost benefit analysis, military appreciations or the like, supports observations by other observers of policymaking. For example, Yehezkel Dror argues that the limited knowledge of policymakers (and indeed the changing nature of goals) constricts the ability to conduct rational processes. He went on to argue that rational processes must be replaced by something else, such as judgement, intuition or heuristics.[102] This phenomenon has been observed in the East Timor case, as key decisions such as the Howard Letter were taken without

---

Personal View', in Richard Tanter, Mark Selden and Stephen Shalom (eds), *Bitter Flowers, Sweet Flowers: East Timor, Indonesia and the World Community*, Rowman and Littlefield, Lanham, MD, 2001, p. 62). See also the earlier discussion about how the United Nations needed five months to deploy a peacekeeping force.

101   Interview with Ashton Calvert.

102   Yehezkel Dror, *Public Policymaking Reexamined*, Chandler Publishing Company, Scranton, NJ, 1968, p. 158.

a strict reliance on a rational-comprehensive analytical method. Experience, judgement and understanding of somewhat intangible national objectives seem to have played the dominant role in this instance.

There is also an argument that results, not processes, are important in policy analysis.[103] After all, it is possible for an individual to conduct this phase alone and come up with a suitable answer. However, reliance on the 'heroic individual' has limits and represents a significant gamble. In this case, the flaws were shown in the apparent lack of effort applied by the Australian Government to influence the Tripartite Talks, and unforeseen implications of policy action such as the Howard Letter. These shortcomings echo Irving Janis and Patrick Haney, who identify a strong relationship between poor process and unfavourable outcomes.[104] It would therefore seem best to design and use a good analytical process, and then adapt it to fit the situation.

It is difficult to overlook the central role played by ministers in analysis during a crisis. In this case, there were occasions where the prime minister brought newly-emerging issues straight to the NSCC, and the ministers themselves became analysts as they discussed the latest occurrences. They did so based on their general knowledge of the situation and their detailed knowledge of the most recent events. This involvement should not be seen as an aberration, according to Hugh White:

> It's the PM [prime minister] who has been onto the phone to Kofi Annan overnight, and while someone would have written up a record it won't have been widely distributed. So the people down lower won't know about what the PM said to Kofi Annan, and they certainly won't know what ministers said to each other.[105]

Ministerial advisers are another important group of insiders during the policy analysis phase. At times, ministers are briefed by their advisers on important proposals, and the advisers are expected to identify the political and policy implications and merits of each. The proximity of advisers also gives them an

---

103   This is probably an argument that Howard himself would make. In his analysis of Howard's leadership style, Paul Kelly notes that 'he thinks like a practitioner who judges governance more by its policy and political outcomes than as a system in its own right'. See Paul Kelly, 'How Howard Governs', in Nick Cater (ed.), *The Howard Factor: A Decade that Changed the Nation*, Melbourne University Press, Carlton, 2006, p. 4.
104   Irving L. Janis, *Crucial Decisions: Leadership in Policymaking and Crisis Management*, The Free Press, New York, 1989, pp. 126–34; and Patrick Haney, *Organizing for Foreign Policy Crises: Presidents, Advisers and the Management of Decision Making*, University of Michigan Press, Ann Arbor, 1997, pp. 124–25.
105   Interview with Hugh White. Eliot Cohen also demonstrates the importance of political leaders in analysis (*Supreme Command: soldiers, statesmen and leadership in wartime*, Simon and Schuster, London, 2003).

opportunity to influence the minister's thinking, often at critical times. How advisers use their position is often up to the minister's preferences, the advisor's personality and the confidence between departments and the advisers.[106]

The earlier discussion of bodies such as Defence's East Timor Policy Unit (ETPU) and the Taylor Committee, and the discussion of the iterative and fast-paced nature of policymaking in this section also show that structures and systems designed to conduct policy analysis in routine situations are not necessarily suited to coping with crises. Instead, organisations may prefer to establish small groups to focus on the issue and provide analysis directly to senior leaders.

However, a number of people interviewed for this study were either openly critical or unsure whether such *ad hoc* arrangements actually made a positive contribution to policymaking. Some felt the creation of new bodies created overlaps and extra work for already strained policy organisations. Further, people who joined the process late in the crisis often spoke of the 'steep learning curve' as they adjusted to both their assigned role and the issues involved in the crisis. Both these negative points raise real questions about whether creating new policy organisations in the midst of a crisis are likely to deliver reliable results.

The different assumptions made by DFAT and Defence, particularly in regards to balancing the competing 'signals' that would be sent by overt military preparations, provides a good example of the influence of dominant frameworks. However, that such different positions were accommodated in this case shows that 'dominant' need not be 'deterministic': strong political leadership can work to stop these frameworks from becoming a source of destructive competition. Dominant frameworks can have other influences though. In this case, the lack of preparation for nation-building tasks may be attributable to the ADF's overwhelming focus on the evacuation and intervention missions as its first priorities. Conversely, a lack of understanding about responsibilities between Australia and the United Nations during a very hectic period could also explain why some assumptions appear to have been made about the international response to the East Timor crisis.

This evidence allows the 'typical' characteristics for this phase to be modified for crisis policymaking:

- Where the ability to conduct rational-comprehensive analysis is limited in a crisis, decision-makers turn to trusted sources of advice or become their own

---

106   Interviews with 051-06 and Aldo Borgu. The role of advisers was not consistent across ministerial offices. One described his minister's disdain for advisers trying to 'second guess' the department (Interview with 064-07).

analysts. This can change the structure of policymaking and which actors will be influential;

- Policy issues are rarely analysed as individual, discrete problems, and the nature of competition between issues and interests, and the consequent influence on the issue at hand, makes analysis iterative;

- Policy insiders dominate; and

- Where dominant frameworks exist, they are likely to be noticeable where there is no clear lead for a crisis.

Policy Instruments

The third phase of the policy cycle involves considering the means, called policy instruments, to achieve the government's ends. The main characteristics of this phase in Bridgman and Davis's model are:

- The instruments most used in Australia include financial, legal, advocacy and government action; and

- There are limitations upon what the government can do with its policy instruments.[107]

Of the instruments used in crises, it should be no surprise that diplomatic and military instruments are more prominent than those identified for domestic policy issues. However, this case also shows how the Australian Government used instruments beyond those normally considered in the context of national security, such as the electoral commission. This case study also confirms that the utility of a given policy instrument is highly situational, not least for its potential to precipitate detrimental consequences if used. More worryingly, some parts of the military instrument would not have been ready or sustainable for offshore operations had they been needed to conduct a more intense combat campaign.

Australian policy instruments

Diplomacy was an essential policy instrument, and the Australian Government used both DFAT and Defence extensively for diplomatic purposes during this crisis. As on other occasions, DFAT used its embassies, delegations and informal contacts with a number of agencies and individuals to advocate Australia's position. DFAT was also the most prominent Australian organisation used

---

107   Bridgman and Davis, *The Australian Policy Handbook*, pp. 70–77.

in consultations with East Timorese, Indonesian and UN leaders in the early period. These consultations included the work by DFAT officials in June 1998 and the visits to Jakarta, New York and Washington by Downer and his senior officials.[108] DFAT also facilitated a range of other forums, such as intra-Timorese reconciliation meetings and later a 'Group of Friends' on East Timor.[109]

While DFAT played the major role in planning and executing the diplomatic effort, Defence's part was important in terms of engaging the Indonesians and regional neighbours in 1999. These activities included indirect advocacy during a joint Australia-Indonesia forum from

9–11 March,[110] and direct approaches by Air Marshal Doug Riding and Allan Behm to senior TNI leaders in June. Defence's diplomacy also extended to practical areas, such as the efforts made in September 1999 by the acting Deputy Secretary Strategy and Intelligence, Martin Brady, to establish cooperative modes between the Indonesian military and ADF; and the regional tour by the Vice Chief of the Defence Force, Doug Riding, to build support for INTERFET. In addition, Defence's attachés in Indonesia, Brigadier Jim Molan and Colonel Ken Brownrigg, played key roles in putting Australia's position to the TNI and establishing a relationship with Indonesian forces in East Timor so that INTERFET could operate without coming into conflict with Indonesian units.[111]

Other instruments make direct contributions to diplomatic efforts—and they can detract from diplomacy as well. For example, cash donations to the UN Transitional Administration in East Timor (UNTAET) and financial support for intra-East Timorese dialogue supported the broad diplomatic messages of reconciliation, while demonstrations of ADF units and equipment displayed

---

108   These were some of the 120 representations made to the Indonesian Government over East Timor during 1998–99, according to John Dauth in his testimony to Foreign Affairs, Defence and Trade References Committee, *Economic, social and political conditions in East Timor*, 13 August 1999, available at <http://www.aph.gov.au/hansard>, accessed 6 December 2006, p. 220.

109   Further aims and results of diplomacy will be discussed later in the section on 'Consultation'. The Group of Friends was an informal meeting of concerned UN member states. This group, which included Japan and New Zealand, began meeting after the ballot announcement in an attempt to build a coalition for intervention (see James Cotton, East Timor, *Australia and Regional Order: intervention and its aftermath in Southeast Asia*, Routledge, London, 2004, p. 95).

110   This forum, known as the CDF-Pangab Forum after the respective military leaders, was instituted after the 1995 Agreement on Maintaining Security between Australia and Indonesia. The March 1999 forum was held in Jakarta, and discussed the role of military forces in democratic societies—see Bilveer Singh, *Defense Relations Between Australia and Indonesia in the Post-Cold War Era*, Greenwood, Westport, CT, 2002, p. 126; and Defence Public Affairs, 'Australian/Indonesian Bi-lateral Military Forum', Media Release DPAO 062/99 dated 5 March 1999, available at <http://www.defence.gov.au>, accessed 17 November 2007.

111   See Alan Ryan, *Primary responsibilities and primary risks: Australian Defence Force participation in the International Force East Timor*, Land Warfare Studies Centre, Duntroon, Canberra, 2000, p. 40; James Cotton, *East Timor, Australia and Regional Order*, p. 121; Paul Daley, 'Gunning for the General', *Bulletin*, 30 June 2004; and interviews with Allan Behm and Martin Brady. See also Bob Breen, *Mission Accomplished—East Timor*, Allen & Unwin, Crows Nest, NSW, 2000, pp. 7–14 for the role of Defence's attachés in Operation *Spitfire* and the initial deployment of INTERFET.

Australia's will and capability to use force if necessary.[112] It is also important to note the role of political leaders in diplomacy. Aside from Downer's efforts, the prime minister was involved in some direct diplomacy through the December 1998 letter to President Habibie, the Bali Summit of April 1999, the Asia-Pacific Economic Cooperation meeting of September that same year, and the negotiations to establish INTERFET.

While its role in diplomacy was clearly valuable, the ADF's main contribution in this crisis came from its ability to deploy and sustain combat forces offshore as part of an international coalition. This capability was complemented by the ADF's ability to lead the coalition force, provide significant logistic support and integrate intelligence from Australian and international sources. When added together, these capabilities allowed the Australian Government to act quickly and decisively after receiving the UN mandate for INTERFET in mid-September.

Australia's alliance with the United States was another important policy instrument. While there no evidence of consultation between the Australian and US Governments about the Howard Letter, developing a shared policy line was clearly important to Australia by February 1999. This imperative was reflected by DFAT secretary Ashton Calvert's visit to Washington, DC, for talks with his US counterparts in the Department of State. Australian political leaders and officials also continued to promote the need for US engagement, most notably with US Pacific Command (USPACOM) and through counterparts in the US Government.[113] The US Government also used its weight to gain Indonesian acceptance for the intervention at a critical time. Once the decision to commit forces was made the United States provided important support to the mission, most visibly through strategic lift and the Marine force positioned off Timor.

While Australia did not to employ all of its economic instruments in this crisis (a discussion that will be taken up later in this section), development aid and targeted financial assistance were prominent. As mentioned earlier, AusAID directed funds to meeting short- and longer-term humanitarian problems, as well as funding immediate initiatives to support policy. These initiatives extended to providing financial and technical assistance to NGOs working in East Timor.

---

112   For example, Allan Behm mentioned the way senior Indonesian officers were reminded of the Australia's long-range bomber capability during visits to Australia, while sensitive intelligence was 'sanitised' (had its source hidden) so blunt messages could be conveyed to senior TNI officers (see also Daley, 'Gunning'; and Interview with 005-06, a former senior ADF officer).

113   Interview with Bob Treloar. He also noted how many of the talks with USPACOM were conducted relatively informally, as 'staff talks' rather than as 'policy talks'. Earl Hailston (the former senior planner for USPACOM) also noted the close relationship between USPACOM and Defence, and stated that he was allowed to maintain closer contact with the Australians than he might have been allowed to do with the military forces of other nations. Recounting his discussions with US Defense Secretary Bill Cohen, John Moore recalled being told that 'Timor was your [Australia's] baby' and that ANZUS did not automatically apply, although consultation did occur without a formal invocation of the treaty.

AusAID also provided technical assistance to policymaking by dispatching assessment teams when requested and organising direct humanitarian assistance on occasions.[114]

The employment of instruments is not without risk, and indeed it is possible for one instrument to work against the needs of another. The latter problem was seen in the conflicting needs of diplomacy and military readiness. As mentioned earlier, the preparation of 1st Brigade had the potential to convey messages that ran counter to other efforts; in this case, to DFAT's preferred policy line that Indonesia would be trusted to manage security and the East Timorese would be encouraged to compromise.[115] That Defence went ahead with preparing 1st Brigade for deployment was a risk, but one that proved worthwhile given the events of September 1999.

The willingness to accept some financial risk to fund the mission was another significant element of Australia's policy response in September. Under normal circumstances, the United Nations establishes elaborate measures to determine funding arrangements for contributions to peacekeeping forces. But these mechanisms take time to build and some nations were reluctant to commit without confirmed funding arrangements. In this case, the Australian Government accepted the risk and paid the deployment costs of some participants, and underwrote a range of other costs until the UN Trust Fund was fully operational. This move was instrumental in keeping negotiations going with a number of countries during INTERFET's early days, and helped to ensure that the force included a broad range of nationalities.[116]

Australia's willingness to bear additional costs also helped to allay concerns and avoid potential ill-feeling with contributing nations. The value of this approach was shown when some contributing nations delivered their forces to Australia without essential military equipment.[117] The necessary equipment was duly loaned by the ADF, and the contingents were able to deploy with minimal delays. When the time came to reconcile the loans, these stores were given as a gift to avoid creating animosity between Australia and the contributing nations.[118]

---

114 Interview with Steve Darvill. These assessment missions also included one to Darwin to assess its ability to support UN operations.

115 See Department of Foreign Affairs and Trade, *East Timor in Transition 1998–2000: An Australian Policy Challenge*, pp. 44–45, for the coordinated ministerial response to Indonesia's announcement about the ballot, and the desire to avoid discussing a potential peacekeeping effort.

116 Interview with Steve Ayling. See also Brigadier Steve Ayling and Sarah Guise, 'UNTAC and INTERFET—A Comparative Analysis', *Australian Defence Force Journal*, no. 150, 2001, p. 51; and Ryan, *Primary responsibilities and primary risks: Australian Defence Force participation in the International Force East Timor*, pp. 43–45.

117 Ryan, *Primary responsibilities and primary risks: Australian Defence Force participation in the International Force East Timor*, p. 52.

118 Australian National Audit Office, *Management of Australian Defence Force Deployments to East Timor*, Commonwealth of Australia, Canberra, 2002, paragraphs 2.61–2.62.

This case also shows how a number of departments and agencies contribute different abilities to create additional policy instruments for crises. For example, the AEC helped the United Nations to establish the legal and procedural framework for the electoral process, established systems for voter registration, developed and procured ballot materials, developed training courses and briefing packages, and facilitated voting for East Timorese expatriates in Australia.[119] According to Corina Perelli, these services made a significant contribution to the ballot's outcome.[120] The AFP was important to providing UNAMET with an ability to diffuse problems through the moral authority of international police.[121] And, while less prominent as an 'instrument' in this case, the intelligence community could have employed—or perhaps did employ—some capacity for covert operations and communications disruption.[122]

Other instruments that the government might want to call upon are owned and operated by the private and community sectors. For example, Australia's main telecommunications company, Telstra, assisted the ADF and the fledgling authority in East Timor by providing on-the-ground communications support in Dili.[123] Other examples included the use of commercial shipping to support the INTERFET deployment and the use of a commercial provider for aeromedical evacuation during UNTAET.[124] Further examples are found in the way commercial and non-government organisations helped AusAID to implement its humanitarian program as suppliers and providers of goods and services.[125] These few examples show that the ownership of some policy instruments had clearly moved from government hands by 1999, but the government could—at a price—harness more instruments for policy than it actually owned.

119   Australian Electoral Commission, 'Submission to the Senate Foreign Affairs, Defence and Trade References Committee: Australian Electoral Commission Support for the East Timor Consultation Ballot', Commonwealth of Australia, Canberra, 1999, pp. 2–8.

120   Corina Perelli was the senior UN election official for UNAMET. Her view was quoted in Australian Electoral Commission, 'Submission to the Senate Foreign Affairs, Defence and Trade References Committee: Australian Electoral Commission Support for the East Timor Consultation Ballot', pp. 1–2.

121   Andrew Hughes thought the AFP's mechanisms for getting support were satisfactory, but spoke of the difficulty with balancing his personal responsibilities for domestic and international crime tasks and this crisis (Interview, 5 September 2005). Tim Dahlstrom spoke of the strain creating the second and subsequent rotations were (or would have been) for the AFP, and the importance of being able to draw upon state police forces to expand their own resources (Interview, 16 August 2005).

122   Ian Dudgeon outlines the roles and capabilities of Australian intelligence agencies in his paper, 'Intelligence Support to the Development and Implementation of Foreign Policies and Strategies', *Security Challenges*, vol. 2, no. 2, July 2006, especially pp. 75–79. He notes the changes to the mandate of the Australian Secret Intelligence Service (ASIS) over time, and it can be inferred from his description that ASIS did not have a covert action capability in 1999. The Defence Signals Directorate is not expressly prohibited from covert operations (such as computer network attack) by legislation, according to Dudgeon (p. 76). Whether this capability was used in 1999 (and indeed, the extent to which it may have existed at the time) cannot be identified through the sources used in this study.

123   Air Vice-Marshal R Treloar, in evidence to Senate Foreign Affairs, Defence and Trade Committee, *Consideration of Additional Estimates (Department of Defence)*, 6 December 1999, p. 67.

124   Breen, *Mission Accomplished—East Timor*, p. 150; and Interview with Kerry Clarke.

125   Interviews with Steve Darvill and Scott Dawson.

Limitations on instruments

Some Australian policy instruments were not used in this crisis. In some instances they were not perceived as useful, or their use would have created significant negative repercussions. On some occasions, the instruments were not suited to the specific task, perhaps because they have limitations or lack the ability to deal with conditions as they exist. Taken together, these reasons show why the utility of policy instruments will always be highly situational in a crisis.

In the first instance, the government did not view information as a vital element of national power or think deeply about how to employ this instrument systematically.[126] While there were some specific instances where information was applied to achieve national objectives, such as the Riding/Behm visit to TNI leaders, the government missed others. According to Defence, an opportunity to shape the opinion of regional audiences about the intervention was missed, and many people were left to develop a negative perception of Australia's actions.[127] These perceptions were also influenced by anti-INTERFET media reporting in Indonesia,[128] including a magazine article that appeared on 24 September 1999 where Howard did not dispute a journalist's assertion that Australia was the United States' 'deputy sheriff' in the region.[129] This story (and image) was roundly criticised in the regional media and created credibility problems for Australia among some of its neighbours.[130]

---

126   The application of information operations is discussed in John Blaxland, *Information-era Manoeuvre: The Australian-led Mission to East Timor*, Working Paper 118, Land Warfare Studies Centre, Canberra, 2002; and Kent Beasley, *Information Operations during Operation Stabilise in East Timor*, Working Paper 120, Land Warfare Studies Centre, Canberra, 2002. Defence's use of the media in 1999 is discussed in more detail in Chapter 7.

127   Australian National Audit Office, *Management of Australian Defence Force Deployments to East Timor*, paragraphs 5.85–5.86. This claim was refuted by DFAT (in the same ANAO report) and Interview with 066-07 (Canberra, 18 December 2007), but a number of articles in regional newspapers provide support. For a sample of the negative reaction, see Zainul Arifin, 'Asean should take the lead in East Timor peacekeeping, says PM', *New Straits Times*, 1 October 1999; Kalinga Seneviratne, 'Australia casts an eye on Timor's oil', *Straits Times*, 24 September 1999; Aleksius Jemadu, 'Can Australia sever ties with Indonesia?', *Jakarta Post*, 20 September 1999; and more neutral statements in newspapers such as *Nation*, 'Editorial—Howard must clarify foreign-policy goals', 29 September 1999. In contrast, some in the region supported Australia's role in the mission—for example, see 'Editorial—Distractions in the Timor issue', *Bangkok Post*, 30 September 1999. Interviewee 066-07 is a Defence official with knowledge of public affairs activities in 1999.

128   Indonesian press reaction to INTERFET, and especially Australia's role in it, included references to Australian brutality and motivation, and asked questions about whether Australia would attack other parts of Indonesia. This reaction is summarised in Kathleen Brahney, 'East Timor: INTERFET Mission Sparks Continued Debate', United States Information Agency—Foreign Media Reaction, 15 October 1999, available at <http://www.globalsecurity.org>, accessed 2 January 2008.

129   See Fred Brenchley, 'The Howard Defence Doctrine', *Bulletin*, 28 September 1999, pp. 22–24.

130   For examples of regional reactions, see Trevor Datson, 'Australian PM popular at home, blasted in Asia', *Reuters News*, 28 September 1999; Agence France-Presse, 'Malaysian politicians slam "Howard Doctrine"', 24 September 1999; and Agence Presse-France, 'Thailand pans Australian PM over plan to be America's "deputy" in Asia', 24 September 1999.

There were also differing perceptions about the efficacy of applying broader economic instruments to force the Indonesian Government to accept peacekeepers before or after the ballot. While Downer and Defence Minister John Moore made mention of the international community's involvement in the Indonesian economy in media interviews,[131] sanctions were not seen as a viable instrument by Australian policymakers at any time in 1999. This attracted significant criticism from academics who argued that economically vulnerable Indonesia was in no condition to resist international pressure, and gave credit to the International Monetary Fund (IMF) and World Bank for eventually convincing Indonesia to accept INTERFET.[132] Maley takes this further by arguing that economic pressure might have convinced the Indonesian Government to accept a neutral military force in East Timor before the popular consultation.[133] There were some forceful responses to this proposition by Australian policymakers:

> We tested the waters as much as we could, and what economic levers did we have? We wanted to bring the Indonesians along, we didn't want to get their backs up and have problems ...[134]

> These points were made by people who had never met President Habibie. We didn't have levers on him. Sanctions are traditionally pretty ineffective and we didn't have available to us more refined 'smart sanctions'. Habibie's mind was not going to be changed by such measures, in any case, or by Australia.[135]

> ... Indonesia was on its knees as a result of the Asian Economic Crisis at the time, they were reacting badly to the IMF intervention ... but at the time we were getting ready to deploy INTERFET, people were actually dying in large numbers on the ground. How long do economic levers take to work?[136]

> I would be skeptical about the economic levers argument, as I am not sure what levers we had. Economic levers tend to work [only] in the long-term, and they work on everybody—not just the government—

---

131 Defence Public Affairs, 'Transcript, Hon John Moore, MP & Hon Alexander Downer', Commonwealth Offices, Melbourne, 6 September 1999, available at <http://www.minister.defence.gov.au>, accessed 12 December 2007.

132 Maley, 'Australia and the East Timor Crisis', pp. 157–58; and James Cotton, 'Against the Grain: The East Timor Intervention', *Survival*, vol. 43, no. 1, 2001, pp. 132–33.

133 Maley, 'Australia and the East Timor Crisis', p. 157; and his testimony to Foreign Affairs, Defence and Trade References Committee, *East Timor in Transition 1998–2000: An Australian Policy Challenge*, 13 August 1999, p. 863.

134 Interview with 024-05.

135 Interview with 032-05.

136 Interview with Michael Scrafton.

when you apply them. It would have been very hard to change short-term Indonesian policies with economic means. ... Indonesians have always been happy to take the hit and wait it out.[137]

When asked whether Australia had considered asking the IMF to pressure Indonesia into allowing a peacekeeping force before the consultation, or whether this option was even discussed, Paul Barratt responded:

Not that I am aware of ... in the Asian meltdown we had sought to ameliorate the worst excesses of the IMF. Downer went into bat on behalf of Indonesia, and I think that was the right way to play it.[138]

This exchange shows that Australian policymakers clearly thought that bringing economic pressure on Indonesia was either impossible or potentially detrimental, or both. What is interesting is that the potential experts on economic power, the Treasury or DOFA, were not clearly engaged in policymaking about East Timor. When asked about their participation, no interviewee described Treasury or DOFA attendance at any of the main interdepartmental working groups, or even any significant consultation, except about funding. This example, in particular, shows that governments make judgements about when and where to apply their instruments. It also shows that just because a government has certain instruments, these instruments are not necessarily available to further policy objectives. Nor will instruments—in this case, using diplomacy alone to convince the Indonesians to accept peacekeepers—always achieve the intended results.

Defence did not use its entire range of military options during INTERFET. Some weapons, such as tanks, were not justified by the level of threat and were potentially damaging to East Timor's underdeveloped road network. Others, such as Australia's F-111 strategic bombers, were used only as a subtle threat. According to one report, these aircraft remained fuelled and armed at the Royal Australian Air Force base Tindal, near Katherine in northern Australia.[139] While this move was not announced, it is an example of how not using an instrument can still have an effect—if the adversary detects the signal.

Policy instruments can also be limited by political decisions. Although the evidence to identify exactly why is not yet publicly available, there are strong indications that the Australian Government chose not to use economic sanctions

---

137   Interview with Frank Lewincamp.

138   Interview with Paul Barratt. These institutions eventually played a role when World Bank President James Wolfensohn expressed concern about the violence to President Habibie (see Steven Mufson, 'World Bank Chief Warns Indonesia On Militias', *Washington Post*, 12 September 1999). The International Monetary Fund also expressed concern about the violence before cancelling their planned visit (see William Murray, 'The Situation in Indonesia and the IMF', International Monetary Fund, 16 September 1999, available at <http://www.imf.org>, accessed 6 February 2006).

139   Andrew Fowler, 'Flying Blind', *4 Corners*, ABC Television (Australia), 29 October 2007.

because it did not want to start a war or a lasting conflict with Indonesia over East Timor, or jeopardise Indonesia's move towards democracy. It is also possible that the Australian Government may have shied away from overt pressure in order to preserve the bilateral trade relationship. While Indonesia was only Australia's tenth-largest trading partner in 1999, any break in the economic relationship might have caused economic discomfort in Australia as well as Indonesia. These types of political, economic and electoral factors weigh heavily upon political decision-makers, potentially more than the risk of violence in a foreign jurisdiction.[140]

Foreign governments might also restrict the use of some policy instruments. For example, AusAID's Scott Dawson spoke about how the Australian Government's ability to sponsor NGO activities in East Timor before September 1999 was constrained by the Indonesian Government:

> There were fairly strict controls about who could work in East Timor which were run out of the foreign ministry and state security apparatus in Jakarta, and that kind of limited the sorts of partnerships that we could make with Australian non-government organisations. None of that [control] existed post-ballot, and ... we were able to make more use of the linkages between church-based NGOs in Australia and church-based NGOs in East Timor.[141]

This type of constraint is usually dictated by sovereignty—states are within their (political) rights to determine who enters their borders and, once there, the activities of those group or individuals. Accepting these conditions is sometimes the price donors must pay to operate in difficult situations.

Policy instruments also have physical limits such as reach, sustainability, survivability and readiness. The ability to use a given instrument at the place or time where it will achieve the desired effect—described as 'reach'—is especially relevant to this case. While Australia has police, military forces, election officials and aid workers, these capabilities must move outside their normal operating areas and be able to work in the appropriate location if they are to contribute as a policy instrument. For example, it was soon apparent that the AFP's communications, air transport and logistics were very limited—although these

---

140 The imperative for preventing any major disruption can be extrapolated from the level of bilateral trade (then A$5bn), in the amount of Australian investment in Indonesia (A$6bn), in the loans made by the Australian Government to Indonesia after the 1997 economic crisis (A$1bn), and in the number of Indonesian students who travel to Australia to study (17 000 people in 2000). See Department of Foreign Affairs and Trade, *Direction of Trade Time Series, 2000-01 One Hundred Years of Trade*, Commonwealth of Australia, Canberra, 2002, p. 2 and p. 4; Stephen Sherlock, *Indonesia's Dangerous Transition: The Politics of Recovery and Democratisation*, Australian Parliamentary Library Research Paper 18, Australian Department of the Parliamentary Library, Canberra, 1999; and Department of Foreign Affairs and Trade, *Advancing the National Interest*, Commonwealth of Australia, Canberra, 2003, Chapter 5.

141 Interview with Scott Dawson.

shortcomings were ameliorated by other agencies or commercial contracts. Other AFP limitations included difficulties with preparing and training large groups of police for peacekeeping duties; however, these shortcomings were overcome through cooperation with other agencies.[142] The ability to protect instruments while deployed may be another limitation, which was seen in the way the AEC was reportedly unwilling to send staff into East Timor due to safety concerns.[143]

Deficiencies in logistics, lift, combat equipment and communications were also identified within Defence.[144] Significant concerns were raised about the amount of body armour and night vision equipment available to the deploying forces,[145] and about the ability to rotate infantry units.[146] However, other possible deficiencies did not become obvious because the operation's scale and intensity prevented 'survivability' from coming to attention. It should also be noted that the ADF did not deploy its full range of military capabilities to East Timor. Tank units, medium artillery and strike bombers all remained outside the territory and its airspace. These units were not deployed for a range of reasons, including the absence of a real military need. Despite having some ability to contribute more firepower to the mission, there seemed to be some consensus that the ADF was lucky it did not have to face a more heavily armed or determined enemy.[147]

'Readiness' also relates to the physical limits of capability. However, it is a separate issue because some instruments may have appropriate physical characteristics, but not be employable immediately. This limitation is especially apparent with military forces. While the ADF showed itself to be a flexible instrument, different elements within the force required considerable lead-time to prepare for missions. This need complicated the relationship between DFAT and Defence in early 1999, because (as mentioned earlier) military preparations ran against the declared policy position that Indonesia was responsible for security in East Timor.[148]

Readiness limitations are also apparent with aid instruments. For example, AusAID did not fund NGOs to maintain an ability to mount new operations quickly in 1999—it only provided funding in return for service when the crisis

---

142   Interviews with Kerry Clarke and Tim Dahlstrom.

143   Interview with 012-05.

144   For more detailed accounts of ADF deficiencies, see Australian National Audit Office, *Management of Australian Defence Force Deployments to East Timor*, Chapter 4; and Ryan, *Primary responsibilities and primary risks: Australian Defence Force participation in the International Force East Timor*, Chapter 3.

145   Deborah Snow and Peter Cole-Adams, 'Army Borrows Uncle Sam's Flak Jackets', *Sydney Morning Herald*, 24 September 1999, p. 1.

146   Other problems with sustaining enabling components, such as the Army's Training Command, were also observed—see Joint Standing Committee on Foreign Affairs Defence and Trade, *From Phantom to Force: Towards a More Efficient and Effective Army*, Commonwealth of Australia, Canberra, 2000, pp. 73–75.

147   Ryan, *Primary responsibilities and primary risks: Australian Defence Force participation in the International Force East Timor*, p. 76.

148   Interviews with Chris Barrie, Paul Barratt and Hugh White.

broke. As a result, it often took valuable time to bring NGO relief capabilities to a state where they could be deployed, while it also took time to negotiate the terms of AusAID support.[149]

Observations about policy instruments

As no two crises are exactly the same, the Australian Government maintains a range of instruments to achieve national security goals. Indeed, the use of many different departments and agencies, and the attempt to coordinate their activities, makes East Timor a prototype of a modern, whole-of-government approach to crisis.[150] In this case, the front-line instruments went beyond the traditional diplomatic and economic means to include the technical expertise of the AEC (and later Customs), and the authority of the AFP. It was also notable that one of the main instruments, the ADF, only provided background intelligence, logistic support, and a role in the diplomatic effort until the crisis became acute. Another interesting factor was the way commercial assets were integrated into the response, albeit in a limited way and only after significant policy effort. This adds another dimension to the understanding of the means available to pursue national objectives.

Of course, just because a government has a viable instrument does not mean that instrument should be used. For example, economic sanctions might have forced the Indonesian Government to accept a peacekeeping force before the ballot. However, there was real potential for sanctions to create negative economic and political consequences for Australia, and to possibly disrupt Indonesia's nascent democracy. Officials need to identify the chances of negative consequences when they develop options to recommend to government.

In other cases, governments may need to accept limitations imposed by other sovereign governments to maintain the ability to work on issues. In this case, Indonesia's limitations on which NGOs could or could not work in East Timor may have been objectionable, but acceptance was the price of providing other forms of Australian assistance. In situations such as this, governments might need to use other instruments as levers to remove or reduce those restrictions.

The practical limitations on instruments also mean that policymakers must consult closely with operators and specialist advisers when options are being developed. This is especially important where there is a difference between what an instrument can do in theory, and what it can do when factors such as survivability, readiness, sustainability and reach are considered. A case should

---

149 Interview with Scott Dawson, who also noted that AusAID now funds some NGOs to maintain emergency relief capabilities at high readiness.
150 The Bougainville operation of 1997 pre-dates Timor and provides some portent of the way policy instruments could be used together, although it was on a smaller scale and few instruments were marshalled.

be made for including Treasury on key committees, such as the SPCG, and of including the Secretary of Treasury on the NSCC. Such representation would ensure that important policy instruments are included in national planning at the earliest possible time.

The typical characteristics identified by Bridgman and Davis for the Policy Instruments phase need little modification for crisis policymaking. However, they can be slightly revised to highlight the types of instruments used in national security situations. This leads to a restatement of the characteristics for crisis policymaking in this phase as:

- The instruments most used by the Australian Government in times of crisis are diplomacy, alliances, military force, economic levers (including foreign aid), information, international law, and (sometimes) social levers; and

- The utility of foreign and defence policy instruments is highly situational in a crisis.

Chapter 4
Bringing Policy Advice Together

While advice may be well-developed after the initiating phases of the cycle, policymakers generally see advantage in exposing that advice to others before seeking decisions. Chapter 4 examines how international and domestic audiences are brought into the policy cycle through consultation, and other internal government actors through coordination. This chapter follows the format used in Chapter 3 and, once again, each section is drawn together by a short observation covering the main points about that phase in lieu of a conclusion for the chapter.

Consultation

The Consultation phase involves testing policy with audiences outside the originating policymaking department. For Peter Bridgman and Glyn Davis, consultation responds to democratic pressure because people 'want a say between elections'.[1] Consultation is expected to increase public involvement and, in turn, increase policy legitimacy. The phase has two typical characteristics:

- Citizens demand a say in policy between elections, and sometimes, consultation is mandatory; and

- Consultation occurs across a continuum from information to control.[2]

Bridgman and Davis' consultation continuum (see Figure 3) spans information (the minimum where people are simply told of decisions), through increasing interaction between government and stakeholders, to control where governments allow citizens to make decisions through referenda.[3] This section shows that the consultation phase in a crisis differs greatly from the typical—so much so that a modified continuum has been developed to show the options for consultation during a crisis. It also shows how consultation can reduce the government's freedom on action in crisis.

---

1 Peter Bridgman and Glyn Davis, *The Australian Policy Handbook*, 3rd edn, Allen and Unwin, Sydney, 2004, p. 78.
2 Bridgman and Davis, *The Australian Policy Handbook*, p. 78 and pp. 80–82.
3 Bridgman and Davis, *The Australian Policy Handbook*, pp. 80–82.

Figure 3: The Consultation Continuum[4]

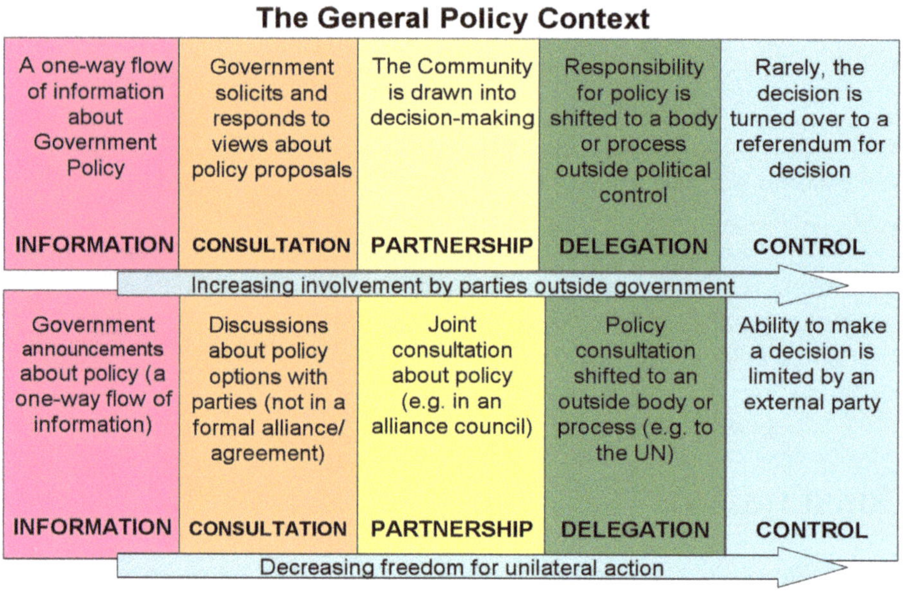

The General Policy Context

A one-way flow of information about Government Policy	Government solicits and responds to views about policy proposals	The Community is drawn into decision-making	Responsibility for policy is shifted to a body or process outside political control	Rarely, the decision is turned over to a referendum for decision
INFORMATION	**CONSULTATION**	**PARTNERSHIP**	**DELEGATION**	**CONTROL**

Increasing involvement by parties outside government ⟹

Government announcements about policy (a one-way flow of information)	Discussions about policy options with parties (not in a formal alliance/ agreement)	Joint consultation about policy (e.g. in an alliance council)	Policy consultation shifted to an outside body or process (e.g. to the UN)	Ability to make a decision is limited by an external party
INFORMATION	**CONSULTATION**	**PARTNERSHIP**	**DELEGATION**	**CONTROL**

Decreasing freedom for unilateral action ⟹

Consultation with international actors

The Australian Government consulted a range of international actors in 1998–99, with different entities being important at different stages. Early in the crisis, most consultation was conducted with the Indonesian Government, East Timorese community leaders and Portugal. In all three cases, the Australian Government was operating at the 'discussion' point along the Bridgman and Davis continuum—there was an attempt to identify the positions of the various parties and, sometimes, to convince them to change their policy preferences. Australia adopted a similar position with other major actors early in 1999, particularly those who might provide support to the popular consultation and future nation-building operation in East Timor. This position moved further to the right on the continuum as the crisis became acute, before reaching 'delegation' and 'control' as the international community decided on action to restore stability. This section explores how the modes of Australian Government consultation changed during 1999, before moving to consultation during the period of acute crisis.

Prior to September 1999, Australia's consultation with Indonesia aimed at firstly determining the attitudes of the key Indonesian actors—such as the Ministry of Foreign Affairs, the military and the new president—and then towards convincing the Indonesians to uphold their agreement to maintain security

---

4   Adapted from Bridgman and Davis, *The Australian Policy Handbook*, pp. 82–87.

during the popular consultation. These discussions were conducted mainly through Australia's embassy in Jakarta, and included a number of visits by Foreign Minister Alexander Downer and meetings with Indonesian leaders. Other ministers, including Defence Minister John Moore and Deputy Prime Minister Tim Fischer, also engaged Indonesian leaders and sought to exchange opinions on the situation.[5] The main thrust of these discussions went towards convincing the Indonesian Government to undertake a more meaningful dialogue with East Timorese leaders.[6]

After the Howard Letter was leaked and the Indonesian Cabinet decided to conduct the ballot, Australian consultation mainly concerned security in East Timor. This discussion ran on two tracks. The first concerned diplomatic efforts to convince the Indonesian Government to discharge their responsibility for security in East Timor, while the second track involved occasional attempts to get the Indonesians to agree to accept a peacekeeping presence for the ballot. This second track culminated with the Bali Summit between Prime Minister John Howard and President B.J. Habibie on 27 April 1999. This meeting, which occurred during the period where the Indonesian Government was considering the final tripartite agreement, marked the last time Australia pressed for peacekeepers before the consultation.[7] After this, the main theme of Australia's formal and informal representations switched to reminding the Indonesians of their commitment to maintain security.[8]

While the Department of Foreign Affairs and Trade (DFAT)'s efforts to consult with Indonesia were covered in the Policy Instruments phase (see Chapter 3), there were also informal and 'off-line' consultations throughout the crisis. These contacts provided an advantage in this sensitive situation, largely because they could be explained as second-tier or unofficial.[9] The Australian Federal Police (AFP) had good relations with Indonesia's police, and they used these links effectively in 1999 and after.[10] Significant discussions at the military-to-military level also occurred. These included a formal seminar about civil-military relations in March 1999, which allowed the apolitical Australian military to

---

5   Interviews with Tim Fischer and John Moore. These exchanges included a round of formal ministerial discussion on 24–25 February 1999.

6   Department of Foreign Affairs and Trade, *East Timor in Transition 1998–2000: An Australian Policy Challenge*, Commonwealth of Australia, Canberra, 2001, pp. 25–26.

7   See Chapter 2, footnote 55.

8   David Goldsworthy, 'East Timor,' in David Goldsworthy and Peter Edwards (eds), *Facing north: a century of Australian engagement with Asia*, Melbourne University Press, Carlton, Vic, 2003, pp. 232–33; and Department of Foreign Affairs and Trade, *East Timor in Transition 1998–2000: An Australian Policy Challenge*, pp. 98–99 and pp. 109–111.

9   For example, note the representations by Downer to the Indonesian Government, as recorded in Department of Foreign Affairs and Trade, *East Timor in Transition 1998–2000: An Australian Policy Challenge*, p. 109 and p. 114.

10   Interview with Adrien Whiddett.

discuss the role of military organisations in democracies with their Indonesian counterparts. Informal contacts were also important. Interviewee 046-06 recalled one such exchange with high-ranking Indonesian officers in 1998:

> There was always that issue of Australia's apparent support for the freedom of East Timor and agitation was going on in Australia at the time. We talked about it, typically off line. They were concerned that we had a predilection for supporting various groups[11]

These military-to-military discussions became sharp at one point, when a senior military leader and Defence official were dispatched to Jakarta to provide their counterparts with evidence of Indonesian military complicity with the East Timorese militias.[12] Consultation like this provided ways to pass diplomatic messages, and to effect important coordination.

DFAT also met with East Timorese leaders from mid-1998. These included visits by Ambassador John McCarthy to the province during 12–16 June, informal consultations about the future of East Timor from June 1998 and financial support to intra-Timorese reconciliation.[13] Other contacts between senior Australians and influential Timorese also occurred, such as the meeting between Downer and Bishop Carlos Belo in Melbourne in February 1999.[14] These discussions were, on one level, simply attempts to gauge the opinion of potentially influential people. However, the manner in which the consultation occurred, and the central proposition expressed to Xanana Gusmão during this time,[15] indicated that Australian consultation was designed to shape East Timorese opinion toward a more moderate and unified position.

Portuguese leaders were also consulted in an attempt to persuade them towards Australia's views. As the former colonial power, Portugal was a member of the UN-sponsored Tripartite Talks, and a *de facto* representative of East Timorese opinion. On one occasion, Downer rebuffed the demand for an immediate recognition of East Timorese independence by Portuguese Foreign Minister Jamie Gama. Instead, Downer argued for a staged process, citing the examples of other peace processes in the region.[16] Further meetings were held between the

---

11 Interview with 046-06.

12 This meeting was discussed in Chapter 1.

13 Department of Foreign Affairs and Trade, *East Timor in Transition 1998–2000: An Australian Policy Challenge*, pp. 20–23, pp. 26–29 and pp. 101–102.

14 Bishop Carlos Bello, a Nobel Laureate, was the Catholic Bishop for Dili in 1998–99. Interviewee 064-07 recalls that Bishop Bello accurately predicted the result of the popular consultation at that early stage.

15 In 1998, Xanana Gusmão was an imprisoned but influential East Timorese resistance leader. He later became independent East Timor's first President. Australia's ambassador to Jakarta had 'regular contact' with Gusmão in 1998, and this helped the Australian Government to obtain a clearer picture of Gusmão's views (Department of Foreign Affairs and Trade, *East Timor in Transition 1998–2000: An Australian Policy Challenge*, p. 27).

16 Greg Hunt, 'Timor peace plan more palatable after dinner', *Australian*, 14 January 1999, p. 1.

foreign ministers, with the aim being to coordinate the two nation's positions on East Timor. During a meeting on 27 February 1999, Downer stressed the need to convince the East Timorese to support the process, clearly hoping the Portuguese would use their influence toward this end.[17]

The Australian Government also consulted intensively with the United Nations, especially with those officials responsible for organising the ballot. These consultations included the March 1999 discussions with Francesc Vendrell's UN assessment team. While this meeting was an exchange of views at one level, the Australian delegation took it as an opportunity to influence UN views on East Timor and Indonesia. Australia-UN consultation continued throughout 1999, with frequent visits to UN Headquarters by a DFAT–Defence team and a series of policy 'non-papers'. Matthew Skoien said these 'non-papers' were provided to the United Nations for use in their own processes:

> Non-papers ... did not have a heading or footer, and no title. They were pages of information, advice and policy options that were consistent with Australia's interests that he [Brigadier Smith] would send off to New York. They would often come back as a UN document. ... That was one way we were able to walk that line of not being formally involved but still influencing heavily.[18]

These were all common techniques within the UN system to help talks progress without implying commitment,[19] and were clearly useful in a situation where considerable sensitivity was required during consultation.

Contact between Australia and the UN Department of Peace Keeping Operations (DPKO) and Department of Political Affairs (DPA) had very subtle and sensitive aims. Significant work was done to convince these departments to use Darwin (rather than Denpassar in Bali) as the key logistic base for the United Nations Mission in East Timor (UNAMET)—a decision that proved beneficial when the peacekeeping force was subsequently required.[20] It was clear to Australian policymakers that the DPKO did not have the staff to conduct detailed appreciations of the situation or to design the necessary force for an operation. In addition, the DPKO was operating in an uncertain environment where pre-emptive contingency planning for a peacekeeping force, in the absence of an assured mandate, created diplomatic challenges with no assurances of troop commitments. In order to reduce this problem, Australia sent a group of defence

---

17   Department of Foreign Affairs and Trade, *East Timor in Transition*, pp. 46–47. See also Goldsworthy, 'East Timor', p. 233 who cites NAA, A9737, 92/051651, Cablegram O.PA6346, Paris to Canberra, 2 March 1999 for detail of this discussion.
18   Interview with Matthew Skoien.
19   Ali Alatas, *The Pebble in the Shoe: The Diplomatic Struggle for East Timor*, Aksara Karunia, Jakarta, 2006, p. 113.
20   Interview with 007-05.

planners to assist the under-strength Military Planning Staff at the DPKO in September 1999 to design a potential structure for a follow-on peacekeeping force. The team also helped the DPKO gauge the willingness of member states to make troop contributions. This cooperation was not only about consultation; it was done to ensure that Australia did not maintain the lead in East Timor for longer than necessary.[21]

AusAID also tried to engage the DPA (and the US Department of State) around mid-1999 to discuss post-ballot structures for governance, possible international contributions, and Australia's role in that contribution. However, the discussions lacked the specificity of detailed planning and were constrained by the inability to prejudge the outcome. As a result, AusAID 'spent a fair bit of time around those sorts of issues—not all of which were very productive at the end of the day', according to Scott Dawson.[22] These discussions with the United Nations were more than attempts to convince; they began to take on characteristics of partnership as UNAMET was launched and the popular consultation drew closer.

Australia also conducted discussions with other potential partners. In the case of New Zealand, the aim was to maintain their interest in supporting Australia with forces at a later date. The purpose of these discussions was to create a sense of partnership, because the New Zealanders were considered valuable coalition partners due to their assessed willingness to engage in offensive military operations under a UN mandate.[23]

From the point of view of both the Australian Government and the Australian Defence Force (ADF), the most important line of consultation was occurring with the United States. Formal consultation started early in 1999 with an exchange of views between DFAT's Secretary, Dr Ashton Calvert, and Stanley Roth of the US Department of State. This meeting provides an insight into the aims of Australian consultation at this time. It also shows the differences between US and Australian views about the likelihood of a peacekeeping mission, and of options to influence the situation.[24] The similarities in policy positions were still strong, however, especially on key points such as alerting the Indonesians to their security responsibilities and their assessment of Habibie's 'unreal'

---

21   Interviews with 007-05 and 062-07.

22   Interview with Scott Dawson.

23   Interview with Allan Behm.

24   The official record of this meeting was leaked in 1999. See Department of Foreign Affairs and Trade, 'Calvert-Roth Meeting, February 1999', copy in author's possession, paragraphs 10–12. The divergence is somewhat ambiguous in this account of the conversation as Calvert and Roth were discussing the same hypothetical situation in different timeframes. As a result, it is likely Roth was playing a 'devil's advocate' role rather than representing official US policy, as Paul Kelly reports (Paul Kelly, *The March of the Patriots: The Struggle for Modern Australia*, Melbourne University Press, Carlton, Vic, 2009, pp. 495-96).

deadline.[25] Occurring early in the crisis, this conversation shows how the Australian Government was clearly moving towards the 'partnership' point of the Bridgman and Davis continuum as it sought to influence the US Government to develop a position that was complementary to Australia's view.

Consultation between Australian ministers and officials and their US counterparts continued throughout the year. This consultation was complicated because different parts of the US Government held different views on the how the United States would act if the situation in East Timor required intervention. General John Castellaw of USPACOM provided an insight into how Washington—meaning the US Departments of State and Defense—were thinking at the time:

> I had the opportunity to host John Hamre, who was the Deputy Secretary [of Defense] and he gave an insight into how [the United States viewed the East Timor situation]. I would say that we viewed this very reluctantly. If you look at that period there we are talking about, 1999, we had come out of Desert Storm and we were still doing no-fly zones in Iraq. We'd done Bosnia-Herzegovina and Kosovo. ... So Hamre said, quite frankly, we were tired by this time in the decade and the Clinton Administration was [tired] too. It became apparent to me, as we were getting pressure to reduce the numbers involved that the policymakers and senior leadership were very reluctant to get involved in the effort.[26]

Despite this indicator, USPACOM—the key US military arm in the Pacific—continued contingency planning for a large involvement in East Timor.[27] For some in Australia, this gave the impression of there being two US positions: one of anticipation of action in Hawaii, and the other of significant reluctance in Washington, DC. This difference was noted by senior ministers and it became the subject of media speculation after mid-year leaks.[28] However, others such as Calvert took USPACOM's activities in a different context:

> It was pretended, in terms of some of the media commentary, [that] they [the United States] were ready to do peacekeeping ... and with just a bit of extra urging [the Australian Government] would have gotten them

---

25 Department of Foreign Affairs and Trade, 'Calvert Roth Meeting', paragraphs 7–9.

26 Interview with John Castellaw. This view was consistent with that expressed by Earl Hailston and a number of Australians including Chris Barrie and Bob Treloar. See also Goldsworthy, 'East Timor', pp. 234–35.

27 Interviews with Earl Hailston, John Castellaw, Bob Treloar and Ashton Calvert. The contingencies considered at this time by USPACOM ranged from low-level evacuations up to a multinational peacekeeping intervention—the figure of 15 000 US troops was mentioned in the Australian Parliament (Stephen Martin, MP, House of Representatives, *Votes and Proceedings*, vol. 55, 11 August 1999, p. 8419).

28 Interview with John Moore. For examples of how the media portrayed this difference, see Paul Daley, 'Timor: We Snub Offer To Send In The Marines', *Sunday Age*, 1 August 1999, p. 1; and Paul Daley, 'Rift Denied With US Over Timor', *Age*, 3 August 1999, p. 3. Don Greenlees and Robert Garran, *Deliverance: The Inside Story of East Timor's Fight for Freedom*, Allen and Unwin, Crows Nest, NSW, 2002, pp. 240–48, describe the reluctance of influential leaders in Congress to commit troops.

there. My understanding was this was not the case. They [USPACOM] certainly had no authority from Washington for peacekeeping. What they were doing was ... military contingency planning for one or both of those scenarios.[29]

Consultation can be politically dangerous when confidential information is leaked. In this case, the revelations contained in the Australian press were politically embarrassing because they created the perception of differences between the positions of the Australian and US Governments, and obliquely between Washington and USPACOM.[30] Leaks also created problems further down the line, according to Bob Treloar: '[The leaks about USPACOM planning] caused some grief and severe compartmentalisation of [ADF] planning processes. Compartmentalisation is an anathema to good planning and preparedness of the troops. It undermines confidence ... and morale.'[31]

The discussions between Australian and USPACOM staff were conducted though liaison officers, videoconferences and visits. These exchanges had a number of aims including comparing each party's understanding of the situation, reviewing the type of contingencies that might arise, and outlining possible military options. The power of this consultation at the operational level was built on very strong bonds between senior USPACOM officers and their ADF counterparts, and resulted in a close and shared understanding between the two organisations by the middle of 1999.[32] Castellaw described the relationship in this way:

> We understood completely how the Australian Army operated, and they understood how we operated. We trained together, planned together, played together. ... We were friends and we enjoyed working with each other. We had a shared view of how planning and operations were conducted. I think you are looking at one of the very, very few situations where US forces were willing to subordinate themselves to another country's military leadership.[33]

However, consultation across the political and military levels was not always so easy to manage despite the alliance and a high degree of familiarity among many of the key leaders. The size and complexity of the US Government seemed

---

29   Interview with Ashton Calvert.
30   Refer to Daley, 'Timor: We Snub Offer', which broke this story. This report drew a denial from Foreign Minister Downer (Sean Aylmer, 'Timor: Downer Says There's No Rift With US', *Australian Financial Review*, 2 August 1999, p. 7). Give the absence of access to US planning documents, it is difficult to determine whether an actual difference between Washington and PACOM existed.
31   Interview with Bob Treloar.
32   Interviews with Bob Treloar, Allan Behm and John Castellaw.
33   Interview with John Castellaw. He was referring to Major General Peter Cosgrove, then Commander of the 1st Australian Division and future commander INTERFET, and Colonel Mark Kelly, Cosgrove's Chief of Staff.

to be one contributing factor. For one interviewee, this crisis exposed a lack of understanding of among Australian officials of the US political system. While the relationships were strong, particularly with USPACOM and the US intelligence community, there was a lack of understanding about how Washington—particularly the US Department of Defense—worked.[34]

Other factors also complicated Australia-US consultation. Marian Wilkinson reported the difference of opinion about the Indonesian military's capacity to maintain security throughout the ballot, and Australia's reluctance to provide the United States with intelligence due to a need to protect 'sensitive Australian intelligence sources'.[35] So while there was clearly some level of misunderstanding between the Australians and their US counterparts before the ballot, the work done throughout 1999 still resulted in a high degree of cooperation between Defence and USPACOM in particular. This work proved beneficial once the crisis became acute in September 1999.

As the situation in East Timor grew into a violent crisis, Australia's consultation—often led by Prime Minister John Howard—aimed to secure international support for an intervention force with an appropriate mandate.[36] The trend for consultation was clearly now towards 'partnership', although it could be argued that Australian consultation had become 'delegation' as the UN Security Council (UNSC)'s decision became crucial to Australian policy in mid-September.

The Australian Government continued to make use of its good relations with key UN bodies as the crisis developed. Howard was in direct contact with UN Secretary-General Kofi Annan, which was crucial because the aim of Australian diplomacy at the time was to create support for a robust Chapter VII (of the UN Charter) mandate. It is easy to forget that such a mandate was not assured, even after significant international opinion came to favour intervention. One interviewee talked about the importance of continued consultation with UN members, such as the Russians, who may have vetoed any UN operation.[37] At this point, Australia's consultation almost became 'delegation' as the government refused to be part of a peacekeeping force without a UN mandate, clear US support and Indonesian permission.[38]

---

34 Interview with 051-06.

35 Marian Wilkinson, 'Why we kept Timor secrets from the US', *Sydney Morning Herald*, 13 August 1999, p. 1. The view of separation between Australia and the United States was taken up in Parliament by opposition member Laurie Brereton and challenged by Foreign Minister Downer (*Sydney Morning Herald*, 'What force in East Timor', 11 August 1999, p. 14).

36 James Cotton, East *Timor, Australia and Regional Order: intervention and its aftermath in Southeast Asia*, Routledge, London, 2004, p. 121.

37 Interview with Michael Scrafton. In the end, the Russian Federation indicated a willingness to 'expeditiously consider additional measures to resolve the situation in East Timor.' (Department of Foreign Affairs and Trade, *East Timor in Transition 1998–2000: An Australian Policy Challenge*, p. 252).

38 These conditions (or close variations) were described in numerous public statements, including Defence Public Affairs, 'Transcript, Hon. John Moore, MP & Hon. Alexander Downer', Commonwealth Offices,

Given these conditions, and the rising public support for intervention described in Chapter 3, it is possible to see a situation where the desire for consultation could have unhinged Australia's preferred policy line during the acute crisis. For instance, if a permanent member exercised their veto against the Chapter VII mandate, Australia (and others in the international community) would have needed another mechanism to legitimise any operation into East Timor. That did not happen of course and, given the support of all permanent members, this scenario was most unlikely.

The form of US support was only assured after a series of meetings between Australian and US officials from 6–9 September 1999. These meetings included at least two videoconferences which discussed the detailed concept for the operation and the likely US contribution.[39] While there was clear political support for ending the violence (the president and a number of senior officials made direct approaches to their Indonesian counterparts during this time),[40] the United States was unwilling to commit combat troops to the mission unless the situation became dramatically worse.[41] This surprised ministers who thought they knew US leaders well and thought they understood the Australia, New Zealand and United States Security Treaty (ANZUS). John Moore recounted one such instance:

> I spoke to Bill Cohen, who I knew before. ... The answer from Cohen was 'it is your baby'. I said that you need to help—it's part of ANZUS. But he said it is all yours. I asked what he would do, and he said he'll have to think about it. He said they would give us intelligence, and he would get back to us. But he said precisely, 'no troops'.[42]

This sparked further consultative efforts on multiple fronts:

> When I [John Moore] spoke to Howard about the fact that we were getting absolutely nowhere with [Bill] Cohen on the matter, I said I was

---

Melbourne, 6 September 1999, available at <http://www.minister.defence.gov.au>, accessed 12 December 2007; Department of Foreign Affairs and Trade, *East Timor in Transition1998–2000: An Australian Policy Challenge*, p. 133; and Interview with Chris Barrie.

39   Goldsworthy, 'East Timor', pp. 248–49.

40   These approaches are outlined in Greenlees and Garran, *Deliverance: The Inside Story of East Timor's Fight for Freedom*, pp. 240–48, and included calls by then US Secretary of State Madeline Albright, Secretary of Defense William Cohen, Chairman of the Joint Chiefs and General Henry Shelton. Commander Then USPACOM Admiral Denis Blair also made a short and reputedly pointed visit to General Wiranto on 8 September 1999. President Bill Clinton made a number of approaches to President B.J. Habibie, including the direct call for Indonesia to accept a peacekeeping force on 10 September (Associated Press, 'U.S. Suspends Military Relations with Indonesia', *The Augusta Chronicle*, 10 September 1999, p. A09).

41   Interview with John Castellaw. John Moore recalled how he asked Bill Cohen for an assurance that US troops would provide additional support if the situation became 'murky', which the US Defense secretary agreed to do. Goldsworthy claims the US decision not to deploy combat troops on the ground with INTERFET was made clear to the Australians on 9 September (Goldsworthy, 'East Timor', p. 249).

42   Interview with John Moore.

astonished. He said that APEC [the Asia Pacific Economic Cooperation meeting] is on in Auckland, and I'll speak to [US President Bill] Clinton. Downer went off to New York, and he was going to chase around there. Nothing came of that. When Howard spoke to Clinton, Clinton said he would have to do something for us. So I rang Cohen again and Cohen rang back. He said he'd come out to Australia to meet me in Cairns.[43]

The importance of obtaining support for the International Force in East Timor (INTERFET) from Southeast Asian nations was quickly understood, and Australia used a range of methods to ensure such consultation occurred quickly. The 9–12 September 1999 APEC meeting in Auckland was critical to this effort, as it brought many key regional leaders together. But, as the earlier discussion of Air Marshal Doug Riding's regional tour in September shows, not all consultation was successful to the extent initially anticipated. In Malaysia's case, early discussions with Australian diplomats indicated that a significant leadership role and a sizeable troop contribution would be forthcoming.[44] Malaysia's ultimate decision not to participate provides an example of where domestic political issues and concern for international relationships intrude on consultation.[45] Other ASEAN nations also needed to balance competing concerns. Singapore's decision calculus included local sensitivities about sending conscripts overseas, and a desire to avoid offending Indonesia or Australia.[46] The Philippines Government was concerned for the danger to its Catholic neighbours, but also wanted to maintain a good relationship with Indonesia. This led to the dispatch of a 'humanitarian task force' from the armed forces of the Philippines to East Timor, and a medical team to West Timor.[47] That 22 nations eventually joined the coalition speaks for a significant success of this consultation, even if it did not achieve exactly its desired outcome.

Consultation continued with Indonesia, with the aim of establishing the modalities for deconflicting INTERFET and TNI operation in Dili. Martin Brady attended talks with senior TNI leaders to achieve this outcome:

---

43   Interview with John Moore.
44   Some have also pointed to the importance placed in not 'offending' Indonesia and to the Association of Southeast Asian state's (ASEAN) doctrine of 'non-interference' (Interview with Ashton Calvert, and Alan Ryan, *Primary responsibilities and primary risks: Australian Defence Force participation in the International Force East Timor*, Land Warfare Studies Centre, Duntroon, Canberra, 2000, p. 41).
45   It is hard to separate this outcome from other factors, such as the poisonous relationship between then Prime Minister Mahathir and Australia and concern over command and funding arrangements (Interviews with 051-06 and 046-06. See also Ryan, *Primary responsibilities and primary risks: Australian Defence Force participation in the International Force East Timor*, pp. 40–42 and Goldsworthy, 'East Timor', p. 251)
46   Interviews with 051-06 and 046-06; and Goldsworthy, 'East Timor', pp. 251–52.
47   Goldsworthy, 'East Timor', p. 252.

> We wanted to de-conflict their operations, so we had three days of talks [at the United Nations in New York] to manage the matter in great detail. It also gave them a sense of partnership, and might have even helped in the long run. We never talked about it publicly, and it never came up.[48]

On the aid front, consultation moved quickly once the humanitarian task became clear and the need to create a new government from scratch was known. In this case, AusAID was able to provide immediate assistance and create an interim development strategy. Their work before the popular consultation provided a springboard for this. Established links with the United Nations and United States also helped, even though new players from these organisations entered the scene.[49]

Domestic consultation

At best, there were two indirect methods of consultation with domestic audiences during this crisis. The first, which has been mentioned earlier and will be taken up again in Chapter 5, was Parliament's Foreign Affairs, Defence and Trade References Committee enquiry into East Timor.[50] This committee heard testimony from many individuals, community groups and officials during its hearings, and these provided a broad picture of what the Australian community thought about the situation in East Timor. Second, the government had access to polling data about the crisis at frequent intervals.[51] However, because neither constitutes a solicitation of opinion by the executive, or discussions before decisions are taken, they cannot be considered consultation in the sense proposed by Bridgman and Davis.

While falling well short of the consultation measures used during other crises (such as during 1941–42 when the Australian Government formed a bipartisan Advisory War Council[52]), the government still provided information directly to the opposition about their policy on East Timor. This contact followed

---

48 Interview with Martin Brady. Interviewee 007-05 also recounted the importance of these talks, and of the important work done by Australia's mission to the UN during the crisis.

49 Interview with Scott Dawson.

50 Foreign Affairs, Defence and Trade References Committee, *Final Report into the Inquiry into East Timor*, 2000.

51 Newspoll conducted a survey on 12 September 1999 that asked voters directly about the government's handling of the crisis (available at <http://www.newspoll.com.au>, accessed 26 August 2006). Roy Morgan Research also asked voters about their perceptions of the government and the opposition three times during September–October 1999, and made comment on voters' positive views of how the prime minister was handling the crisis ('Labor Stretches Two-Party Preferred Lead As Troops Go In To East Timor', Finding No. 3240, 12 October 1999, available at <http://www.roymorgan.com>, accessed 26 August 2006).

52 The Advisory War Council was a compromise arrangement to ensure unity of decision-making after the Labor Opposition declined Prime Minister Menzies' invitation to join a 'national government' (see David Day, *The Politics of War: Australia at War 1939–45 from Churchill to MacArthur*, HarperCollins Publishers, Pymble, 2003, p. 86; and David Horner, *Inside the War Cabinet: Directing Australia's War Effort 1939–45*, Allen and Unwin, St Leonards, NSW, 1996, pp. 20–21).

convention where the Australian Government seeks to create a bipartisan view of policy by discussing major commitments, such as the deployment of troops, with the Opposition. This may also extend to allowing Opposition leaders to read intelligence reports and receive briefings from officials. However, these briefings were one-way communication according to then Opposition leader, Kim Beazley:

> The opposition is not consulted on national security. The opposition is often quite intensively briefed, but we are not seen as part of the decision-making process. On some occasions, such as when it is necessary for us to facilitate a piece of legislation [through Parliament] you get engaged, but that's up to the prime minister ... [with regard to East Timor specifically] ... I was briefed occasionally [as opposition leader], but our defence and foreign affairs spokesmen were briefed all the time. Very regularly. It was much more intense than now.[53]

Despite this, the opposition was given advance notice of the major deployments, such as the commitment of UNTAET and INTERFET, but not other major initiatives, such as the Howard Letter. Beazley's final remark shows that this convention may not be applied consistently, or at least applied as consistently as the alternative government might like.

Secrecy and consultation

The principle of strict secrecy was applied in this crisis although, as the comments above about leaks showed, it was not always maintained. Despite these breaches, four main reasons for maintaining secrecy can be identified in this case. The first involves protecting a policy position while it is being developed. The Howard Letter was a good example of how well secrecy could be applied, and how secrecy can prevent an initiative from being pre-empted by other parties or derailed by opponents. A second, related reason is to allow one side to make preparations for an activity without alerting possible opponents or the public. This helps to maintain the element of surprise; it may also allow the government to act without scrutiny during sensitive activities. A third reason for secrecy involves protecting confidences; this is why the Calvert–Roth cable was classified, and why its leaking embarrassed the Australian Government. Lastly, secrecy helps protect intelligence sources and methods.[54] This need

---

53 Interview with Kim Beazley.
54 For instances where information about intelligence activities came into the public domain, see Paul Daley, 'Spy effort stepped up in Timor', *Age*, 20 March 1999, p. 5; Paul Daley, 'Armed with information, now what?', *Age*, 29 May 1999, p.4; and Ian Hunter, 'Elite forces scouted island from April', *Sydney Morning Herald*, 11 October 1999, p. 11.

explains why the Riding/Behm mission to Jakarta in June 1999 was very risky, for it involved an admission that Australian intelligence had access to sensitive Indonesian information.[55]

These advantages allow governments to feel justified about maintaining secrecy in crises. However, it may be more difficult to maintain secrecy in the future. While measures can be taken to avoid leaks, these are not foolproof and come at a cost for efficiency and internal cohesion. More importantly, the public's increasing access to information, analysis and opinion is likely to place pressure on the government's narrative in a future crisis. While some activists and the media tried to produce a different story to promote immediate intervention during the acute crisis, the Australian Government was not forced to act prematurely and the public remained broadly satisfied with the government's actions in September 1999.[56]

Observations about consultation

This examination of the Consultation phase shows some continuity with the 'typical' characteristics, but also significant differences that are attributable to the nature of national security crises. Consultation during the crisis also spanned Bridgman and Davis' continuum, and showed clearly that governments can cede control over national security policy to outsiders during a crisis.

In this case, consultation efforts did not involve the government engaging the public in any real way. Instead, the main consultation was between the Australian Government and foreign entities, especially the governments of the United States, Indonesia, Portugal and New Zealand; and non-government agencies and agents including the United Nations and East Timorese leaders. Most of this consultation took place in the space between information and partnership on the Bridgman and Davis continuum. The Australian Government used this space to obtain views about policy options (generally in terms of others' aims and positions), convince others of the merits of the Australian case and develop aligned positions with important actors.

Interaction with specific entities later in the crisis showed consultation in the form of delegation, verging on control. In this case, the Australian Government was only willing to act decisively to stabilise East Timor if their desired

---

55   Greenlees and Garran, *Deliverance: The Inside Story of East Timor's Fight for Freedom*, pp. 166–68.

56   For examples of media encouragement, see Paul Kelly, 'From the Lips of Prime Ministers: Diplomacy at the Crossroads', *Australian*, 15 September 1999, p. 13; and Andrew Bolt, 'Don't Expect Praise', *Herald Sun* (Melbourne), 16 September 1999, p. 18. Of course, critics also assailed the government for its handling of the crisis (for example, see Greg Sheridan, 'The Burden is Here to Stay', *Australian*, 17 September 1999, p. 15). For the public's reaction, Newspoll's 12 September 1999 questions shows opinions evenly split between support for the government's actions and opinion that the government was not doing enough (see <http://www.newspoll.com.au>, accessed 26 September 2006).

conditions for intervention were met by Indonesia, the United Nations and others. This movement along the consultation continuum showed the real limits of the Australian Government's agency in this crisis, and demonstrated the importance of creating space for future activity through constant attention to relationship building. Such space was needed because the Australian Government was unwilling to create a deeper conflict with Indonesia by pressing ahead unilaterally. It therefore relied on bringing others to a similar way of thinking about the problem, using both the post-ballot violence and the pattern of diplomatic contact that had been developed over the previous—and indeed, many—years.

Bridgman and Davis consider consultation as intrinsically good for policy development because it increases policy legitimacy and acceptance, and this case provides examples where consultation was beneficial to Australia. It is clear, for instance, that consultation reduces friction in policymaking because it allows the government to understand the policy positions of others and provide opportunities to devise strategies to overcome possible friction. For example, the limited consultation between the Australian Government and the Opposition served to build sufficient consensus for the government's action without letting the opposition share the credit for the decisions. While this consultation may only come late in the crisis or appear perfunctory, it remains an important step for winning bipartisan support, especially for military action, in a crisis. The value of consulting with international leaders was also shown in this crisis. Although the consultation undertaken at the APEC meeting in Auckland imposed a short delay in the process, it was clearly worth using this opportunity to gain international support for intervention.

The Howard Letter shows the risk when consultation is not undertaken. After the government's new policy position became known, wider and more focused consultation began with a broader range of actors. Since some actors held opinions that differed from those of Australia, the government found that it needed to do significant work to close the gaps in views (notably with the United States over the likely outcomes and the applicability of the ANZUS Treaty) as the pressure to act increased throughout the year.

Regardless of the potential for gains and cost avoidance, consultation is not automatically beneficial in crises because it can actually decrease the chances of success. First, consultation increases the time it takes to make a decision by increasing the number of actors involved, potentially allowing other parties to take the initiative or resulting in missed opportunities. Second, consultation also gives opponents time to take pre-emptive action or marshal opinion against a policy. This desire to limit the potential for damaging criticism or debate was one reason why knowledge of the Howard Letter was confined to a very small group and not shared with allies. Third, consultation also increases the chances of allowing other parties to know one's intentions. Thus the compromise of policy intentions during consultation can jeopardise surprise and reduce trust among potential partners. These reasons provide support for anticipating a continued role for the characteristic of secrecy in crisis policymaking.

This examination of the Consultation phase shows that the typical characteristics can be modified for crisis policymaking as follows:

- All consultation options are used with overseas interlocutors (who are primarily other governments and major international organisations), with information, discussion, partnership and delegation commonly occurring;

- Consultation between the government and the public usually takes the form of a one-way passage of information; and

- Much consultation occurs in secret.

Coordination

The Coordination phase aims to achieve 'tolerable compatibility' across government activities in an attempt to minimise harmful inconsistencies. This phase is characterised by the way coordination is institutionalised through structures and routine processes.[57] However, there is more to coordination than this, and other influences—often described as bureaucratic politics—can also interfere. Two characteristics for the Coordination phase can be identified from Bridgman and Davis:

- Governments will describe structures and routines that suit their particular preferences and best thinking for the time, the task at hand, and external factors.

- Coordination is conducted in a competitive environment.[58]

This section examines how the structures and routines described in Chapter 1 actually worked in this crisis, while pointing to the importance of informal practices that bind this system together. The thorny question of bureaucratic politics is then broached, for it provides evidence to show that collegiality prevailed over harmful competition in this case.

---

57   Bridgman and Davis, *The Australian Policy Handbook*, pp. 93–97.
58   Bridgman and Davis, *The Australian Policy Handbook*, pp. 93–104.

Structures and routines for coordination

Structure is often used to promote coordination where tasks are complex and require different types of specialised knowledge, or where conflicts of interest can occur.[59] In this case, structural changes were made to clarify roles, to improve dialogue between departments and to meet the tangible challenges of this crisis. However, opinions about the role of central agencies—which Bridgman and Davis see as essential to coordination—and the effectiveness of those changes were varied. The role of political leadership in coordination is also underplayed and deserves separate consideration.

Early interdepartmental dialogue became formalised in a number of different ways by April 1999. Further to existing committees and forming new ones (such as Bill Paterson's Committee), departments extended standing invitations to other agencies for internal planning meetings (such as Defence's East Timor Working Group and, sometimes, the Strategic Command Group), while joint delegations travelled to places such as the United Nations and Washington. DFAT helped to tie these structural changes together by exercising a leading role in the period before INTERFET's deployment. This involved being the focal point for Cabinet submissions, leadership of a variety of interdepartmental delegations, raising a consular crisis centre with *ad hoc* staffing, and retaining the chair of the Strategic Policy Coordination Group (SPCG).

The nature of the acute crisis in September tested these existing coordination structures and created a need for new ones. One of the main changes to interdepartmental coordination came as the National Security Committee of Cabinet (NSCC) began to operate on a daily basis, and the main coordinating role of the SPCG passed to the Taylor Committee.[60] While it could be argued that such arrangements could have been put in place before the crisis, some interviewees remarked that it was either difficult to foresee some aspects of what happened (such as leading the international force), or that the need to create new bodies would not have arisen if the violence had not triggered a rapid international intervention.[61]

Opinions varied on the effectiveness of the new arrangements, particularly the Taylor Committee. While the Department of Prime Minister and Cabinet (DPM&C)'s role in coordination was widely acknowledged, many also recognised that existing coordination mechanisms were not delivering as well as they should. But some close to the committee (although outside it) were sceptical about its role and effectiveness. Some commented that the Taylor Committee

---

59   Anthony Downs, *Inside Bureaucracy*, RAND/Little, Brown and Company, Boston, 1968, pp. 50–53.
60   Interviewee 051-06 observed that the informal processes of the SPCG made it unsuited to managing a crisis and noted broader concerns about the need to coordinate better at the official level. For background, see the section in Chapter 2 titled 'Acute crisis and response'.
61   Interviews with Chris Barrie, 024-05 and 028-05.

became too bureaucratic and inflexible, or that it existed on the fringe of the action.[62] Others such as Hugh White and General Michael Keating did not consider *ad hoc* solutions suitable in any case:

> It seemed to me that the establishment of this new mechanism under [D]PM&C, to replace other mechanisms that I think were working satisfactorily, was a mistaken move and a move that was made more about bureaucratic politics than good advice to government.[63]

> I'm not so sure about the 'wrong output from the SPCG' line [as justifying the need for the Taylor Committee]: if you don't like the output, (leaders should) tell the SPCG to create the right output, rather than create another body.[64]

Other interviewees, often those closely involved in the committee, were more supportive—perhaps because they had a different view of the committee's mandate:

> The whole support to government stepped up eight or ten notches as a consequence of Allan's committee. A lot of it was due to having the function, and a lot was Allan's ability to manage it.[65]

> The [Taylor] Committee ... kept the discipline if you like. ... It wasn't a high-powered policymaking body, it was there to coordinate. To smoothe the wheels.[66]

> ... to some degree the creation of another committee was amusing at the time. But with hindsight, what we didn't realise at the time, was that we were learning. So when we found something wasn't working, we formed the Taylor Committee. It wasn't the case that we just stuck with something. We moved onto a different model ...[67]

> The Taylor Committee came after a very hectic year and an acute crisis. It was time to find a way to step back, draw a breath and find a way to develop some medium- and long-term policy options for the relationship with Indonesia.[68]

The adoption of new methods to coordinate policy shows, as Aldo Borgu said in his interview, that the government as a whole was learning as it went. The

---

62 Interviews with Aldo Borgu, 009-05, Michael Scrafton and 032-05.
63 Interview with Hugh White.
64 Interview with Michael Keating.
65 Interview with Michael Scrafton.
66 Interview with 014-05.
67 Interview with Aldo Borgu.
68 Interview with Ashton Calvert.

key officials learned quickly (or knew from experience) about the potential disconnects that could occur in the existing structures and the weaknesses in those mechanisms, so they made changes. In one interpretation, this shows that a highly adaptive mindset is necessary to keep the activities of a large number of agencies coordinated in a national security crisis. It also shows that involving ministers and senior officials in crisis simulations may help them to learn before an event, and so reduce the chance of mid-crisis change. In another interpretation, decisions to form new bodies in the midst of a crisis can be simply part of an ongoing conflict where agencies jockey for power.

One prescription for avoiding conflict over responsibilities (or turf) is role clarity. A lack of role clarity, should it exist, can have consequences including conflict, nugatory work at lower levels, and work at 'cross purposes with people running different agendas'.[69] While some activities needed active de-confliction and demarcation, Australian Government agencies seem to possess a good idea about what they were required to do during this crisis. For example, the coordination role played by DPM&C was understood and not disputed, as was DFAT's leading role in the pre-crisis meetings with external actors and Cabinet submissions. This is not to claim that the division of responsibilities was always clear, and some instances of where people are uncertain about processes or rules should be expected in any new situation. However, Alan Ryan's assessment that 'the issue of how departmental responsibilities were divided was never fully resolved' seems to overstate the difficulties faced in this case.[70]

Having a way to settle disputes over responsibility quickly, authoritatively and with minimal work is therefore essential to successful coordination. The method used in this crisis can best be likened to a series of courts. Small problems between departments, generally technical ones linked to different interpretations of policy or legislation, may get resolved in lower-level committees (like that chaired by Bill Paterson) or in discussions between officials. If not solved here, problems would be elevated to more senior committees including the SPCG and the Secretaries Committee on National Security (SCNS). The final court was the NSCC, but the ministers would be displeased if a matter reached them that could have been resolved at lower levels.[71]

Agencies were very aware of their responsibilities, but still willing to cede some at different times. One example involved Defence conducting important diplomatic tasks instead of DFAT (as discussed in Chapter 3). Understanding what counterpart organisations actually do is another way of ameliorating

---

69   Interview with Bob Treloar.
70   Ryan, *Primary responsibilities and primary risks: Australian Defence Force participation in the International Force East Timor*, p. 39.
71   In his interview, Tim Fischer recounted the prime minister's intolerance towards 'protecting fiefdoms' and airing interdepartmental conflicts in the NSCC.

conflict.[72] The less-formal interactions between DFAT and Defence's Strategic Command Division staff mentioned by Michael Keating were attempts to promote this understanding.

Providing a forum to reconcile issues is another way of inducing role clarity and reducing the problem of turf battles. According to Interviewee 052-06, the SCNS played an important role as it allowed a 'fairly robust discussion' between the departmental secretaries. Issues that could not be resolved here would be referred to the ministers. All were aware that such a move would provide additional, unwelcome work for the minister that could be viewed as a failure on their part.

The role of the central agencies of DPM&C and Treasury is interesting because this case provides an important distinction between the view of coordination presented by Bridgman and Davis, and this particular instance of crisis policymaking. According to Bridgman and Davis, the central agencies 'work to resist fragmentation by providing consistent rules and processes'.[73] Their view receives wide support in other literature, including work that ascribes a key role to the British Treasury.[74]

This case provides partial support for the usual interpretation of the roles played by central agencies. On balance, DPM&C played its established role throughout.[75] It was involved in developing the broad direction for policy (such as its involvement in drafting the Howard Letter), while performing its usual tasks of advising the prime minister and guiding Cabinet business. DPM&C's main new intervention in the process—forming Bill Paterson's group—was also a fairly normal response to this kind of matter. While no doubt useful, this committee played a relatively small part in coordination compared to others such as the SPCG (which included DPM&C representation), DFAT's East Timor Task Force and Defence's East Timor Working Group.[76] Consequently, DPM&C did not assume a leading position (and still an indirect leadership role) until the acute crisis. On the other hand, the other major central agency, the Treasury, was only a minor player. It limited its involvement mainly to matters of expenditure, although it would have played a key role in the question of the 'Timor Tax'.

---

72 Interview with Adrien Whiddett.

73 Bridgman and Davis, *The Australian Policy Handbook*, p. 97.

74 These works include Hugh Heclo and Aaron Wildavsky, *The Private Government of Public Money: Community and Policy inside British Politics*, MacMillan, London, 1974; and Martin Smith, *The Core Executive in Britain*, MacMillan Press, Basingstoke, 1999.

75 Interviewee 052-06 noted how DPM&C handled their role 'as normal' though International Division and, later, the Taylor Committee.

76 Both DFAT's and Defence's coordinating committees met far more frequently than Paterson's group, and often included representatives from the same organisations.

Political leadership through the NSCC was another structural element of coordination with a deeper relevance. The view of the NSCC as the bridge for national security policy was mentioned in Chapter 1, as this is the place where authoritative commands were issued and, sometimes, where gaps between departments were closed. When asked about how coordination looked from the political level, Interviewee 048-06 commented that it was 'better than normal' because daily NSCC meetings during the acute crisis imposed discipline on the bureaucracy; there was less room for conflict because answers were needed the next day. But routine was not the only factor. The strong solidarity of the NSCC was important for preventing gaps opening between departments.[77] This also led to a strong distaste for conflict or competition between departments among the senior ministers and indeed senior leaders. As Tim Fischer noted, anything more than 'a touch of light banter' would have resulted in a censure from the prime minister and secretary of DPM&C.[78] The distinctive flow-on effect of this attitude will be discussed later in this section.

Ministerial staffs were also involved in coordination through their role in keeping their minister aligned with the prime minister and other ministers. This role extended to keeping ministers aware of departmental activities— whether by reading submissions, calling senior departmental officers or even sometimes attending senior departmental meetings. Advisers would also help to coordinate activity by describing 'the minister's thinking' on various issues. Of these advisers, the prime minister's international adviser played a crucial part as a conduit of information to, and from, the prime minister.[79]

Routines also help to coordinate activities by making actions consistent and predictable.[80] Thus DPM&C's *Cabinet Handbook* outlines a number of routines that ensure coordination occurs before submissions are presented to Cabinet.[81] These processes are supported—in theory at least—by strong links between the norm of coordination, the concept of collective responsibility of Cabinet, and the strong desire to prevent surprises from emerging at the Cabinet table or in discussion between senior officials.[82]

While formal Cabinet submissions seem to have been infrequent in this case, it was usual for other documents and draft cables to be circulated to relevant

---

77   While John Moore thought the relationships between key ministers were very good (Interview, 29 November 2006), other interviewees thought competition between the prime minister and Treasurer Peter Costello could be observed.

78   Interviewee 051-06 also said that the prime minister would not tolerate poor cooperation.

79   Interview with Aldo Borgu.

80   Glyn Davis, *A Government of Routines: Executive Coordination in an Australian State*, Centre for Australian Public Sector Management/MacMillan, South Melbourne, 1995, pp. 24–26.

81   B. Guy Peters, 'Managing horizontal government: The politics of co-ordination', *Public Administration*, vol. 76, no. 2, 1998, p. 41.

82   Interview with 052-06.

stakeholders before final submission. The small size of the policy community undoubtedly helped to make this process relatively smooth.[83] Of the major instruments used to support routines, it was the time-honoured methods of meetings, telephone calls and—although a relatively recent innovation at the time—email that helped make the processes work at the speed required.[84]

Despite this, and noting that uncertainty still exists over what was discussed at the 1 December 1998 NSCC meeting, the East Timor crisis appears to have begun with an instance of poor coordination. Paul Barratt recalled his words to the Secretary of DPM&C on 22 December:

> I said to Max [Moore-Wilton] that I had just heard about the letter to Habibie and that we weren't consulted on that letter. I said that we had consultative processes coming out our ears, and they are rigorously enforced, insisted upon, except when it matters.[85]

The effect of this lack of coordination was felt deeply within Defence. On top of the frustration expressed by Hugh White at the 15 January 1999 SPCG meeting (as discussed in Chapter 2), Defence planners were forced into a situation where a range of practical options needed to be devised quickly. The ADF itself needed to conduct a crash program of resource redistribution and training to bring sufficient forces to readiness for deployment.

Other problems—many of which were discussed earlier in Chapters 2 and 3—continued to flow from the initial decision not to consult or coordinate on the policy shift concerning East Timor. In particular, it was clear that DFAT's preferred policy line of early 1999, which aimed to prevent a major rupture in Australian-Indonesian relations, could have been compromised by Defence's need to prepare forces for operations. The problem was further embodied in the different ways both departments viewed the possible course of the crisis, and their different concepts of 'worst case'.[86]

While a number of instances have been discussed already, communication between departments posed additional problems. On one hand, it might be difficult to find the person who could make a decision in a large place like Defence, and work-arounds or a range of entry points might be needed if difficulties were encountered with specific people.[87] There were also times where

---

83   Interviews with 028-05 and 032-05.

84   Most interviewees spoke of the importance of direct communication to coordination. For example, Adrien Whiddett spoke of regular liaison meetings and telephone calls, Andrew Hughes spoke of the need for a central crisis room, and Allan Behm spoke of the way email could be used effectively when people asked themselves who really needed to know the information.

85   Interview with Paul Barratt.

86   Interviews with Allan Behm, Peter Briggs and 035-05.

87   Interviews with 014-05, 028-05, Andrew Hughes and Major General John Hartley (Canberra, 27 September 2005). Hartley was Land Commander Australia in 1999. As such, he was responsible for preparing

people found themselves talking in different languages: another interviewee thought a 'Babel Fish' was needed to interpret between the government and the ADF on some occasions.[88] But even if such a device existed, there would still be a range of other problems confronting coordination, such as secrecy, compartmentalisation, policy ambiguity and the turf battles associated with bureaucratic politics.

Collegiality trumps turf

Structures and processes are clearly important to coordination, but they may not be sufficient. As the popularity of bureaucratic politics as an explanation for intra-governmental behaviour shows, there is a deep-seated view that government agencies act in their own self-interests and this creates competitive or even conflictual relationships.[89] While it is possible to observe instances of conflict and competition between departments in this case, these instances were relatively minor and immaterial to the outcome. Instead, this case provides support for the view that relationships between government departments in a crisis are more collegial and reliant upon informal aspects of coordination such as relationships and trust.[90]

Strong personal relationships, a willingness to approach the work with a collegial attitude, and the small size of the group involved in the case and their frequent experience of working together,[91] were cited as important factors for coordination in a number of interviews:

> I think [relationships are] critical ... especially at the SES [Senior Executive Service] level in the Commonwealth, and even the states.[92]

Australian land forces for deployment and providing advice to the Chief of Army and COMAST.

88   Interview with 009-05. A 'Babel Fish' is a mythical animal that instantly translates any language into another.

89   For a sample of the Australian literature on role of bureaucratic politics in foreign and defence policy, see Russell Trood, 'Bureaucratic politics and foreign policy', in F.A. Mediansky (ed.), *Australian Foreign Policy into the New Millennium*, MacMillan Education Australia, South Melbourne, 1997; Nancy Viviani, 'The Official Formulation of Foreign Policy', in F.A. Mediansky and A.C. Palfreeman (eds), *In pursuit of national interests: Australian Foreign Policy in the 1990s*, Pergamon Press, Sydney, 1998; Christopher Waters, 'The Great Debates: H.V. Evatt and the Department of External Affairs', in Joan Beaumont, Christopher Waters, David Lowe and Gary Woodard (eds), *Ministers, Mandarins and Diplomats: Australian Foreign Policy Making 1941–1969*, Melbourne University Press, Carlton, Vic, 2003, pp. 54–58; Geoffrey Hawker, RFI Smith, and Patrick Weller, *Politics and Policy in Australia*, Queensland University Press, St Lucia, 1979, Chapter 7; Gary Smith, Dave Cox and Scott Burchill, *Australia in the world: an introduction to Australian foreign policy*, Oxford University Press, Melbourne, 1996, p. 45; and Des Ball, *The Politics of Australian Defence Decision Making*, Reference Paper No. 183, Strategic and Defence Studies Centre, The Australian National University, Canberra, 1991, p. 46.

90   This view is also shared by Allan Gyngell and Michael Wesley, *Making Australian Foreign Policy*, Cambridge University Press, Cambridge, 2003, pp. 40–42 and p. 253.

91   Interviewees 020-05, 051-06 and 032-05 commented on the way the small group involved in national security policy was a particular advantage for Canberra.

92   Interview with Adrien Whiddett.

That our senior ministers, senior bureaucrats and senior military have worked with each other in the past means they can talk with each other on the phone and fix problems. That was a great advantage in 1999.[93]

[Relationships] were very important. Did I go about building them? No, I didn't. They came about through a process that I don't think exists any more. I went though a series of jobs that put me into professional contact with military officers who were coming up through the system ...[94]

I knew most of the people. One of the points I would make is that coordination in Australia is easier in the security area than in any other major country that I am aware of because ... [for example] all of the other heads of the intelligence agencies had been contemporaries, or near contemporaries in DFAT in the [19]60s and [19]70s. So we knew one another. We could just pick up the phone. We were around the lake. It was not difficult to coordinate at all.[95]

Trust also allowed action to occur faster, and the familiarity gained during ordinary times often bred confidence between people.[96] While relationships usually worked better where they had been established, newcomers were not excluded. This was most notable in departments or agencies that posted people into and away from Canberra—especially DFAT, the ADF and the AFP. In these instances, it was normal for people recently appointed to jobs in Canberra to either bring someone with established relationships with them to meetings, or seek to develop relationships quickly. On some occasions however, newly arrived or promoted senior officials would delegate (for a short period) the function of working with other stakeholders to a close subordinate who had been in position longer. When the time came to build one's own network, officials generally did so through the formal structure of meetings and committees. Beyond that, people grew their relationships through telephone calls, emails and informal discussions.[97]

In other situations, people with wide-ranging ties could be used as intermediaries, using the trust they had developed in different organisations to bridge gaps:

---

93   Interview with 029-05.
94   Interview with Michael Scrafton.
95   Interview with 014-05.
96   Interview with 021-05 (Canberra, 12 August 2005). Interviewee 021-05 was a former senior Defence intelligence official.
97   Interviews with 012-05, Kerry Clarke, 020-05, Martin Brady, 024-05, Michael Keating and Andrew Hughes.

I think one role that I played was that I was seen to be a reasonably sensible player from both the bureaucratic and political side of the house, which was kind of to lend a bit of confidence in both areas that their concerns were being taken care of.[98]

The key [to understanding the positions of other ministers] was the Defence and Foreign Affairs Adviser to the Prime Minister, Michael Thawley ... he understood defence, he understood foreign affairs ... and he was an enormous support to me when I started at Defence.[99]

Thus trust was clearly important to coordination in this case, and it seems to have been more widespread—to different degrees, but widespread nonetheless—at the more senior levels in government. Thus relationships within Cabinet, and between officials and ministers in the NSCC, were important to maintaining cooperation throughout.[100] At other times, strong relationships and trust had not been formed at lower levels and this could be a problem: 'That level of relationship didn't necessarily exist further down the chain—that it was more compartmentalised both within and between organisations.'[101]

It was not all plain sailing though, and a few interviewees reported minor instances of disagreement and even conflict between individuals.[102] Matthew Skoien went as far as to speak of animosity between Defence and DFAT at some levels, especially at first. However, the same interviewee also said that:

When people realised what needed to happen, they just got on and worked together ... and made things happen despite other issues and problems. So when the group was brought together and given some imprimatur to do something, I think, that even if the government structures and formalities weren't there, individually we all got on and worked well together.[103]

This experience was echoed by Interviewee 033-06, who said that working together in a crisis soon overcame attitudes whereby people were departmental

---

98   Interview with 009-05.

99   Interview with John Moore.

100   John Moore described his strong trust in one of his senior officials, and how this influenced his way of working. Daryl Williams identified the need to trust people because he, as a minister, did not have all the information. Hugh White observed the long way many officials had to come in 1996 to overcome the new government's mistrust of their relationship with the previous government.

101   Interview with Andrew Hughes.

102   Interviews with Paul Barratt, 012-05, Michael Keating and Andrew Hughes all cited instances where disagreement or conflict occurred. However, none recalled this as a major impediment to policymaking.

103   Interview with Matthew Skoien. Interviewee 062-07 thought that some DFAT officials had a poor understanding of ADF officers and tended to underestimate their knowledge.

representatives first, and team members second.[104] This view of good working relationships was also seen in instances where parts of different organisations worked together. For example:

> I don't recall any animosity. Strategic Command had been working extensively with relevant DFAT teams—joint briefings on what we did and why, and at social gatherings including dinners and drinks—before and after I arrived ... All this was to our favour after the crisis started.[105]

This kind of divergence in opinions about working relationships shows how perceptions of conflict can vary according to where you sit, and can be strongly influenced by personalities. In other words, conflict may occur as a result of institutional pressures, but conflict also occurs because individuals simply allow it.

Observations about coordination

This case supports the importance placed upon structures and routines in coordination by Bridgman and Davis. However, the evidence of this case adds weight to the collegial interpretation of coordination over the competitive, bureaucratic politics view.

This case shows the importance being flexible enough to change structures and routines when the situation warrants. Such flexibility was shown in 1999 in the way different committees and staff organisations were formed to cope with the increased policy workload and the imperative of keeping activity aligned. The way some important committees, especially SCNS and the SPCG to a lesser extent, were sidelined during the acute phase also shows an instance where structures were adapted to the situation. Flexibility was also displayed in the way departments invited others to meetings, and generally used their input to improve policy advice. This shows the value of being pragmatic in times of crisis, and making changes where essential.

The extent of structural and process change does not mean that the policymaking process was entirely deficient, or that it was entirely unable to cope with the demands of the day. Some of the existing structures, particularly the NSCC, served the Australian Government well. It is also important to acknowledge that politicians and senior officials were able to change structures, while the people involved adapted to the situation quickly and made the new structures work under considerable pressure. As a result, the case shows that adaptation in crisis should not be feared if people are sufficiently flexible to cope with

---

104 Interviewee 062-07 also noted the importance of establishing himself as part of the team when sent to work in another department.
105 Interview with Kerry Clarke.

new demands. However, relying upon continual adaptation as the method of structuring for crisis also contains risks which could be minimised if well-considered and practised alternative structures and processes are available to deal possible crises.

The East Timor crisis also points to other important factors for coordination. This case shows that big is not necessarily better: the relatively small size of the Canberra bureaucracy can help to improve policy responses to new situations. Even more importantly, this case highlights the importance of informal aspects such as relationships and trust to coordination.

Some authors place these informal aspects at the centre of coordination. For example, Donald Chisholm argues that informal bargaining, norms or networks based on friendship or technical expertise are powerful devices under some conditions.[106] However, these informal mechanisms are not given enough attention, often because they are considered as illegal, unhealthy or designed to achieve personal—rather than organisational—goals. Chisholm promotes a contrary view to the orthodoxy and instead describes informal networks as flexible, adaptive, coherent and problem-oriented.[107] The importance of informal aspects was reasonably well-understood by practitioners and often mentioned in interviews, but they are not mentioned by Bridgman and Davis. This case supports the need to encourage informal coordination methods, while noting the importance of formal structures that provide these methods with an overarching legitimacy.

The importance of established relationships does not mean that 'newcomers' find it difficult to break into the tight circle of national security policymakers. That the posting cycle for most Departments continued during the crisis meant that new people were continually being changed in the very senior echelons—particularly in DFAT and Defence—and these newcomers needed to adapt quickly to both the demands of their new jobs and the issues at hand. These factors show the need to develop a resilient personnel system, as Paul Barratt stressed in his interview:

> It is also important that the organisation is not too personality dependent. Like a person could get run over by a bus on the way home from work, and you should never be in a situation where the organisation is going to fall over. It is a badly run organisation that would let that happen.[108]

---

106   Donald Chisholm, *Coordination without Hierarchy: informal structures in multiorganisational systems*, University of California Press, Berkley, 1989, pp. 11–12 and p. 39.
107   Chisholm, *Coordination without Hierarchy: informal structures in multiorganisational systems*, p. 12 and pp. 27–28.
108   Interview with Paul Barratt.

The norm of 'no surprises', role clarity, interpersonal relationships and trust created an air of collegiality in national security policymaking in this case. This characteristic is generally omitted from the literature concerning policymaking, especially where bureaucratic politics is offered as an explanation for behaviour or outcomes.

Indeed, most of the comments about coordination in the interviews conducted for this study describe a far more collegial approach to policymaking than the theory of bureaucratic politics would allow. Differences—which certainly existed—occurred at the margins, and these should be expected. However, a number of factors may have worked to lessen conflict, such as the small size of the bureaucracy, the urgent nature of the crisis, the relatively clear division of responsibilities, political leadership and the significant interpersonal relationships between key players.

It is entirely possible that collegiality is a transitory phenomenon. The body of literature concerning the role of bureaucratic politics in foreign and defence policy means this view was widely held in Australia from the 1950s until the 1990s. In this case, however, a collegial attitude can be seen in the way officials emphasised the importance of respecting the roles of others, 'getting on' and maintaining relationships. These norms were backed by a strong political will to finish the task. However, it is possible that a future government may not be as cohesive as the NSCC of 1999, or as able to exert its will over interdepartmental rivalries. Future collegiality should not be assumed, and governments will need to take active steps to promote trust and cooperation, and reduce the rewards for destructively competitive behaviour.

There are clearly some differences between the 'typical' characteristics and those seen during crises. As a result, the characteristics of the Coordination phase in crisis policymaking will be thus changed:

- Governments describe structures and routines that suit their particular preferences and best thinking for the time, the task at hand, and external factors; and

- Coordination is basically collegial, but the potential for conflict should not be ignored.

Ministers have been involved in policymaking at various stages of the cycle; they have been important to identifying issues, have participated in analysis and even conducted consultation. Their influence has also been felt in coordination. The next chapter examines the point where ministers become central to policymaking, namely the Decision phase. But that point is not the end of the story because decisions must be implemented and, in theory at least, evaluated. The task of examining these last three policy cycle phases is taken up in Chapter 5.

Chapter 5
Decision and Beyond

This chapter completes the study of Australian policymaking during the 1999 East Timor crisis by examining the last three phases of the policy cycle: Decision, Implementation and Evaluation. This chapter follows the format of the previous two.

Decision

The Decision phase is the pivotal point of the cycle where the analysts' work is judged by the authoritative actors in the cycle—in this case, the prime minister and the National Security Committee of Cabinet (NSCC). The characteristics proposed by Peter Bridgman and Glyn Davis for the Decision phase are:

- Cabinet is dominant;

- Officials, when invited, answer questions of a technical nature and leave the room before decisions are taken; and

- Cabinet conventions are based on collective responsibility, secrecy, and recorded decisions.[1]

This phase is pivotal; but it is also opaque. While anecdotal evidence is often provided in memoirs, the press and interviews such as those undertaken for this study, the vital documents that record cabinet decisions are secured from the public for thirty years. The revealing records of cabinet conversations, which are contained in cabinet notebooks, are withheld for fifty years. Further, the processes or factors considered in the day-to-day decisions of political leaders often go unrecorded. Together, this lack of good evidence makes it difficult for an outsider to understand decisions processes in this case (and others as well). As Paul Barratt remarked: 'Getting inside the minister-to-minister relationship is a hard veil for anyone to penetrate.'[2]

As a result, this section offers insights about the factors that led to specific decisions in the East Timor crisis. Further evidence, such as Cabinet notebooks and Cabinet submissions, will be needed to reconstruct the discussions between

---

1   Peter Bridgman and Glyn Davis, *The Australian Policy Handbook*,

3rd edn, Allen and Unwin, Sydney, 2004, pp. 106–109.
2   Interview with Paul Barratt.

Australia's senior leaders. Meanwhile, the interviews collected for this case study provide some evidence to begin understanding the Decision phase's characteristics.

Dominant prime minister and involved committee

While Cabinet remained the final authority for decisions, it is more useful to focus on the dominant role of the prime minister and the main Cabinet committee, the NSCC. As noted earlier, the membership and processes of the NSCC are different to Cabinet and other committees in that officials are invited to sit with politicians. The NSCC also has considerable formal power because its decisions are recorded as Cabinet decisions (although that power is not absolute as the NSCC refers some matters to the full Cabinet). This power was used extensively in 1999 by the NSCC, and it seems that only decisions concerning the final or in-principle decisions regarding the deployment of police or military forces to East Timor were referred to Cabinet.[3] This freedom to commit the government and direct activity allowed the prime minister and the NSCC to be the dominant decision-makers in this case.

There are three other reasons for this dominance. The first relates to then Prime Minister John Howard's personal authority. Electoral success clearly played a role in generating this authority, while being at the centre of the government meant that most key decisions were brokered through his office. These factors were enhanced by Howard's personality and his colleagues' trust. This was activated through his meticulous attention to process and inclusive pattern of consultation; he learned the value of carrying his colleagues with him from observing other prime ministers.[4] But the prime minister was also his own man:

> Anyone who takes the prime minister (Howard) to be a patsy for anyone else is seriously mistaken. He would make his own decisions, and he often went against other ministers or officials. ... No committee that Howard chairs runs by consensus. It runs by trying to get agreement— and that doesn't mean that Howard has made up his mind (beforehand)— but when he has made up his mind there is no doubt that he gets what he wants.[5]

---

3   John Moore also described the autonomy generally received in defence and national security matters from Cabinet, and neither Tim Fischer nor he could recall a situation where Cabinet overturned an NSCC decision.
4   Interviews with John Moore and 051-06. Interviewee 052-06 noted how the prime minister used NSCC as a tool to keep his key ministers involved. Other commentators noted John Howard's dominant and personalised role. For examples, see John Birmingham, 'A Time For War: The Re-birth of Australia's Military Culture', *Quarterly Essay*, no. 20, 2006, pp. 42–43; and Greg Sheridan, 'All the World's a Stage', in Nick Cater (ed.), *The Howard Factor: A Decade that Changed the Nation*, The University of Melbourne Press, Carlton, 2006, p. 159.
5   Interview with Chris Barrie.

These factors of delegation, process and personality helped Howard to lead authoritatively during crisis, but another factor was also important. The second reason was that the grouping of Howard, Treasurer Peter Costello, Foreign Minister Alexander Downer and Deputy Prime Minister (and National Party leader) John Anderson meant that the NSCC contained Cabinet's key leaders.[6] When Defence Minister John Moore—who had a reputation as an internal powerbroker—was added, it is not surprising that the NSCC was able to dominate national security decision-making at that time.

This group relied on precedent to operate as it did. Former deputy Prime Minister Tim Fischer likened this to the authority given to the Expenditure Review Committee in the budget process, but there was also an intangible factor: 'I think there was a feeling of comfort [in Cabinet] that if the NSCC had looked at it in detail then it did not need to be unpicked.'[7]

This confidence was born partly from the status of the individual members, and partly from success in managing other major issues, such as the Asian Economic Crisis.[8] When coupled with their access to information and close contact with senior officials, the NSCC had the means and authority to act within Cabinet's very broad guidelines and a degree of latitude to make new policy if needed.

Procedural factors were the third additional reason to explain the NSCC's dominance. One important contributor was the NSCC's ability to meet daily (and frequently twice daily) during the acute stage of this crisis.[9] This meant that NSCC ministers were kept apprised of breaking issues and agencies raised matters for decision in a timely fashion.[10] Other factors that promoted the NSCC's role included access to briefings, the ability to question senior officials in depth and together (noting ministers would not usually be able to quiz the senior officials from departments other than their own), and the ability to conduct consultative and coordination tasks themselves. Taken together, these procedural factors gave the national security ministers a high degree of awareness and involvement in the crisis. It also allowed them to move the NSCC from being a decision-making body alone towards being a body for decision and management.

Dominance has pitfalls though. It is also possible that a dominant group can suffer from a cognitive defect, such as bias or groupthink. While the

---

6   John Anderson replaced Tim Fischer in July 1999.
7   Interview with Tim Fischer.
8   Interviews with Chris Barrie and Aldo Borgu. The Asian Economic Crisis refers to the series of interconnected financial meltdowns that afflicted some Asian countries, including Indonesia, in 1997–98.
9   It is hard to determine the actual frequency of full Cabinet meetings during the acute phase of the crisis, but most interviewees could not recall meetings more frequently than weekly during September 1999.
10   Interview with 048-06.

methodology used in this study was not suited to identifying these types of problems, it is possible to see how the NSCC could get sidetracked on important, but nonetheless second-order issues. Hugh White provided an example:

> Minister Downer made his 'coalition of the willing' remark on [the weekend]. NSCC met on Monday and did not discuss it—they focused on the safety of consular officials in Dili instead. They got to the coalition statement on Tuesday, [the same day] Habibie was in press saying it would not happen.[11]

These remarks were widely reported,[12] and the notion was quickly and explicitly rejected by President B.J. Habibie.[13] Yet this apparent diplomatic disagreement did not ultimately have a major impact on other important factors, such as international support for Australia's leadership role. In White's opinion, that was a close call. While consular official safety is important, the focus on this issue to the exclusion of major matters such as international relationships and national credibility prevented the NSCC from developing a unified view on coalition development at this delicate moment. It also prevented the NSCC from considering how best to clarify what might have been interpreted as a call to arms against Indonesia. 'It was lucky that we had the initiative,' said White.[14]

Howard also used other mechanisms for decision-making in this crisis. Of these, unilateral decisions were the least used and seem limited only to times where he was discussing fast-moving events with international leaders.[15] More commonly, Howard would discuss important emerging issues with Downer and Moore.[16] Other important consultations occurred between ministerial advisers, and between ministerial advisers and the prime minister's office. Interviewee 051-06 characterised such discussions as a normal way of doing business, especially in a system where ministers have substantial authority to act in their own right and direct control over principal instruments. Since these discussions tended to foreshadow subsequent NSCC discussions and decisions, the committee's central role was preserved.[17]

---

11 Interview with Hugh White, who was referring to Alexander Downer's doorstop interview on 4 September 1999 (see Geoffrey Barker, 'Australian foreign minister on possible peacekeeping force', Radio Australia, 4 September 1999).

12 Paul Daley, 'Troops Could Go Within Days', *Sunday Age*, 5 September 1999.

13 Shaun Anthony, 'Jakarta blocks Canberra's call for armed intervention', *West Australian*, 6 September 1999.

14 Interview with Hugh White.

15 Hugh White recounts the interaction between John Howard and UN Secretary-General Kofi Anan as one instance, although Howard was probably working within the NSCC's agreed course at the time.

16 Defence Minister John Moore acknowledged that a 'sub group' of Ministers, not the full NSCC, would be meeting on the night of 6 September 1999 to discuss the Timor Crisis (see Defence Public Affairs, 'Transcript, Hon John Moore, MP & Hon Alexander Downer', Commonwealth Offices, Melbourne, 6 September 1999, available at <http://www.minister.defence.gov.au>, accessed 12 December 2007).

17 Interview with John Moore. Interviews with Tim Fischer, 051-06, 048-06 and 064-07 also described the important role of informal contact between ministers and the facilitating role of their advisory staff.

Closely involved officials

The emergent role for the NSCC was influenced by the growing trust between the political leaders and their senior officials during 1999. In 1998, it was common for officials to attend the NSCC, but to not always stay for the entire meeting; at times, they would be asked to leave when matters got 'political'. There would also be occasions where officials were not invited at all.[18]

This situation changed in 1999, where senior officials, the prime minister's international adviser and (frequently) less-senior officials and ministerial staff attended most, if not all, NSCC meetings and stayed throughout.[19] According to one interviewee, this was indicative of the government learning that the bureaucracy was not full of 'old Laborites', but of seasoned public servants who were experienced in national security matters.[20] At other times, it was a reflection of fast-moving events.

The privilege of attending the complete NSCC meeting provided those senior officials with a better understanding of the reasons for decisions, and an opportunity to comment as the discussion progressed toward decision. It did not, however, mean that the officials participated in the decision, for 'you always knew they were the decision-makers and we were the advisers'.[21] The close involvement was reflected by Chris Barrie, Hugh White and Paul Barratt, who described the NSCC's atmosphere as one of open discussion or even 'collegiality'.[22] These descriptions speak of a high degree of trust between the NSCC ministers and their senior officials during this crisis.

A conventional Cabinet?

While Cabinet's conventions were observed, some were bent to fit the particular requirements of the events of 1999. Of these, secrecy and collective responsibility remained intact, although the latter was modified in that the NSCC—rather than the full Cabinet—took most major operational decisions.

Compromises were made in other areas as well. First, the NSCC took many briefs verbally, bypassing the normal process of written submissions and coordinating comments. This potential weakness was ameliorated by the Taylor Committee's work, as it consulted across government relatively quickly when preparing its submissions. Another factor that ameliorated concerns about the lack of formal

---

18   Interview with John Moore.

19   Interviews with Hugh White and Paul Barratt.

20   Interview with Chris Barrie. This point was supported in interviews with Daryl Williams, Tim Fischer and John Moore.

21   Interview with Paul Barratt.

22   Interviews with Hugh White, Chris Barrie and Paul Barratt. Daryl Williams also described how the prime minister invited his international adviser to make policy contributions in the NSCC (Interview, 17 March 2007).

process was the members' willingness to accept an occasional surprise: 'No one was too precious about having uncleared matters (tabled), especially once the tempo of events increased.'[23] This was a particularly telling compromise, for it ran against the norm of 'no surprises', and adds support to the 'collegial' view expressed in earlier.

The close involvement of ministers and senior officials in the details of the crisis was another factor that modified normal processes and promoted faster decision-making. According to Hugh White:

> One of the ways that people get crisis management machinery wrong is that they assume that, in a crisis, ministers still have limited time and limited attention because they are getting around a whole lot of other things. That's not what happens. ... In a crisis, the only people who understand the situation are the ministers. And the people lower down know less and less about what is going on.[24]

This highly abbreviated and closed form of decision-making meant that normal processes—involving formal consultation, briefing papers and preliminary committee meetings—became less important as the crisis progressed. One factor enabling this was the tendency for ministers and officials effectively to stop work on most other tasks. They read cables (reports from overseas missions), intelligence briefings and other submissions more carefully and more often— and developed a deeper understanding of the situation. In this sense, most NSCC members became both the 'desk officer' and the decision-maker during this crisis.[25]

It is one thing to make decisions; it is another to communicate decisions so people charged with implementation can do so faithfully. With the limited information contained in formal minutes, a short space of time between meetings and the hyper-busy schedules generated by crisis, officials rely upon understanding the decision-makers' intent.[26] The guidance provided by the NSCC was considered satisfactory by a number of interviewees—and, importantly, none complained about an inability to understand the NSCC's intent.[27] Scott Dawson from AusAID thought:

---

23 Interview with Chris Barrie.
24 Interview with Hugh White.
25 Interview with Hugh White.
26 Intent describes the outcomes desired by political leaders. Intent may be more encompassing in practice, for politicians may also choose to stipulate how the outcome is to be achieved, and not just what should be achieved. An understanding of intent enables subordinates to adjust their plans to the emerging situation, or to take action where guidance is incomplete or ambiguous.
27 Chris Barrie, Hugh White and Michael Scrafton made particular mention of the importance of intent in their interviews.

[A Cabinet decision was] a pretty clear statement ... after the ministers agreed it. So in that sense we had a clear statement of intent. ... I don't recall too much difficulty that he [our minister] had with anything that we sent to him, and [cabinet and ministerial submissions] were written in a way designed to give us a mandate to go ahead and do things.[28]

However, many senior leaders had only a general understanding of their minister's detailed requirements and relied upon their understanding of the context of events to develop directives to their subordinates:

We had some very clear understandings of what a number of key objectives had to be. ... I think in these broad terms we had an understanding of the key challenges and particularly what to avoid.[29]

... You might get word from the minister that this [issue] was being canvassed. You would also look for the Cabinet document to find things for [us]. You certainly had a hankering of what it was about before [NSCC decisions] came and you would know what was coming.[30]

Other ministers, notably Downer, would have regular meetings with task force officials to hear their views directly:

Every two weeks we would brief Downer on how the ETTF [DFAT's East Timor Task Force] was tracking. This was an informal, fireside chat ... there was no agenda, it was very much a 'so what have you got for me.' ... Downer would say what he had to say, [and] offer guidance or not.[31]

These few comments show that while intent is transmitted in a number of ways, the most important factors for understanding intent was a knowledge of the minister's or senior official's long-term goals and preferences, an understanding of where others stood on an issue, some ability to extrapolate once new information came to hand, and a willingness to ask follow-up questions.[32] But a clearly stated intent was not always easy to obtain, as Aldo Borgu noted:

The minister was under no illusions that he necessarily knew what he wanted, so he was fairly reliant upon the department for advice on issues. He would give broad parameters, but given Moore's style he was not the

---

28 Interview with Scott Dawson.
29 Interview with 009-05.
30 Interview with Adrien Whiddett.
31 Interview with 062-07.
32 Interviewee 051-06 described the value the prime minister and other ministers placed on knowing the opinions and preferences of other main actors before decisions were made.

sort of person who communicated by reams of paper. His style was to talk to people and talk through issues, and he would have someone from the office involved. He would say 'you tell me what'.[33]

Consequently, subordinates still worked hard to identify the intent of a decision before they passed instructions to others. However, this management approach may be a blessing: after all, it would be a poor minister who provided a misleading intent to their officials.

Observations about decision

While making definitive observations about the substance of decisions during the East Timor crisis remains difficult, it is possible to discuss the way the Decision phase worked. For one, the prime minister's dominance is clear. Howard's chairmanship of the NSCC gave him the final say in decisions, but his style was not unilateral: he preferred to operate with and through his key committee. As a result, the existence of a strong leader, and indeed a strong leadership core, meant most decisions were made through the NSCC without constant or even frequent reference to Cabinet. When the focus of ministers upon the issue is added, the NSCC acted as a highly responsive committee that managed the crisis—particularly the acute stage—to achieve the main objectives of the day (see p. 58).

The NSCC's effectiveness was shown by the way their intent was grasped by those officials responsible for implementing policy. For example, the NSCC's position on a number of critical issues was well understood, such as the conditions for Australian involvement and the desire to avoid war with Indonesia. In addition, the close interaction between senior officials and political leaders ensured that if the NSCC did not provide all of the necessary direction, the officials could follow their intent. This need for officials to interpret guidance, understand the broader context of issues, and make changes as the situation demands is clearly an essential aspect of crisis policymaking.

While these changes involved some temporary bending of particular Cabinet conventions, one important convention concerning the separation of political decision-makers and their official advisers was applied less stringently in 1999.[34] That the nation's political leaders overcame the real (or perceived) suspicion of their senior public servants, and trusted their officials to remain throughout the NSCC meetings, was important to making decision-making faster and more

---

33   Interview with Aldo Borgu.
34   Allowing officials to sit through NSCC meetings might be interpreted as a reversion to Australian practice during the Second World War, where officials frequently sat with Cabinet ministers on important war-related committees. See Martin Painter and Bernard Carey, *Politics Between Departments: The fragmentation of executive control in Australian government*, University of Queensland Press, Brisbane, 1979, pp. 100–104.

responsive than might otherwise have been possible. This shows a highly pragmatic streak at play, which means that a Decision phase like the one used in 1999 may not be repeatable under other conditions and leaders.

As a result, the Decision phase in crisis is slightly different to the typical. It is therefore worth characterising this phase in terms of:

- The prime minister is dominant.

- Cabinet conventions are based on collective responsibility, secrecy, and recorded decisions; and

- Officials, when invited, may remain during all discussion; but in general they answer questions of a technical nature and leave the Cabinet room before decisions are taken.

Implementation

Implementation is the penultimate phase of the policy cycle, where 'the machinery of government smoothly implements the Cabinet's wish—in theory'.[35] The two main characteristics of implementation identified by Bridgman and Davis were:

- Implementation is considered throughout the policy cycle; and

- The more agencies involved, the more difficult implementation becomes.[36]

Since this study takes a Canberra-centric view of national security policymaking, there is no intention to discuss here the activities of the diplomats, election officials, police, military personnel or aid workers who actually served in East Timor or elsewhere.[37] However, issues such as the way forces were assigned to the International Force in East Timor (INTERFET), how aid was organised and how the media was managed from Canberra are germane to this discussion.

Considered throughout the policy cycle

Implementation occurred throughout 1999, often in parallel with earlier parts of the policy cycle. One particularly good example of this was the Australian

---

35 Bridgman and Davis, *The Australian Policy Handbook*, p. 119.
36 Bridgman and Davis, *The Australian Policy Handbook*, pp. 119–21.
37 A number of other authors have undertaken this task, including Bob Breen, *Mission Accomplished—East Timor*, Allen & Unwin, Crows Nest, NSW, 2000, for an ADF perspective; Neil Sugget, *See the Road Well: Shaping East Timor's Frontier*, Pandanus Books, Canberra, 2005, for the perspective of Customs officials after early 2000; Lansell Taudevin, *East Timor: Too Little Too Late*, Duffy and Snellgrove, Sydney, 1999, for an aid worker's perspective; and Richard Tanter, Mark Selden and Stephen Shalom (eds), *Bitter flowers, sweet flowers: East Timor, Indonesia, and the world community*, Rowman & Littlefield Publishers, Boulder, CO, 2001, for a number of papers about UNAMET's activities.

preparation for dealing with an independent East Timor, which included establishing a direct connection between humanitarian aid and East Timor, and by establishing a consulate in Dili.[38] A second instance displaying simultaneity between consultation and implementation can be seen in the way Australia prepared forces for peace operations—widely interpreted as peace operations in East Timor—while the Australian Government insisted that Indonesia remained responsible for security. These examples show how considerable amounts of policy may need to be developed after implementation begins.

In another respect, those implementing policy may be writing aspects of that policy at the same time. This situation was evident during the period when the INTERFET coalition was formed. Officials exercised a significant deal of discretion at this time, offering carrots and some small sticks in order to entice decisions from potential contributors. On one occasion, INTERFET Branch made it known that attachés from non-contributing nations accredited to Canberra would soon be excluded from the classified operational briefs. As one foreign government, in particular, was horrified at the thought of being excluded from the 'inner circle', INTERFET Branch and their attaché kept the conversation open and this eventually led to a contribution of forces to INTERFET.[39]

Structures and processes need to be in place to support implementation. One example is the need for appropriate financial arrangements to support novel solutions to policy problems. As AusAID found in this case, budgets and annual allocations can actually work against implementation by delaying activity or by precluding certain options. Despite these impediments, the agency juggled rules and realities—sometimes by using 'creative accounting' measures such as trust funds or moving funds between appropriations—to ensure that the desired policy was implemented.[40] These points highlight the importance of legitimate and understood financial processes that are flexible enough to make funds available when they are needed to support implementation.

One interesting aspect of implementation in this case was the way the strong political imperative behind INTERFET allowed, or perhaps forced, officials to take risks that might have been unacceptable under other circumstances. This was especially noticeable in the way officials accepted a large degree of

---

38   For example, DFAT listed a range of implementation activities and aid programs in relation to East Timor in their March 1999 submission (Department of Foreign Affairs and Trade and AusAID, *Submission to the Senate Foreign Affairs, Defence and Trade References Committee Inquiry into East Timor*, Senate Foreign Affairs, Defence and Trade References Committee, *Additional Information, Volume 5*, Commonwealth of Australia, Canberra, 1999, pp. 047–048 and pp. 056–062).

39   Interview with Steve Ayling.

40   Steve Darvill described how one agency wrote a contract for helicopters to support UNTAET from June to August 1999 (Interview, 5 July 2005). While sufficient funds were available for the full contract, this money would be 'lost' at the end of the financial year—and they were not permitted to commit the Commonwealth unless they had an approved budget. At this stage, AusAID created a new 'trust fund' so that the money could be held beyond the formal financial year.

financial risk in order to facilitate (or entice) non-Anglo-Saxon contributors to INTERFET.[41] In some instances, Australian officials showed significant initiative by agreeing to pay for capital equipment items and to underwrite compensation benefits for a number of contributors as a way of getting their rapid agreement to make a contribution.[42]

Implementation was also essential to supporting the political message in other ways. Early in the United Nations Mission in East Timor (UNAMET) deployment, the Department of Foreign Affairs and Trade (DFAT) and AusAID recognised the importance of getting UN humanitarian agencies involved, and showing the people of East Timor that Australia was supporting them. This required some novel and risky implementation measures according to Steve Darvill of AusAID:

> Again, it was that kind of practical stuff [that was needed]. ... I was phoning around trying to get rice. And Ralph [an AusAID official] essentially went to Woolies and emptied their warehouse of rice, so that day there was stuff to drop. Back here I was phoning rice growers, and working out how to get it there. So I was on the bus on the way home, negotiating for a 747 [aircraft]. It was expensive, but we had to make things happen. There was a political message that we had to get out there.[43]

Desperate times often call for creative thinking and unusual measures.

The use of the media during crisis is another aspect of implementation, and one that attracted criticism from a number of interviewees. One important use was the way Australian leaders employed the media to make sense of the crisis for the Australian public.[44] During September 1999 alone, Prime Minister John Howard gave 53 separate media interviews and speeches that helped him to explain the situation to domestic (and sometimes international) audiences. He used these opportunities to explain the events in East Timor, outline the reasons for Australia's commitment, stress Australia's role as being both in-line with the international community and in-line with Australia's responsibilities, and to reduce growing domestic animosity against Indonesia. He did not, however, miss the opportunity to highlight the government's political achievements and how these contributed to the operation's success.[45] Other ministers also

---

41   Interview with Steve Ayling.

42   This example financial risk was discussed in the earlier discussion of policy instruments in Chapter 5.

43   Interview with Steve Darvill. The risk of this hurried activity was shown when a food airdrop injured a small boy (see 'Refugee boy crushed by East Timor airdrop', *Birmingham Post*, 30 September 1999, p. 9).

44   See Paul 't Hart, K Tindall and C Brown, 'Success and failure in crisis leadership: Advisory capacity and presidential performance in the 9/11 and Katrina crises', unpublished paper, 2007, pp. 7–8.

45   For example, Howard linked the government's economic management to the operation in East Timor (John Howard, 'Address to the ACT Division of the Liberal Party', 29 September 1999, available at <http://www.pm.gov.au>, accessed 10 April 2006).

provided press briefings or spoke to other audiences; the Defence minister made 23 announcements about the East Timor operation and the Foreign minister made at least 31 announcements—the majority of these in the period 6–10 September 1999.[46] The Australian commander in East Timor, Major General Peter Cosgrove, also played an important part in developing the narrative and providing a reassuring message to people in Australia and internationally.[47] However, it was the prime minister who carried the bulk of the message to the Australian people and presented the government's preferred view of this crisis.

Getting this message out is not simple, and there are significant limitations in using the media as a tool to support policy implementation. First, having an independent media reflect the government's preferred view is no easy task. This difficulty is magnified when the target of influence is a foreign population, and their domestic media is the only viable way of reaching them. One interviewee, who was involved in Defence's public affairs organisation in 1999, recounted the analysis undertaken to identify how to get messages to the Indonesian people in particular, and the Southeast Asian public more generally. He cited the real challenge with getting balancing messages through media outlets that were either controlled by foreign governments, or highly sympathetic to their government's position.[48] He also noted the decline of funding for Radio Australia and Australia Television International during this period, but added the audience for this type of media was relatively small. He thought suggestions that foreign media could be manipulated were fanciful, but recounted the way positive messages were sent to specific audiences in Japan to encourage their support.[49]

The second difficulty relates to the tools available to an organisation such as Defence public affairs. The formal tools—press releases and media alerts—often provide the news 'filling' for the daily newspapers. However, they have limited utility if the media wants other stories or is simply unwilling to accept the view presented to it. Also, public statements need to be carefully managed to ensure all remain 'on message'. Transcripts of media interviews and speeches by Prime Minister Howard, Foreign Minister Downer and Defence Minister Moore all showed high degrees of consistency in their messages about the international mandate, relationship with Indonesia, and will of the East Timorese people when discussing the intervention. Keeping these messages coordinated was a major

---

46   This workload compelled the minister of defence to assign a second adviser to the media liaison role to keep track of the requests and allow the primary media adviser to maintain close contact with the prime minister's office (Interview with 048-06).

47   Interview with Chris Barrie.

48   A problem noted in James Cotton, *East Timor, Australia and Regional Order: intervention and its aftermath in Southeast Asia*, Routledge, London, 2004, pp. 121–22; and Department of Foreign Affairs and Trade, *East Timor in Transition 1998-2000: An Australian Policy Challenge*, Commonwealth of Australia, Canberra, 2001, p. 145.

49   Interview with 066-07, who has knowledge of Defence public affairs planning in 1999.

task that required real ingenuity given the technology of 1999. In one instance, the system of synchronising near simultaneous briefings in Dili, Darwin and Canberra involved taping conferences and then playing them down the satellite phone line to the next conference location.[50]

Third, it was also difficult to be 'proactive' due to political sensitivities (as discussed earlier) and the complexity of engaging with a sceptical media. Interviewee 066-07 recounted one attempt where Defence arranged for a very senior ADF officer to speak to an influential Indonesian journalist about a range of topics, with the aim of showing Australia's benign intentions and friendly attitude towards Indonesia. By his recollection, this attempt was only marginally successful and almost back-fired as the journalist interpreted a casual remark in a negative way. On other occasions, the desire to get fresh news footage from East Timor to the international media could have resulted in negative images of the Australian intervention being sent into the public domain. This led to some photographs being confiscated to protect operational security and Australia's image. Engaging with the media to implement policy is clearly an important, but complex, aspect of implementation.

Other interviewees criticised the Australian Government for being less than effective in using the media to further their interests. The attempts to influence regional perceptions about Australia, as mentioned in Chapter 4, are one example. However, the broader problem concerned the difficulty with using information as a policy instrument. For example, Allan Behm said:

> My view was that you should use the international media, among other things, to present your position and the operational character of your deployment in the best possible light, and the opposition's in the worst possible light. But we did none of that. We didn't engage anybody to work over the *New Straits Times* or the Jakarta newspapers, we didn't seed stories about the Indonesian generals—and we could have run terrible smear campaigns because we knew all about them and how corrupt they were. We could have had that stuff flashed all round the world, and undermined the credibility of the Indonesian military and Kopassus. I think this was a great lacuna in respect out of our IW [Information Warfare] policy toward East Timor.[51]

---

50   Interview with 066-07.

51   Interview with Allan Behm. Michael Scrafton (Interview, 5 August 2005) also described the difficulties of implementing an 'information operations campaign' at the strategic level. There was more success at the operational level: see Kent Beasley, *Information Operations during Operation Stabilise in East Timor*, Working Paper no. 120, Land Warfare Studies Centre, Duntroon, Canberra 2002; and John Blaxland, *Information-era Manoeuvre: The Australian-led Mission to East Timor*, Working Paper no. 118, Land Warfare Studies Centre, Duntroon, Canberra, 2002.

Matthew Skoien also pointed to tactical reasons for not using the media to explain Australia's position:

> If only the media knew that in fact we were doing more than anyone else in the world to prepare and be ready to guide consideration in the UN and US; but we wouldn't, couldn't speak out about it ... [if] it had looked that we were preparing an Australian peacekeeping force before the ballot or anything like that, we feared that Indonesia would say they would only go ahead with this if Australia took no part. That would have been our worst outcome.[52]

These conflicting views of whether or how to use the media highlight a profoundly difficult choice faced by policymakers. In these situations, they must confront the need to gather support for initiatives and remain accountable, while balancing the need to restrict information for the purposes of achieving policy objectives.

Cooks and broth?

It is not surprising to find that implementation becomes more complex and complicated as the number of participants increase. For example, Steve Darvill recalled how the relatively straightforward task of organising helicopters for UNAMET using a commercial provider was soon complicated as other departments became involved:

> When we hired the helicopters, there was a period where they couldn't go ... from our point of view it was being treated a logistical thing—get them on contract, painted the right colour. ... But having done that, [attention] shifted to the political arena and DFAT went to Jakarta and took this up in the UN with Indonesia.[53]

And:

> The ADF had duty of care for their people, if they fell ill on deployments. They would normally have their hospital go with them, but the Indonesians were not going to have a bar of that, and it fell back onto us to hire a medevac [medical evacuation] facility to sit on the tarmac in Darwin—at great expense—just in case there was a need. I don't know whether it got used much. But that became a kind of political issue with Defence, and DFAT had to play the political dialogue [with Indonesia] to make this happen.[54]

---

52 Interview with Matthew Skoien.
53 Interview with Steve Darvill.
54 Interview with Steve Darvill.

However, the limited capacity of some organisations actually increases the need to involve more players. This was especially seen in the difficulties experienced by the Australian Federal Police (AFP) when deploying overseas. This went beyond having insufficient numbers of police officers, as the AFP also needed support for communication, transport and logistics.[55] It is also important to recognise that civilian firms and charities become critical to implementation when the government either lacks their own capabilities, or needs help to surge for a crisis.[56]

Implementation also influences the way people think about coordination. On the one hand, the act of executing a policy decision can have a unifying effect within large organisations. Some interviewees commented on how people got behind each other during this crisis, while another commented on how single-minded Canberra became once forces were deployed.[57] On the other hand, some had the impression that, once the decision was made, politicians would just leave the departments and agencies to get on with the job; both Major General John Hartley and Interviewee 009-05 cited instances of this:

> On one occasion, [Defence Minister] Moore called General Cosgrove and directed him to call a fresh press conference to announce that INTERFET would conduct operations across the Indonesian border if needed [in 'hot pursuit'[58]]. Moore then called back five minutes later to check to see that the arrangements had been made.[59]

> I think there was still quite a strong entrenched feeling within the military element of the structure—to Dili and beyond quite frankly—that it wasn't appropriate for civilian advisers to be urging them to provide information quickly, and a view that some of this stuff needs to be sat on so that the minister doesn't bugger up 'our operation'.[60]

The complexity involved in implementation was also shown through issues such as the 'hot pursuit' remarks and the shooting at Mota'ain.[61] In both cases, the

---

55   The need for state police was especially acute as the AFP prepared for the second rotation of UNAMET.

56   Some of the specific shortfalls for INTERFET were discussed in Alan Ryan, *Primary responsibilities and primary risks: Australian Defence Force participation in the International Force East Timor*, Land Warfare Studies Centre, Duntroon, Canberra, 2000, p. 39.

57   Interview with Kerry Clarke. In interview, Adrien Whiddett and Matthew Skoien also expressed similar views.

58   For descriptions of this incident, see Ellen Knickmeyer, 'Australia: peacekeepers allowed to cross border in hot pursuit', Associated Press Newswires, 30 September 1999; and Dennis Shannahan, 'Muzzling Moore the hottest pursuit—Australia cannot afford to send any more mixed messages', *Australian*, 2 October 1999, p. 10.

59   Interview with John Hartley.

60   Interview with 009-05.

61   Australian forces exchanged fire with Indonesian border police and troops on 11 October near the border crossing at Mota'ain (see Raphael Epstein, 'Australians and Indonesian forces clash in East Timor', AM (ABC Radio), 11 October 1999, available at <http://www.abc.net.au>, accessed 2 January 2008.

wider range of players and heightened political sensitivity added another layer to considerations that may not have been grasped immediately. As Interviewee 009-05 noted:

> For me, that [problem] will always crystallise around the shooting incident that happened at [Mota'ain] on the border, which we found out about through CNN. ... You know, we had the minister screaming down the phone trying to find out what had gone on. ... I tried COMAST [Commander Australian Theatre, in Sydney] and then I actually rang Dili to find out what was going on. I got some Captain who was quite aghast, and probably rightly so in a sense that here was this wally from headquarters trying to get some information. But what the doctrine manuals said was a fairly trivial tactical incident had the potential to be a serious strategic impediment in the government's policy. It could have brought us frankly to a shooting war with Indonesia. I don't think the Defence system, then or now, has really engaged its mind on how to deal with that issue.[62]

These difficulties also extended to a range of other problems that had a lesser impact on the overall mission. However, it is important to note that the implementation of INTERFET went well, to the point where it was described as successful and a significant achievement by Australia's leaders and by some foreign observers.[63]

Observations about implementation

Asked whether Australia achieved its policy objectives, Hugh White started his answer by listing what he thought were the key four at the start of 1999: East Timor would remain a part of Indonesia, there would be no disruption to Australian-Indonesian relations as a result of East Timor, East Timor would not disrupt TNI-ADF relations, and Australia would not have large parts of the ADF deployed in East Timor. He concluded: 'We got none from four'.[64]

However, the effective implementation of INTERFET in the period of acute crisis ultimately saved the 'strategic bacon'. First, it was the beginning of the end of the humanitarian crisis that had been occurring since 4 September 1999. Second, INTERFET's deployment kept global attention focused on the East

---

62   Interview with 009-05.

63   For examples, see Alexander Downer, 'Australia at Year's End—Retrospect and Prospect', Speech by the Hon. Alexander Downer MP, Minister for Foreign Affairs, at the National Press Club, Canberra, 1 December 1999, available at <http://www.foreignminister.gov.au>, accessed 27 November 2007; Fred Brenchley, 'The Howard Defence Doctrine', *Bulletin*, 28 September 1999; John Howard, 'Statement on East Timor', 23 November 1999, available at <http://www.australianpolitics.com>, accessed 16 April 2006; and Maxine McKew, 'Clinton advisor praises Australian leadership on East Timor', *7.30 Report*, ABC Television, 13 January 2000.

64   Interview with Hugh White.

Timor problem, which gave legitimacy to the cause and additional exposure to encourage more support for it. Third, INTERFET initially operated amid TNI forces, and then maintained a separation between themselves and the Indonesians across a difficult border and so averted major clashes—and perhaps war. Fourth, INTERFET provided enough stability for the UN transitional administration to begin work on creating an independent East Timor. Thus, successful implementation led to an objective desired by many—although not enjoyed by everyone who should have shared in it. The successful mission also allowed the Australian Government to weather significant media and political criticism over its handling of the crisis. Although the critics were fast to point out the shortcomings and the lives lost in the crisis, the Australian Government was able to respond by acknowledging some faults while pointing to the world's newest free nation. It was the Australian Government's position that resonated most with Australian voters.[65]

Unlike the impression provided by the policy cycle, policy in a crisis is unlikely to be a single decision followed by a single action. Instead, a range of decisions are made and implemented over time, with later decisions being influenced by the impact of measures implemented earlier. In this case, formal Cabinet or NSCC decisions were not the only progenitor of actions; even routine cables from DFAT posts elicited some form of action in Canberra that contributed to policy implementation.

The importance of structures and processes, intent, creative thinking and risk all came though in this case. Structures and processes are generally considered essential to spending money; public servants in Australia cannot, in layman's terms, commit public funds without an approved budget and the authority to spend that money. However, some impediments can be overcome (legally) if political support is present and if the officials have a clear understanding of what is needed to meet the intent of the decision-makers. Armed with some confidence, officials can then devise alternatives and even accept risk in areas ranging from funding to media engagement.

Given the wide range of problems that arise in any crisis, a variety of players must be involved in implementation and they need to be consulted early. This case showed how the agencies traditionally responsible for national security policy in Australia—DFAT, Defence and the Department of Prime Minister and Cabinet (DPM&C)—needed important support from those normally associated with domestic aspects of security, particularly the AFP. It also identifies that some agencies, such as AusAID and the Australian Electoral Commission, were

---

65   See the polling on attitudes to the Timor crisis in Ian McAllister, *Attitude Matters: Public opinion in Australia towards defence and security*, Australian Strategic Policy Institute, Canberra, 2004, pp. 23–24. The Howard Government would be returned twice more in 2001 and 2004.

only partially aware of their role in national security at all. This crisis also reinforces the need to consult operational agencies at the start of planning, and to practise responses before crises occur.

This case has not provided strong evidence to alter the typical characteristics of the policy cycle to account for crisis conditions. Consequently, the characteristics of the Implementation phase of crisis policymaking remain as:

- Implementation is considered throughout the policy cycle; and

- The more agencies involved, the more difficult implementation becomes.

Evaluation

The Evaluation phase provides the nominal end of the policy cycle, where the utility of policy is questioned and a new cycle of analysis begins. Two characteristics of evaluation are:

- If conducted at all, evaluation typically occurs after the policy has been implemented in full; and

- Policy advice is not systemically evaluated.[66]

An examination of these sources finds that the characteristics of policymaking described by Bridgman and Davis generally hold true for this crisis, although there are some small differences. This section also shows that if evaluation is difficult, then a spirit of self-criticism is essential.

Evaluation only after implementation is complete

Of the clearly identifiable evaluation efforts that took place around the East Timor crisis, most occurred afterwards. Of these, two formal evaluations were conducted after the event, but these covered only limited aspects of the crisis and the government's response. The first, an Australian National Audit Office (ANAO) report about the ADF's deployment into East Timor, was unusual.[67] While a broad range of Defence activities have been subjected to ANAO scrutiny over time (64 Defence-specific reports were delivered in the period 1996–2007), the vast majority of these focused on procurement or other management functions. In this case, the ANAO chose to look at an operational activity and made recommendations on issues that included training standards, public affairs planning and preparedness issues. AusAID also participated in a

---

66   Bridgman and Davis, *The Australian Policy Handbook*, pp. 131–33.
67   Australian National Audit Office, *Management of Australian Defence Force Deployments to East Timor*, Commonwealth of Australia, Canberra, 2002.

formal UN evaluation of the humanitarian response, and regular assessments of transitional administration programs. These evaluations were conducted on a six-monthly basis and provided to donor countries before major meetings.[68]

Defence conducted internal evaluations of its policy processes during the crisis. Allan Behm's report into Defence command arrangements is still classified, but he recounted some aspects of the report for this study. His report was developed after interviews with key members of Defence, some outsiders, and his own observations of Defence during the crisis. Interestingly, he developed two versions of the report: a 'vanilla' draft for external (government) readers and a more candid version for an internal audience. The internal version was reputedly a very blunt assessment of Defence's organisational deficiencies, and it included recommendations to change the structure of Defence headquarters. However, even supposedly objective assessments can be controversial and may not lead to any action: according to Behm, no recommendations to improve coordination were implemented as of early 2005 (although the results of others, such as a separate review of ADF command and control in 2003, did result in some change).[69] According to another source, some of the data captured by Behm was different to what people were saying at the time and resulted in a mismatch between feedback then and criticism later.[70]

On top of Behm's formal evaluation, Defence's Strategic Command Group conducted an informal yet frank evaluation of its own performance. In this, the Service chiefs reportedly expressed their concern about the way command and control was effected, especially the limited role given to Commander Australian Theatre and his headquarters.[71] Other interviewees from within and outside Defence spoke of learning lessons from previous events and operations and how these were applied during the East Timor crisis. This shows, at least, a willingness among officials to test current or likely events against experience.[72]

Three other modes of evaluation were certainly ongoing throughout the crisis, but it is difficult to pinpoint their influence on policymaking. The first, and most important, was the way politicians and officials evaluate events themselves. While evidence to prove self-criticism is very scarce (aside from personal accounts), some hints of criticism and reflection may be found in the way structures were changed mid-crisis. While other reasons may have been influential, the decision

68   Interview with Scott Dawson. These reports can be read at World Bank, 'Trust Fund for East Timor', available at <http://web.worldbank.org>, accessed 12 July 2007. For the United Nations' evaluation of the 1999 humanitarian program see Chris Hurford and Margareta Wahlstrom, *OCHA and the East Timor Crisis*, Office for the Coordination of Humanitarian Affairs, November 20001, available at <http://ochaonline.un.org>, accessed 12 July 2007.
69   Interview with Kerry Clarke.
70   Interview with Frank Lewincamp.
71   Interview with Frank Lewincamp.
72   Interviews with Scott Dawson, Frank Lewincamp and John Hartley.

to create new organisations within DPM&C and Defence to manage different aspects of the crisis can be interpreted as learning, and perhaps contemporary criticism of the policymaking process.[73]

One group that did not have a formal review of their performance was the NSCC. Former Attorney-General Daryl Williams noted that ministers are 'constantly reassessing as things move on', but 'there's not that much time available to sit down and do an academic review of what's gone on before. But in the moving forward exercise, you are reassessing as you go'.[74]

This seems unlikely to change because ministers will always be confronted with new issues. It is also unlikely to change because it would require a willingness on the part of ministers to initiate reviews of their own performance voluntarily— and there's no evidence to show that ministers would expose their collective or individual performances to what would become politically-charged scrutiny. But while internal review and 'lessons learnt' processes can be difficult to conduct when time is short, they offer at least one way of learning from experience.

Parliamentary committees can play a role in evaluation—but none had a measurable effect on policymaking in 1999. Of the two parliamentary bodies operating in 1999, the Foreign Affairs, Defence and Trade References Committee (FADTRC) was the most focused on this crisis through its hearings on the social, political and economic conditions in East Timor. FADTRC often probed officials with questions about government policy, the history of the case, the facts of the emerging crisis, and details of Australia's assistance to East Timor. However, its interim report, tabled soon after INTERFET deployed, only contained recommendations concerning the future of Radio Australia and a request for a committee visit to the territory.[75] FADTRC's final recommendations were similarly slim. Aside from another request to visit Indonesia, the only policy-relevant recommendation concerned East Timorese access to oil from the Timor Gap.[76] None of these recommendations can be interpreted as offering an evaluation of policymaking.

The Senate Estimates process is another forum where evaluation can occur. The purpose of this process is to examine the operations of government by considering 'estimates of government expenditure referred to Senate legislation

---

73 Interviewee 051-06 mentioned the concerns being reflected about coordination and their role in the decision to establish the Taylor Committee.

74 Interview with Daryl Williams.

75 Foreign Affairs Defence and Trade References Committee, *Interim Report on East Timor*, Senator John Hogg (Chair), Commonwealth of Australia, Canberra, 1999, paragraphs 3.54 and 3.57.

76 Foreign Affairs Defence and Trade References Committee, *Final Report into the Inquiry into East Timor*, Senator J Hogg (Chair), Commonwealth of Australia, Canberra, 2000, p. 74 and p. 200.

committees as part of the annual budget cycle'.[77] This mechanism provided an opportunity for senators to ask detailed questions of public servants and, in so doing, scrutinise the government and its performance. In 1999–2000, most of the issues raised in this committee related to the costs of the Timor campaign, the effects of the campaign on other areas of Defence, and questions about issues such as reserve forces and equipment.[78] There were some questions about readiness, as well as Indonesian activities and the TNI-ADF relationship.

That neither committee—FADTRC or Senate Estimates—appeared to contribute to evaluation highlights the difficulties faced by Parliament. While committees can have access to departmental officers and ask questions of them, the depth of questioning generally depends upon the expertise of the individual senator and their staff. This format also creates a competitive atmosphere where officials aim to provide complete answers, while providing only enough information to answer the specific question. Nor can officials discuss classified information in this forum or offer personal opinions about events or policy. These shortcomings make Parliamentary committees unsuitable for the type of reflection or self-criticism that aids evaluation.

Policy advice not systematically evaluated

There are four likely ways to systematically evaluate crisis policymaking in Australia: a formal (perhaps judicial) evaluation by an external agency on the performance of the system and people within it; internal departmental evaluations; special or periodic inquiries by Parliament; or 'whole-of-government' evaluations by a central agency. It is also possible that a deep, individual evaluation by a well-placed minister or senior official—which could be described as 'self-critique'—might also act as an informal evaluation method.

Despite the different types of evaluation listed above, there was no evidence of a systematic evaluation of policymaking during or after the East Timor crisis. Of the identified evaluation efforts, Behm's report on defence command arrangements provides one instance of systemic evaluation, albeit one focused on a single department. The other major evaluation by the ANAO crossed departmental lines to a small extent, but it was focused on the management of the deployment.[79] While both are examples of evaluation, they fall well short of a government-wide process that would be useful for evaluating policymaking

---

77 Australian Senate, 'Consideration of Estimates by the Senate's Legislation Committees,' *Senate Brief No. 5*, September 2006, available at <http://www.aph.gov.au>, accessed 25 February 2006.

78 For example, see Senate Foreign Affairs, Defence and Trade Committee, *Consideration of Additional Estimates (Department of Defence)*, 10 February 1999. At least six meetings of this committee discussed East Timor issues in 1999–2000.

79 It should be noted that the ANAO is mandated to examine government agencies, not Cabinet (see Commonwealth of Australia, *Auditor-General Act 1997 (Commonwealth)*, available at <http://www.comlaw.gov.au>, accessed 18 October 2007).

processes and structures. There was also a call for a commission of inquiry was also made by the Opposition spokesperson on foreign affairs, Laurie Brereton, which was unsuccessful.[80]

This should not be surprising. Michael Di Francesco noted that Australian policy departments of the 1990s 'commonly protested that evaluating policy advising activities was impractical since it presented what they saw as insurmountable problems of definition ... and fuelled concerns that, if pressed, assessment would invariably fall back on judgemental factors'.[81] According to Di Francesco, that would reduce evaluation to a highly political activity in a sphere where policy advice was traditionally held to be non-political.

Indeed, the reticence to be open to any external evaluation—particularly in the highly partisan Senate—is well illustrated in this exchange between the FADTRC Chairman, Senator John Hogg of Queensland, and DFAT's John Dauth. According to Hansard, Hogg said:

> Throughout this inquiry, there have been more brickbats than bouquets for DFAT. If you have read the Hansard that will show itself to be fairly true. There has been a claim—and these are my words trying to paraphrase a number of people who have put evidence to us—that DFAT has failed in its advice to the government, in its advice to the Parliament... there have also been claims by some people appearing before us—rightly or wrongly; I am not siding with anyone on the evidence—that there should be an inquiry into DFAT and its shortcomings over a long period of time, whether it be 25 years ago or even today. Do you have a response to that?'

Dauth's response was short: 'No, Senator, I do not'.[82]

There is anecdotal evidence to suggest that the lessons of East Timor informed planning for the next major national security issue, which involved the Sydney Olympics in 2000, and for national security policymaking in general.[83] This type of evaluation is, however, inherently personal and reliant upon a continuing role for key participants in future relevant activities.

Observations about evaluation

The two main characteristics of evaluation developed by Bridgman and Davis are very closely matched to the experience of this case. While the main evaluation

---

80   Laurie Brereton, MP, 'East Timor: Revelations on Four Corners', News Release, 15 February 2000.
81   Michael Di Francesco, 'An Evaluation Crucible: Evaluating Policy Advice in Australian Central Agencies', *Australian Journal of Public Administration*, vol. 59, no. 1, 2000, p. 37.
82   Foreign Affairs, Defence and Trade References Committee, *Economic, social and political conditions in East Timor*, 6 December 1999, p. 39.
83   Interviews with Chris Barrie, Frank Lewincamp, Steve Darvill, Aldo Borgu, 028-05, and 033-05.

efforts occurred after the crisis, none were systematic, cross-government evaluations of policymaking. However, this is not to say that evaluation did not occur at all—at a minimum, evaluation of some type can be inferred from structural change, such as the Paterson and Taylor Committees. These structural changes show that evaluation—at least in the minimal form of self-critique—occurs during the policy cycle.

Evaluation seems more likely to occur after failure, particularly when there is a strong public demand for answers.[84] In this case, voices for change to policymaking structures would likely have been hampered by the overall perception that INTERFET was a successful mission—indeed, about 99 per cent of Australians interviewed in one survey thought the ADF had performed well in East Timor.[85] Speaking against a strongly-held conventional wisdom and demanding a review can be difficult. These difficulties can continue even where well-researched and considered recommendations are provided after evaluation. As this case shows, not all recommendations are acted upon, no matter how prescient or logical they may be.

As a result, the characteristics of the Evaluation phase in a crisis will remain:

- If conducted at all, evaluation typically occurs after the policy has been implemented; and

- Policy advice is not systemically evaluated.

This chapter completes the examination of the East Timor case and its comparison against the proposed characteristics of crisis policymaking in Australia. This examination has shown some continuity between the 'typical' characteristics proposed by Bridgman and Davis, particularly in the role of the prime minister and his executive, in the importance of external actors, and in the complexity of coordination and implementation. But some differences were also identified, particularly in the roles of officials in decision-making and in significant collegiality between departments. Change was also observed in the policymaking structures during the crisis. The final chapter of this study recounts the East Timor crisis' effect on the national security policymaking system in Australia, and identifies what this case tells us about the characteristics of Australian policymaking in national security crises.

---

84   A point made by Interviewee 052-06, and at least partially demonstrated by various formal inquiries since 1999 into the October 2002 Bali Bombings, the Australian Wheat Board's activities in Iraq and that into Australia's intelligence community.

85   Ian McAllister, *Attitude Matters: Public opinion in Australia towards defence and security*, Australian Strategic Policy Institute, Canberra, 2004, pp. 23–24.

Chapter 6

Conclusion: East Timor and the Characteristics of Crisis Policymaking

Influence of the East Timor Crisis

The East Timor crisis had broad effects at many levels. At the global level, the international response to the crisis gave some reason to hope (at the time) that the United Nations could become an effective body for maintaining international order. At the regional level, this crisis changed a range of relationships, particularly those between Indonesia, Australia, the new nation-state of East Timor and their neighbours. Without overstating the effect, the crisis began a new and different period in Australian politics where policy was more self-confident, increasingly interventionalist within the region and even more closely aligned to the United States. The crisis itself also created a major disruption in the Australian–Indonesian relationship that was to last for around six years. The intervention into East Timor further showed the need to reconsider Australia's defence policy after a long period dominated by the Defence of Australia concept.[1] These implications make studying the East Timor crisis especially worthwhile because Australia's strategic environment continues to change in response to broad systemic forces and local problems and issues. The likelihood of new crises emerging in Australia's region makes it essential for the Australian Government to learn from its experience.

The crisis also brought change to four significant areas of policymaking in Australia. First, the East Timor crisis had a significant effect on the structure of national security policymaking. At the beginning of 1999, the linkage between the National Security Committee of Cabinet (NSCC), the Secretaries Committee on National Security (SCNS) and the Strategic Policy Coordination Group (SPCG) was a reasonably strong and well-established one. Indeed, as Peter Briggs pointed out, the linkages were well practised by the end of 1998. However, a different crisis management model emerged in 1999 that saw no real role for

---

1 In simple terms, the 'Defence of Australia' concept stresses defence of the sea-air gap to Australia's north and emphasises the importance of maintaining self-reliant forces to protect Australian territory. It provides an alternative to a 'forward defence' posture that involves basing outside Australia (mainly in Southeast Asia) and force structure priorities that emphasise coalition operations. For a discussion, see Michael Evans, *From Deakin to Dibb: The Army and the Making of Australian Strategy in the 20th Century*, Land Warfare Studies Centre, Duntroon, Canberra, 2001, pp. 17–33.

SCNS—one of the main elements of the formal national security policymaking structure—in the crisis' acute phase, because the overlap in membership between the senior committees and the fast pace of events made SCNS redundant. Its place was taken by the NSCC, which was supported instead by the *ad hoc* Taylor Committee. Similar *ad hoc* restructuring occurred in other Departments—most notably in Defence, where two new organisations were created to manage the new, unusual, sensitive and heavy workload created by the role of coalition leader.

Defence was not the only group to change its structures: the Department of Foreign Affairs and Trade (DFAT) created a small policy group, and AusAID merged parts of its Humanitarian and Indonesia Sections to manage the issue. The Australian Federal Police (AFP) expanded its existing overseas deployment cell dramatically, and then went through the process of raising groups by thinning its existing forces in Australia and calling on the State police forces to provide officers for the United Nations Mission in East Timor. A few years later, the AFP formed an entirely new body, to be called the International Deployment Group, to allow them to respond to similar situations. Of course, others did little to change because they had existing groups to manage their input into this type of activity. For example, the Australian Electoral Commission (AEC) was able to manage most of its contribution through its Overseas Elections Section. On balance though, the formal structure that existed before 1999 was found wanting in some respects, and the established structure for managing a crisis had to be extensively revamped as the situation became more acute.

The second place where the crisis was felt was in the NSCC because, while its function might not have changed, the East Timor crisis changed its operating mode and role. As a result, the NSCC was no longer a purely political committee, run along the same lines as Cabinet—it became a combined committee of politicians and officials that worked together while retaining their traditional responsibilities. In addition, the increased frequency of meetings effectively altered the NSCC's role from decision, to one of management and decision.

Third, East Timor also influenced the way some policy instruments were conceived. While projecting force into the region was long considered a role for the ADF, this was the first time that Australia had led an expeditionary operation in the region since the Borneo campaigns of 1945. Now Australia was actively considering how it could be the largest contributor to future coalitions within the 'arc of instability', should that prove necessary.[2] The AFP also moved to the fore of potential instruments to enhance foreign policy and

---

2 See Department of Defence, *Defence 2000—Our Future Defence Force*, Commonwealth of Australia, Canberra, 2000, p. 48. The term 'arc of instability' captured the prevailing thinking on crises and conflict within Australia's near-neighbourhood in the late-1990's—see Paul Dibb, 'Indonesia: the key to Southeast Asia's security', *International Affairs*, 77, no. 4, 2001, pp. 830–31.

national security, because a number of different crises around the world did not involve large military forces and significant firepower. Instead, they involved criminal-like activity that was best countered through the application of police powers. The role of Australia's foreign aid program was also reconceived during this time, and AusAID became more explicitly focused on security and working with other Commonwealth departments.[3] The Australian Government also saw that it had considerable financial resources that it could use to achieve its objectives. Despite this, other instruments conducted business as usual. For example, DFAT's many overseas missions performed their usual job of liaison, communication and persuasion; and the AEC's Overseas Elections Section performed its assistance role once more.

Finally, a number of new security policy issues emerged directly and indirectly from the East Timor crisis. Now the Australian Government needed policy to manage a new state on its doorstep, while having to reconstruct its relationship with Indonesia. Australia also had to become accustomed to a new, dual image in the region where some viewed Australia as a leader at some level, while others saw Australia as an interventionist state that was especially close to the United States.[4] The East Timor crisis also raised questions about Defence spending and Defence policy: indeed, it marked the start of a period where Defence was a major political issue, and the management of 'national security' became a major issue in the next two elections. More broadly, the East Timor crisis, together with the near-contemporaneous conflict in Kosovo, led to significant questions about humanitarian intervention and the role of the United Nations. According to then Foreign Minister of New Zealand Phil Goff, the success of the East Timor intervention had led some to develop unrealistic expectations about the utility of military intervention in the region's other conflicts.[5] Others described a 'responsibility to protect' people in situations where governments cannot or will not'.[6]

This study has devoted considerable effort to developing insights about crisis policymaking and demonstrating how crisis differs from 'typical' instances of policymaking. The next section completes this work by arranging the characteristics identified in previous chapters into a manageable, essential group.

---

3   Interview with Steve Darvill.

4   A perception re-enforced by the 'Deputy Sheriff' article in an Australian news magazine—see Fred Brenchley, 'The Howard Defence Doctrine', *Bulletin* (Australia), 28 September 1999, pp. 22–24).

5   Phil Goff, 'Opening Address', in Bruce Brown (ed.), *East Timor—The Consequences*, New Zealand Institute of International Affairs, Wellington, 2000, p. 15.

6   See Kofi Annan, *Annual Report to the UN General Assembly*, 20 September 1999, available at <http://www.un.org>, accessed 5 October 2007. The new view of responsibility advocated by Annan was articulated in International Commission on Intervention and State Sovereignty, *The Responsibility to Protect*, International Development Centre, Ottawa, 2001, p. 11.

The Characteristics of Crisis Policymaking

This paper has already discussed some of the shortcomings of the Australian Policy Cycle as a normative or descriptive model for policymaking. However, this cycle has helped to structure the analysis of national security policymaking, and highlight some of the similarities and differences between nominally 'typical' characteristics and the actual conduct of policymaking in this case. These typical characteristics have been modified to reflect the experience of this crisis and are grouped at Table 8 below.

Table 8: The Characteristics of Crisis Policymaking

Phase	Characteristics of Policymaking
Issue Identification	• The prime minister, his national security ministers and their senior officials are the dominant domestic actors in issue identification and, by extension, problem definition.
	• Foreign actors and events (especially governments) have the ability to place issues on the crisis policy agenda when they intend to harm Australian interests, when the interests of Australia's allies and friends are threatened, and when high levels of interdependence mean that threats to others' interests are viewed as threats to Australia.
	• Other domestic actors have a limited ability to identify issues in a crisis.
	• Mass appeal plays a limited role in issue identification.
Policy Analysis	• Where the ability to conduct rational-comprehensive analysis is limited in a crisis, decision-makers turn to trusted sources of advice. This can change both the structure of policymaking and which actors will be influential.
	• Policy issues are rarely analysed as individual, discrete problems, and the nature of competition between issues and interests, and the consequent influence on the issue at hand, makes analysis iterative. Policy insiders dominate.
	• Where dominant frameworks exist, they are likely to be noticeable where there is no clear lead for a crisis.
Policy Instruments	• The instruments most used by the Australian Government in crises are diplomacy, alliances, military force, economic levers (including foreign aid), information, international law, and (sometimes) social levers.
	• The utility of foreign and defence policy instruments is highly situational in a crisis.
Consultation	• All options are used with overseas interlocutors (who are primarily other governments and major international organisations); with information, discussion, partnership and delegation commonly occurring.
	• Consultation between the government and the public usually takes the form of a one-way passage of information.
	• Much consultation occurs in secret.

Coordination	• Governments describe structures and routines that suit their particular preferences and best thinking for the time, the task at hand, and external factors.
	• Coordination is basically collegial, but the potential for conflict should not be ignored.
Decision	• The prime minister is dominant.
	• Cabinet conventions are based on collective responsibility, secrecy, and recorded decisions.
	• Officials, when invited, may remain during all discussion; but, in general, they answer questions of a technical nature and leave the Cabinet room before decisions are taken.
Implementation	• Implementation is considered throughout the policy cycle.
	• The more agencies involved, the more difficult implementation becomes.
Evaluation	• If conducted at all, evaluation typically occurs after the policy has been implemented.
	• Policy advice is not systemically evaluated.

While the 22 characteristics presented here are thorough and suitable for lengthy analysis, this list is not easily used to discuss crisis policymaking under other conditions. These characteristics also overlap in a number of places, and some are more important than others. Refining these 22 points to a smaller group of 5 (identified below) provides a shorthand way to discuss crisis policymaking without compromising the substance of this study.

Dominant executive

The national security executive's dominance of crisis policymaking is evident from its role in issue identification, policy analysis, coordination, consultation and decision. The executive's dominance also allows it to impede or shape evaluation.

The prime minister stands above other ministers in crisis policymaking.[7] Prime ministers maintain this position by using their superior institutional and political resources to provide leadership to the Cabinet, and usually the nation, when a crisis occurs. Of all their political resources, their support in the party room and Parliament's lower house are significant assets. However, their institutional

---

7 This finding provides strong support to a range of other work on Australian foreign policy. For other work that also makes this link, see Peter Edwards, *Prime Ministers and Diplomats: The Making of Australian Foreign Policy 1901–1949*, Oxford University Press, Melbourne, 1983; Russell Trood, 'Prime Ministers and Foreign Policy', in Patrick Weller (ed.), *Menzies to Keating: The Development of Australian Prime Ministership*, Melbourne University Press, Carlton, Vic, 1992; and Allan Gyngell and Michael Wesley, *Making Australian Foreign Policy*, Cambridge University Press, Cambridge, 2003, pp. 97–102.

resources are more important in time of crisis. They have their own sources of advice and choose the method of decision-making; although they must take care to ensure they can gain Cabinet support on major decisions. Another critical advantage is their role as an information hub. In the tight timeframes of a crisis, where communication channels narrow and discussions with overseas interlocutors are of great import, the prime minister has an exclusive view. The prime minister is also the leader who defines the problem to the public and generally acts as the personification of national interests. These advantages and responsibilities mean that they must receive the best possible level of support during a crisis.

The key national security ministers are also important. But while their sources of information, advice and resources are significant, they rarely secure authority over other departments. For example, the minister of defence may be highly influential when the ADF is employed, but the NSCC is unlikely to approve supporting diplomatic or economic activities without the foreign minister's concurrence or a prime-ministerial directive. At times, the foreign minister may be able to act as the lead in a crisis, as Sir Garfield Barwick did in the early stages of *Konfrontasi*.[8] However, this position is easily lost if the prime minister takes a direct interest or loses confidence in the minister.

Australian leaders normally rely heavily on advice from senior officials and ministerial advisers, despite the occasional instances of unilateral decision-making. Under most conditions, senior officials and advisers are highly influential in issue identification, policy analysis, consultation, coordination and implementation. Some play a discreet part in decisions as well. Trust is an essential part of this relationship—as the East Timor case showed: increasing trust between ministers and their officials changed the operating mode of the NSCC. A number of senior officials involved in this case also referred to their close contacts with others, and the positive effect of these relationships on the smooth functioning of the crisis policymaking system.

Collegial approach

This study showed that the Australian crisis policymaking system tends towards a collegial approach, which supports the analysis of foreign policymaking by Allan Gyngell and Michael Wesley.[9] Although interagency conflict occurs, it did not reach the worst excesses of bureaucratic politics during the East Timor

---

8   Barwick's role in the *Konfrontasi* (Confrontation) between Indonesia and the nascent Malaysian state is well described in Gary Woodard, *Asian Alternatives: Australia's Vietnam Decision and Lessons on Going to War*, Melbourne University Press, Carlton, Vic, 2004, pp. 74–78. This view was supported by Interviewee 060–07, a former senior official in Defence who was serving in External Affairs at the time of *Konfrontasi*.
9   Gyngell and Wesley, *Making Australian Foreign Policy*, p. 32.

crisis. This is because role clarity, political direction, agreed processes, personal relationships and trust served to mitigate or resolve conflicting points of view—most of the time.

This collegiate approach has other effects on policymaking. It, together with the pressures of time and secrecy, makes rational-comprehensive approaches to policymaking less valued. Instead, ministers and senior officials tend to use their experience and intuition to make sense of emerging situations where normal policy processes cannot or do not deliver within their perceived time limitations. This informal analytical process sees mot have worked in the East Timor case, but it also meant that the Australian Government did not fully recognise the importance of some issues or events until it was too late to have real influence.

Secretive and closed system

Crisis policymaking is secretive and closed due to time pressures, the system's competitive nature (that is, between protagonists), and the privileged sources of information used. Those same pressures also impose restrictions about who within government has information about future plans, while the use of sensitive intelligence usually prevents national leaders from releasing some kinds of information during a crisis and for some time after the event. While the lack of transparency gives some people cause for concern,[10] even critics concede that secrecy in national security matters is usually in the public interest.[11]

Central role for external actors

While most domestic actors play peripheral roles in crises, foreign governments and other external actors are usually at the centre. At the start, an external actor usually frames the issue by challenging an existing interest. External actors may also help the government meet a challenge by employing their significant resources, such as military forces or economic assets. Close consultation with allies will be necessary in most crises.

Complicated and complex implementation

The significant range of issues involved in any crisis makes policymaking complicated. Identifying the issues at stake is critical, because this directly bears upon the instruments used and the range of actors involved. This

---

10   Carl Oatley, *Australia's National Security Framework: A Look to the Future*, Australian Defence Studies Centre, University of New South Wales, Canberra, 2000, p. 18; and Bertrand Robert and Chris Lajtha, 'A New Approach to Crisis Management', *Journal of Contingencies and Crisis Management*, vol. 10, no. 4, 2002, pp. 181–83.

11   Warwick Funnell, *Government by Fiat: The Retreat from Responsibility*, UNSW Press, Sydney, 2001, p. 190.

increases the importance of having multidisciplinary planning teams and sound written procedures, and of providing opportunities to practice together before a crisis occurs. Such measures will improve the participants' ability to understand the implications of possible events, or anticipate how their policies may be challenged in crises.

The growing number of actors and actions, and reactions among them; the apparent compression of time and space; and the interconnectedness of future national security crises will make implementation increasingly complex.[12] Yet the characteristic of complexity is one that Australian governments have found difficult to manage at times. For example, the failed attempt to create a coordinated counter-subversion plan for Asia in the 1950s shows how difficult it can be to implement effective plans and align departmental efforts.[13]

Seeing order where none exists?

While the Australian Policy Cycle has been used to arrange the discussion of national security policymaking in this crisis, this does not mean that the policy process during 1999 was either controlled or orderly. From the nominal start of the crisis, when Indonesian President B.J. Habibie received Australian Prime Minister John Howard's letter, Australian policymakers were forced to react to event after event—from the Indonesian Cabinet's decision to grant the referendum in January 1999, through to continuing TNI-sponsored violence in East Timor, to the tense time while the international community waited for Habibie to invite the intervention force in September, to the US reluctance to play a major combat role in any intervention and finally to the UN Security Council (UNSC)'s decision to grant a mandate for INTERFET. These actions by external players forced the Australian Government into an essentially reactive posture. Even attempts to be proactive, such as the Bali Summit of late April 1999 or the visit to Indonesia by Air Marshal Doug Riding and Allan Behm in June 1999, seemed unable to exert significant influence on international processes or Indonesian behaviour. As a result, Australia's policy aims changed significantly throughout the year and none of the goals held before March 1999 were still valid or achievable by September of the same year. Further, Australia's modes of consultation had shifted from 'information' and 'partnership' to 'delegation' and even 'control' by September, as policy was essentially reliant upon the willingness of both the UNSC and Habibie to allow the intervention force into East Timor.

---

12   Michael Evans, 'Towards and Australian National Security Strategy: A Conceptual Analysis', *Security Challenges*, vol. 3, no. 4, 2007, p. 117.
13   Christopher Waters, 'A failure of imagination: R.G. Casey and Australian plans for counter-subversion in Asia, 1954–1956', *Australian Journal of Politics and History*, vol. 45, no. 3, 1999, pp. 360–63.

This picture of an 'uncontrollable' policy environment and missed objectives could be used to argue that the policy process failed to deliver on the Government's aims. But such a view promotes unrealistic expectations, for it overlooks the 'multiplayer' nature of policymaking in a crisis, and the very real resources that most players can use to achieve their objectives. It also overlooks one aspect of the outcome, in that the East Timorese people expressed their desire for independence and subsequently achieved this aim. Further, Australia and Indonesia avoided serious violence, and long-term harm does not seem to have been caused the bilateral relationship at the time of writing (which are, admittedly, very low benchmarks of success). While the policymaking situation did not unfold as some might have hoped, there was a reasonable degree of effectiveness present throughout. Rather than hold unrealistic ideals, we should expect policymaking during crises to be messy and rely upon significant flexibility. Achieving such flexibility requires a policymaking process built on sound structures, efficient processes and, ultimately, skilled individuals.

This study has identified five main characteristics that should be considered as Australia reviews its structures, processes and capabilities for crisis policymaking. From this, it is clear that Australia's future crisis policymaking system must continue to change in ways that accord with these characteristics, while retaining an ability to respond to new challenges. Such change will be essential because Australia will face more complex crises in the future, and these crises will involve high stakes for its relationships, sovereignty, public safety and the economy. How the Australian Government organises its policymaking system beforehand will be critical to managing the transformative potential of those events. Making the most of pre-crisis opportunities to improve organisation, information sharing, training and ultimately culture will improve the ability of future policymakers to respond effectively to crisis. This is a critical matter for governments to address, and to review periodically to ensure the continued relevance and robustness of Australia's crisis policymaking system.

Appendix

Text of Prime Minister Howard's Letter to President Habibie:

Prime Minister
Canberra
19 December 1998

My dear President,

It was good to meet you in Kuala Lumpur and hear of the progress you are making with your political and economic reform programme. I have followed with particular interest the development of your plans for elections next year and am pleased that our Electoral Commission has recently been in Indonesia discussing ways in which we can help you with them.

You have an enormous amount on your agenda and East Timor is just one of many pressing issues. But I hope that, recognising our goodwill towards your personally and towards Indonesia, you will permit me to make some suggestions about the East Timor situation.

Your offer of autonomy for East Timor was a bold and clear-sighted step that has opened a window of opportunity both to achieve a peaceful settlement in East Timor and to resolve an issue that has long caused Indonesia difficulties in the inter national community. A settlement would enable you to put the issue behind you. It would make a substantial difference to Indonesia's standing in the world, with the benefits that could bring.

I want to emphasise that Australia's support for Indonesia's sovereignty is unchanged. It has been a longstanding Australian position that the interests of Australia, Indonesia and East Timor are best served by East Timor remaining part of Indonesia. We would of course welcome any peaceful settlement that had the support of both Indonesians and East Timorese and met the interests and aspirations of both.

Observing developments since your offer of autonomy, however, I fear that the boldness of your offer has not been matched with the degree of progress in negotiations which might have been expected. My concerns are that the UN process are not producing the desired results quickly enough, and that, with heightened expectations, attitudes in East Timor are hardening. It would be a real tragedy if the opening you have created is not taken advantage of and the situation worsens in East Timor.

In our view, one reason for the difficulties is that negotiations with the Portuguese do not give an adequate role for the East Timorese themselves. In the end, the issue can be resolved only through direct negotiations between Indonesia and East Timorese leaders. If you can reach agreement directly with the East Timorese, then the international dimensions would take care of themselves, or at least be much easier to deal with.

I would urge you to take this course, and to focus on winning acceptance for your offer from the East Timorese themselves. The best way of achieving this may be for you to enter into direct negotiations with representative leaders from East Timor, including the two East Timorese bishops and Xanana Gusmao.

On the substance of negotiations, the advice I am receiving is that a decisive element of East Timorese opinion is insisting on an act of self-determination. If anything, their position—with a fair degree of international support—seems to be strengthening on this.

It might be worth considering, therefore, a means of addressing the East Timorese desire for an act of self-determination in a manner which avoids an early and final decision on the future status of the province. One way of doing this would be to build into the autonomy package a review mechanism along the lines of the Matignon Accords in New Caledonia. The Matignon Accords have enabled a compromise political solution to be implemented while deferring a referendum on the final status of New Caledonia for many years.

The successful implementation of an autonomy package with a built-in review mechanism would allow time to convince the East Timorese of the benefits of autonomy within the Indonesian Republic.

I take the liberty of making these suggestions, knowing the matter is complex and not pretending to have the solutions. I hope, however, that some of these outside perspectives might be useful to you in your efforts to reach a settlement.

Australia wants very much to see a just and lasting solution to the problem. We believe that a solution in within your grasp if the visionary lead you have given can be followed up effectively and directly with the East Timorese.

If you see any merit in these thoughts I would be happy to talk with you directly about them or have someone discuss them discreetly with you.

We are very willing to do what we can to help.

Yours sincerely

(John Howard)

His Excellency Dr B.J. Habibie
President
Jakarta
Republic of Indonesia

(*Source*: Department of Foreign Affairs and Trade, *East Timor in Transition*, pp. 181–82.)

Bibliography

Books, Journal Articles and Theses

Alatas, Ali, *The Pebble in the Shoe: The Diplomatic Struggle for East Timor*, Aksara Karunia, Jakarta, 2006.

Andrews, Eric M., *The Department of Defence*, Oxford University Press, South Melbourne, 2001.

ANOP Research Services, 'Public Attitudes to Defence: Report of the 1987 National Study on Community Attitudes', Crows Nest, NSW, 1987.

Ayling, Brigadier Steve and Sarah Guise, 'UNTAC and INTERFET—A Comparative Analysis', *Australian Defence Force Journal*, no. 150, 2001, pp. 47–56.

Ayson, Robert, 'The "Arc of Instability" and Australia's Strategic Policy', *Australian Journal of International Affairs*, vol. 61, no. 2, 207, pp. 215–31.

Babbage, Ross, *Preparing Australia's Defence for 2020: Transformation or Reform?*, The Kokoda Papers No. 1, The Kokoda Foundation, Canberra, 2005.

Ball, Desmond, 'Silent Witness: Australian Intelligence and East Timor', in Desmond Ball, James Dunn, Gerry van Klinken, David Bourchier, D Kammen and Richard Tanter (eds), *Masters of Terror: Indonesia's Military and the Violence in East Timor in 1999*, Canberra Papers on Strategy and Defence no. 145, Strategic and Defence Studies Centre, The Australian National University, Canberra, 2002, pp. 239–61.

———, 'The Blind Men and the Elephant: A Critique of Bureaucratic Politics Theory', *Australian Outlook*, vol. 28, no. 1, 1974, pp. 71–92.

Beasley, Kent, *Information Operations during Operation Stabilise in East Timor*, Working Paper no. 120, Land Warfare Studies Centre, Duntroon, Canberra, 2002.

Bell, Coral, *Crises and Policy-makers*, Canberra Studies in World Affairs, no 10, Department of International Relations, The Australian National University, Canberra, 1982.

———, *The Conventions of Crisis: A Study in Diplomatic Management*, Royal Institute of International Affairs, London, 1971.

Beveridge, David, 'Australia's Future Threat Space: Strategic Risks and Vulnerabilities', *Security Challenges*, vol. 2, no. 2, 2006, pp. 43–60.

Birmingham, John, 'A Time For War: The Re-birth of Australia's Military Culture', *Quarterly Essay*, no. 20, 2006.

Blaxland, John, *Information-era Manouevre: The Australian-led Mission to East Timor*, Working Paper no. 118, Land Warfare Studies Centre, Duntroon, Canberra, 2002.

Brabin-Smith, Richard, *The Heartland of Australia's Defence Policies*, SDSC Working Paper no. 396, Strategic and Defence Studies Centre, The Australian National University, Canberra, 2005.

Brändström, Annika, Fredrik Bynander and Paul 't Hart, 'Governing by looking back: Historical analogies and crisis management', *Public Administration*, vol. 82, no. 1, 2004, pp. 191–210.

Brecher, Michael, 'State Behaviour in International Crisis', *Journal of Conflict Resolution*, vol. 23, no. 3, 1979, pp. 446–80.

Brecher, Michael, and Jonathon Wilkenfield, *A Study of Crisis*, University of Michigan Press, Ann Arbor, 1997.

Breen, Bob, *Mission Accomplished—East Timor*, Allen and Unwin, Crows Nest, NSW, 2000.

Brereton, Laurie, 'East Timor: Revelations on Four Corners', News Release, 15 February 2000.

Bridgman, Peter, and Glyn Davis, *The Australian Policy Handbook*, 3rd edn, Allen and Unwin, Sydney, 2004.

Burton, Kate, *Scrutiny or Secrecy? Committee Oversight of Foreign and National Security Policy in the Australian Parliament*, Commonwealth of Australia, Canberra, 2005.

Centre for Democratic Institutions, *Managing Transition in East Timor Workshop*, The Australian National University, 26–29 April 1999.

Cheeseman, Graeme, and Hugh Smith, 'Public consultation or political choreography? The Howard Government's quest for community views on defence policy', *Australian Journal of International Affairs*, vol. 55, no. 1, 2001, pp. 83–100.

Chisholm, Donald, *Coordination without Hierarchy: informal structures in multiorganisational systems*, University of California Press, Berkeley, 1989.

Clausewitz, Carl von, *On War*, trans M. Howard and P. Paret, Princeton University Press, Princeton, 1976.

Cohen, Eliot, *Supreme Command: soldiers, statesmen and leadership in wartime*, Simon and Schuster, London, 2003.

Collins, Lance and Warren Reed, *Plunging Point: Intelligence Failures, Cover-ups and Consequences*, 4th Estate/Harper Collins, Sydney, 2005.

Connery, David, *National Security Community 2020: Six Practical Recommendations for the Australian Government*, The Kokoda Foundation, Canberra, 2007.

Cotton, James, 'Against the Grain: The East Timor Intervention', *Survival*, vol. 43, no. 1, 2001, pp.127–42.

———, 'East Timor and Australia—Twenty-five years of the policy debate', in James Cotton (ed.), *East Timor and Australia*, Australian Defence Studies Centre/Australian Institute of International Affairs, Canberra, 2000, pp. 1–22.

———, *East Timor, Australia and Regional Order: intervention and its aftermath in Southeast Asia*, Routledge, London, 2004.

Daudelin, Jean and Lee J.M. Seymour, 'Peace Operations Finance and the Political Economy of a Way Out', *International Peacekeeping*, vol. 9, no. 2, 2002, pp. 99–117.

Davis, Glyn, *A Government of Routines: Executive Coordination in an Australian State*, Centre for Australian Public Sector Management/MacMillan, South Melbourne, 1995.

Dee, Moreen, '"Coalitions of the Willing" and Humanitarian Intervention: Australia's Involvement with INTERFET', *International Peacekeeping*, vol. 8, no. 3, 2001, pp. 1–20.

Dent, Helen, 'Consultants and the Pubic Service', *Australian Journal of Public Administration*, vol. 61, no. 1, 2002, pp. 108–13.

Deutsch, Karl, 'Crisis Decision-Making: The Information Approach', in Daniel Frei (ed.), *Managing International Crises*, Beverly Hills, Sage Publications, 1982, pp.15–28.

Dibb, Paul, 'A Reply to the Critics of the Defence of Australia', in Paul Dibb, *Essays on Australian Defence*, Canberra Papers on Strategy and Defence no. 161, Strategic and Defence Studies Centre, The Australian National University, Canberra, 2006, pp. 83–85.

————, 'Indonesia: the key to Southeast Asia's security', *International Affairs*, vol. 77, no. 4, 2001, pp. 829–42.

Di Francesco, Michael, 'An Evaluation Crucible: Evaluating Policy Advice in Australian Central Agencies', *Australian Journal of Public Administration*, vol. 59, no. 1, 2000, pp. 36–48.

Downs, Anthony, *Inside Bureaucracy*, RAND/Little, Brown and Company, Boston, 1968.

Dror, Yehezkel, *Policymaking Under Adversity*, Transaction Books, New Brunswick, NJ, 1986.

————, *Public Policymaking Reexamined*, Chandler Publishing Company, Scranton, PA, 1968.

Dudgeon, Ian, 'Intelligence Support to the Development and Implementation of Foreign Policies and Strategies', *Security Challenges*, vol. 2, no. 2, July 2006, pp. 61–80.

Edwards, Meredith, *Social Policy, Public Policy: From Problem to Practice*, Allen and Unwin, Crows Nest, NSW, 2001.

————, *Social Science Research and Public Policy: Narrowing the Divide*, Policy Paper #2, Academy of Social Sciences in Australia, Canberra, 2004.

Edwards, Peter, *Prime Ministers and Diplomats: The Making of Australian Foreign Policy 1901–1949*, Oxford University Press, Melbourne, 1983.

Evans, Michael, *The Tyranny of Dissonance: Australia's Strategic Culture and Way of War 2001–2005*, Land Warfare Studies Centre, Duntroon, Canberra, 2005.

————, 'Towards and Australian National Security Strategy: A Conceptual Analysis', *Security Challenges*, vol. 3, no. 4, 2007, pp. 113–30.

Everett, Sophia, 'The Policy Cycle: Democratic Process or Rational Paradigm Revisited?', *Australian Journal of Public Administration*, vol. 62, no. 2, 2003, pp. 65–70.

Fernandes, Clinton, *Reluctant Saviour: Australia, Indonesia and the independence of East Timor*, Scribe, Melbourne, 2004.

————, 'The Road to INTERFET: Bringing the Politics Back In', *Security Challenges*, vol. 4, no. 3, 2008, pp. 83–98.

Fischer, Tim, *Seven Days in East Timor: Ballots and Bullets*, Allen and Unwin, St Leonards, NSW, 2000.

Franks, Lord Oliver S, *Falklands Island Review: Report of a Committee of Privy Counsellors*, HMSO, London, 1983.

Funnell, Warwick, *Government by Fiat: The Retreat from Responsibility*, UNSW Press, Sydney, 2001.

George, Alexander, 'A Provisional Theory of Crisis Management', in Alexander George (ed.), *Avoiding War: Problems of Crisis Management*, Westview Press, Boulder, CO, 1991, pp. 22–27.

Gerodimos, Roman, 'The UK BSE Crisis as a Failure of Government', *Public Administration*, vol. 82, no. 4, 2004, pp. 911–29.

Gilding, Simeon, 'Delivery of Government Policy in Times of Crisis—A Specific Reflection', paper presented at the Government Policy and Evolution Conference, Canberra, 27 July 2005.

Goff, Phil, 'Opening Address', in B. Brown (ed.), *East Timor—The Consequences*, Wellington, New Zealand Institute of International Affairs, 2000, pp. 216–57.

Goldsworthy, David, 'East Timor,' in Goldsworthy and Peter Edwards (eds), *Facing north: a century of Australian engagement with Asia*, Melbourne University Press, Carlton, Vic, 2003, pp. 216–57.

———, 'Regional Relations,' in Goldsworthy and Peter Edwards (eds), *Facing north: a century of Australian engagement with Asia*, Melbourne University Press, Carlton, Vic, 2003, pp. 130–78.

Greenlees, Don, and Robert Garran, *Deliverance: The Inside Story of East Timor's Fight for Freedom*, Allen and Unwin, Crows Nest, NSW, 2002.

Gyngell, Allan, and Michael Wesley, *Making Australian Foreign Policy*, Cambridge University Press, Cambridge, 2003.

Halperin, Morton, *Bureaucratic politics and foreign policy*, The Brookings Institution, Washington, DC, 1974.

Haney, Patrick, *Organizing for Foreign Policy Crises: Presidents, Advisers and the Management of Decision Making*, University of Michigan Press, Ann Arbor, 1997.

Hawker, Geoffrey, R.F.I. Smith, and Patrick Weller, *Politics and Policy in Australia*, Queensland University Press, St. Lucia, 1979.

Heclo, Hugh, and Aaron Wildavsky, *The Private Government of Public Money: Community and Policy inside British Politics*, MacMillan, London, 1974.

Hermann, Charles, *Crises in Foreign Policy: A Simulation Analysis*, Bobbs-Merrill, Indianapolis, 1969.

———, 'Types of crises and conclusions for crisis management', in Daniel Frei (ed.), *International crises and crisis management*, Saxon House, Westmead, 1978, pp. 29–41.

Hertkorn, Michaela, 'The relevance of perceptions in foreign policy: a German-U.S. perspective', *World Affairs*, vol. 162, no. 2, 2001, pp. 60–71.

Horner, David, *Inside the War Cabinet: Directing Australia's War Effort 1939–45*, Allen and Unwin, St Leonards, NSW, 1996.

Howard, Cosmo, 'The Policy Cycle: A Model of Post Machiavellian Policy Making?', *Australian Journal of Public Administration*, vol. 63, no. 3, 2005, pp. 3–13.

International Commission on Intervention and State Sovereignty, *The Responsibility to Protect*, International Development Centre, Ottawa, 2001.

International Crisis Group, *Resolving Timor-Leste's Crisis*, Asia Report, no. 120, 2006.

Janis, Irving L., *Crucial Decisions: Leadership in Policymaking and Crisis Management*, The Free Press, New York, 1989.

———, *Groupthink: psychological studies of policy decisions and fiascoes*, 2nd edn, Houghton Mifflin, Boston, 1982.

Jenkins, Brian, 'Policy analysis: Models and approaches', in Michael Hill (ed.), *The Policy Process: A Reader*, Harvester Wheatsheaf, Hemel Hempstead, 1993, pp. 34–44.

Keating, Gavin, 'The Machinery of Australian National Security Policy: Changes, Continuing Problems and Possibilities', *Australian Defence Force Journal*, no. 166, 2005, pp. 20–34.

Kelly, Paul, 'How Howard Governs', in Nick Cater (ed.), *The Howard Factor: A Decade that Changed the Nation*, Melbourne University Press, Carlton, Vic, 2006, pp. 3–18.

———, 'Re-thinking Australian Governance: The Howard Legacy', *Australian Journal of Public Administration*, vol. 65, no. 1, 2006, pp. 7–24.

———, *The March of the Patriots: The Struggle for Modern Australia*, Melbourne University Press, Carlton, Vic, 2009, Chapter 35.

Laffin, Martin, 'Public policy making', in Rodney Smith and Lex Watson (eds), *Politics in Australia*, Allen and Unwin, Sydney, 1989, pp. 38–48.

Liberal Party and National Party, *Defence Policy*, 1989 (copy in author's possession).

Lovell, David, Ian McAllister, William Maley and Chandran Kukathas, *The Australian Political System*, 2nd edn, Longman, South Melbourne, 1998.

Maley, Maria, 'The Growing Role of Australian Ministerial Advisers', *Canberra Bulletin of Public Administration*, no. 110, 2003, pp. 1–4.

Maley, William, 'Australia and the East Timor Crisis: Some Critical Comments', *Australian Journal of International Affairs*, vol. 54, no. 2, 2000, pp. 151–61.

Marker, Jamsheed, *East Timor: A Memoir of the Negotiations for Independence*, McFarland and Co., Jefferson, NC, 2003.

McAllister, Ian, *Attitude Matters: Public opinion in Australia towards defence and security*, Australian Strategic Policy Institute, Canberra, 2004.

McConnell, Allan and Alastair Stark, 'Foot-and-Mouth 2001: The Politics of Crisis Management', *Parliamentary Affairs*, vol. 55, no. 4, 2002, pp. 664–81.

Megalogenis, George, *The Longest Decade*, Scribe, Melbourne, 2006.

Oatley, Carl, *Australia's National Security Framework: A Look to the Future*, Australian Defence Studies Centre, University of New South Wales, Canberra, 2000.

Painter, Martin and Bernard Carey, *Politics Between Departments: The fragmentation of executive control in Australian government*, University of Queensland Press, Brisbane, 1979.

Parsons, Wayne, 'Not Just Steering but Weaving: Relevant Knowledge and the Craft of Building Policy Capacity and Coherence', *Australian Journal of Public Administration*, vol. 63, no. 1, 2004, pp. 43–57.

Peters, B. Guy, 'Managing horizontal government: The politics of co-ordination', *Public Administration*, vol. 76, no. 2, 1998, pp. 295–311.

Pitty, Roderick, 'Strategic Engagement', in Peter Edwards and David Goldsworthy (eds), *Facing North: A Century of Australian Engagement with Asia*, Department of Foreign Affairs and Trade, Canberra, 2003, pp. 48–80.

Rhodes, R.A.W., and Patrick Dunleavy, *Prime minister, cabinet, and core executive*, St Martin's Press, New York, 1995.

Robert, Bertrand, and Chris Lajtha, 'A New Approach to Crisis Management', *Journal of Contingencies and Crisis Management*, vol. 10, no. 4, 2002, pp. 181–91.

Robinson, Geoffrey, 'With UNAMET in East Timor—An Historian's Personal View', in Richard Tanter, Mark Selden and Stephen Shalom (eds), *Bitter Flowers, Sweet Flowers: East Timor, Indonesia and the World Community*, Rowman and Littlefield, Lanham, MD, 2001, pp. 55–72.

Rosenthal, Uriel, and Bert Pijnenburg, 'Simulation-orientation scenarios: An alternative approach to crisis decision-making and emergency management', in Uriel Rosenthal and Bert Pijnenburg (eds), *Crisis Management and Decision Making: Simulation Oriented Scenarios*, Kluwer Academic Publishers, Dortrecht, 1991, pp. 1–7.

Rosenthal, Uriel, Paul 't Hart and Alexander Kouzmin, 'The Bureau-Politics of Crisis Management', *Public Administration*, vol. 69, no. 2, 1991, pp. 211–33.

Rosenthal, Uriel, Paul 't Hart and Michael Charles, 'The World of Crises and Crisis Management', in Uriel Rosenthal, Paul 't Hart, and Michael Charles (eds), *Coping With Crises: The Management of Disasters, Riots and Terrorism*, Charles C. Thomas, Springfield, IL, 1989, pp. 5–22.

Ryan, Alan, *Primary responsibilities and primary risks: Australian Defence Force participation in the International Force East Timor*, Land Warfare Studies Centre, Duntroon, Canberra, 2000.

Scheiner, Charles, 'Grassroots in the Field-Observing the East Timor Consultation', in Richard Tanter, Mark Selden and Stephen Shalom (eds), *Bitter Flowers, Sweet Flowers: East Timor, Indonesia and the World Community*, Rowman and Littlefield, Lanham, MD, 2001, pp.109–26.

Sheridan, Greg, 'All the World's a Stage', in Nick Cater (ed.), *The Howard Factor: A Decade that Changed the Nation*, The University of Melbourne Press, Carlton, Vic, 2006, pp. 149–59.

Sherlock, Stephen, *Indonesia's Dangerous Transition: The Politics of Recovery and Democratisation*, Australian Parliamentary Library Research Paper no. 18, Canberra, 1999.

Singh, Bilveer, *Defense Relations Between Australia and Indonesia in the Post-Cold War Era*, Greenwood, Westport, CT, 2002.

Singleton, Gwynneth, Don Aitken, Brian Jinks and John Warhurst, *Australian Political Institutions*, 6th edn, Longman, South Melbourne, 2000.

Smith, Gary, Dave Cox and Scott Burchill, *Australia in the world: an introduction to Australian foreign policy*, Oxford University Press, Melbourne, 1996.

Smith, Hugh, 'Foreign Policy and the Political Process', in Fedor A. Mediansky and A.C. Palfreeman (eds), *In pursuit of national interests: Australian Foreign Policy in the 1990s*, Pergamon Press, Sydney, 1988, pp. 17–44.

———, 'Politics of foreign policy', in Fedor A. Mediansky (ed.), *Australian Foreign Policy into the New Millennium*, MacMillan Education Australia, South Melbourne,1997, pp. 13–32.

Smith, Martin, *The Core Executive in Britain*, MacMillan Press, Basingstoke, Hampshire, 1999.

Sugget, Neil, *See the Road Well: Shaping East Timor's Frontier*, Pandanus Books, Canberra, 2005.

Tanter, Richard, Mark Selden and Stephen Shalom (eds), *Bitter Flowers, Sweet Flowers: East Timor, Indonesia and the World Community*, Rowman and Littlefield, Lanham, MD, 2001.

Taudevin, Lansell, *East Timor: Too Little Too Late*, Duffy and Snellgrove, Sydney, 1999.

Taylor, John, *Indonesia's Forgotten War: The Hidden History of East Timor*, Pluto Press, Leichhardt, NSW, 1991.

Terrill, Greg, *Secrecy and Openness*, Melbourne University Press, South Carlton, Vic, 2000.

Thayer, Carl, 'Australia–Indonesia Relations: The Case of East Timor', paper presented at the *International Conference on Australia and East Asian Security into the 21st Century*, Department of Diplomacy, National Cheng Chi University, Taipei, Taiwan, 8 October 1999.

't Hart, Paul, *Groupthink in government: a study of small groups and policy failure*, Swets and Zeitlinger, Amsterdam, 1990.

't Hart, Paul, K. Tindall and C. Brown, 'Success and failure in crisis leadership: Advisory capacity and presidential performance in the 9/11 and Katrina crises', unpublished paper, 2007, copy in author's possession.

Tiernan, Anne, *Power Without Responsibility*, UNSW Press, Sydney, 2007.

———, 'The Learner: John Howard's System of National Security Advice', *Australian Journal of International Affairs*, vol. 61, no. 4, 2007, pp. 489–505.

Trood, Russell, 'Bureaucratic politics and foreign policy', in Fedor A. Mediansky (ed.), *Australian Foreign Policy into the New Millennium*, MacMillan Education Australia, South Melbourne, 1997, pp. 33–52.

———, 'Prime Ministers and Foreign Policy', in Patrick Weller (ed.), *Menzies to Keating: The Development of Australian Prime Ministership*, Melbourne University Press, Carlton, Vic, 1992, pp. 156–82.

Viviani, Nancy, 'Australia Indonesia Relations—Past, Present and Future', Senate Foreign Affairs, Defence and Trade References Committee, *Additional Information, vol. 2*, Commonwealth of Australia, Canberra, 1999, pp. 2–5.

———, 'The Official Formulation of Foreign Policy', in Fedor A. Mediansky and A.C. Palfreeman (eds), *In pursuit of national interests: Australian Foreign Policy in the 1990s*, Pergamon Press, Sydney, 1998, pp. 45–65.

Walcott, Charles E. and Karen M. Hult, *Governing the White House*, University of Kansas Press, Lawrence, 1995.

Waters, Christopher, 'A failure of imagination: R.G. Casey and Australian plans for counter-subversion in Asia, 1954–1956', *Australian Journal of Politics and History*, vol. 45, no. 3, 1999, pp. 347–61.

Welch, David A., 'The Organizational Process and Bureaucratic Politics Paradigms: Retrospect and Prospect', *International Security*, vol. 17, no. 2, 1992, pp. 112–46.

Weller, Patrick, *Cabinet Government in Australia, 1901–2006*, UNSW Press, Sydney, 2007.

Wheeler, Nicholas and Tim Dunne, 'East Timor and the New Humanitarian Intervention', *International Affairs*, vol. 77, no. 4, 2001, pp. 805–27.

White, Hugh, 'The Road to INTERFET: East Timor—1999', unpublished paper, copy in author's possession, 2007.

Woolcott, Richard, 'The consequences of the crisis over East Timor', in Bruce Brown (ed.), *East Timor—The Consequences*, New Zealand Institute of International Affairs, Wellington, 2000, pp. 25–33.

Australian Government Sources—Documents, Reports, Media Releases and Speeches (Published, Archived and Websites)

Note: The content of most Australian Government websites changed in December 2007 when a new government was elected. While these documents will be archived, some with new addresses, this work was not completed at the date of submission. The websites shown here were correct at the date shown.

AusAID, *Report of the AusAID Fact-Finding Mission to East Timor*, 10–20 March 1999, Commonwealth of Australia, Canberra.

Australian Electoral Commission, *Submission to the Senate Foreign Affairs, Defence and Trade References Committee: Australian Electoral Commission Support for the East Timor Consultation Ballot*, Commonwealth of Australia, Canberra, 1999.

Australian National Audit Office, *Management of Australian Defence Force Deployments to East Timor*, Commonwealth of Australia, Canberra, 2002.

———, 'Publications', no date, available at <http://www.anao.gov.au>, accessed 31 March 2007.

Anderson, John MP, 'East Timor: Peacekeeping', *House of Representatives Official Hansard*, 20 September 1999, p. 9925.

Brereton, Laurie MP, 'East Timor: Peacekeeping', *House of Representatives Official Hansard*, 9 August 1999, p. 8098.

Commonwealth of Australia, *Auditor-General Act 1997 (Commonwealth)*, available at <http://www.comlaw.gov.au/ComLaw/Legislation/ActCompilation1. nsf/0/BB20076E1967426CCA25737700160327/$file/AuditGeneral997.pdf>, accessed 18 October 2007.

———, *Commonwealth of Australia Constitution Act (The Constitution)* 1900, available at <http://www.comlaw.gov.au/comlaw/comlaw.nsf/440c19285 821b109ca256f3a001d59b7/57dea3835d797364ca256f9d0078c087/$FILE/ ConstitutionAct.pdf>, accessed 4 April 2007.

———, *Defence Act (1903)*, available at <http://www.austlii.edu.au/au/legis/ cth/consol_act/da190356/>, accessed 27 December 2007.

———, *Freedom of Information Act 1982 (Commonwealth)*, available at <http:// www.comlaw.gov.au/comlaw/management.nsf/lookupindexpagesbyid/ IP200401430?OpenDocument>, accessed 12 April 2007.

————, *Style manual for authors, editors and printers*, 6th edn, Snooks and Co (rev), John Wiley and Sons Australia, Canberra, 2002.

Defence Public Affairs, 'Australian/Indonesian Bi-lateral Military Forum', Media Release DPAO 062/99 dated 5 March 1999, available at <http://www.defence. gov.au/media/1999/06299.html>, accessed 17 November 2007.

————, 'Hon John Moore—East Timor Update', MIN 271/99, 14 September 1999, available at <http://www.minister.defence.gov.au/1999/27199.html>, accessed 12 December 2007.

————, 'The Hon J Moore, Progress on the Implementation of the Defence Reform Program', Media Release 067/99, Canberra, 11 March 1999.

————, 'Transcript, Hon John Moore, MP & Hon Alexander Downer', Commonwealth Offices, Melbourne, 6 September 1999, available at <http:// www.minister.defence.gov.au/1999/mt0699.htm>, accessed 12 December 2007.

Department of Defence, *Australia's Strategic Policy*, Commonwealth of Australia, Canberra, 1997.

————, *Defence 2000—Our Future Defence Force*, Commonwealth of Australia, Canberra, 2000.

————, 'Department of Defence Submission', Senate Foreign Affairs, Defence and Trade References Committee, *Additional Information, Volume 5*, Commonwealth of Australia, Canberra, 1999, pp. 108–116.

————, 'Global Operations and Exercises', available at <http://www.defence. gov.au/index.htm>, accessed 28 September 2006.

————, *Strategy Planning Framework Handbook*, Defence Publishing Service, Canberra, 2006.

————, *Defending Australia in the Asia-Pacific Century: Force 2030*, Commonwealth of Australia, Canberra, 2009

Department of Foreign Affairs and Trade, *Agreement with Indonesia on Maintaining Security*, Commonwealth of Australia, Canberra, 1995.

————, *Annual Report 2000–2001*, Commonwealth of Australia, Canberra, 2001.

————, *Annual Report 2001–2002*, Commonwealth of Australia, Canberra, 2002.

————, 'Calvert Roth Meeting February 1999', copy in possession of the author.

————, *Direction of Trade Time Series, 2000-01 One Hundred Years of Trade*, Commonwealth of Australia, Canberra, 2002.

———, *East Timor in Transition 1998–2000: An Australian Policy Challenge*, Commonwealth of Australia, Canberra, 2001.

———, *In the National Interest—Australia's Foreign and Trade Policy White Paper*, Commonwealth of Australia, Canberra, 1997.

Department of Foreign Affairs and Trade and AusAID, *Submission to the Senate Foreign Affairs, Defence and Trade References Committee Inquiry into East Timor*, Senate Foreign Affairs, Defence and Trade References Committee, *Additional Information, vol. 5*, Commonwealth of Australia, Canberra, 1999, pp. 044–085.

Downer, Alexander, 'A Long Term Commitment: Australia And East Asia', speech to the Indonesian Council on World Affairs and the Indonesia-Australia Business Council, Borobodur Hotel, Jakarta, 9 July 1998, available at <http://www.dfat.gov.au/media/speeches/foreign/1998/980709_icwa_iabc.html>, accessed 12 April 2006.

———, 'Answers to Questions Without Notice—East Timor Peacekeeping', House of Representatives Official Hansard, 9 August 1999, p. 8174.

———, 'Australia at Year's End—Retrospect and Prospect', speech by the Hon Alexander Downer MP, Minister for Foreign Affairs, at the National Press Club, Canberra, 1 December 1999, available at <http://www.foreignminister.gov.au/speeches/1999/991201_npc.html>, accessed 27 November 2007.

———, 'Australia—Stability in the Asia Pacific', Paper presented at the Harvard Club, New York, 9 June 1998, available at <http://www.foreignminister.gov.au/ speeches/1998/stability-asia_jun98.html>, accessed 27 July 2007.

———, 'Australian Government Historic Policy Shift On East Timor', Media Release 12 January 1999, available at <http://www.dfat.gov.au/media/ releases/ foreign/1999/fa002_99.html>, accessed 12 January 2006.

———, 'CEDA Luncheon Address', 20 July 2000, available at <http://www.dfat.gov.au/media/transcripts/2000/000720_fa_ceda.htm>, accessed 12 April 2006.

———, 'Indonesia's Challenges: How Australia Can Help', paper presented at the International Conference on Indonesian Economic Stabilisation and Recovery, Australian National University, Canberra, 23 November 1998, available at <http://www.foreignminister.gov.au/speeches/1998/981123_indonesia.html>, accessed 12 April 2006.

———, 'International Crisis Resolution: The Example of East Timor', Oxford, 26 January 2000, available at <http://www.dfat.gov.au/media/speeches/foreign/2000/000126_intl_crisis.html>, accessed 23 January 2006.

Foreign Affairs, Defence and Trade References Committee, *Economic, social and political conditions in East Timor*, Hearing of 13 August 1999, available at <http://www.aph.gov.au/hansard/senate/commttee/s2527.pdf>, accessed 6 December 2006.

———, *Economic, social and political conditions in East Timor*, Hearing of 9 September 1999, available at <http://www.aph.gov.au/hansard/senate/commttee/s2555.pdf>, accessed 6 December 2006.

———. *Economic, social and political conditions in East Timor*, Hearing of 6 December 1999, available at <http://www.aph.gov.au/hansard/senate/commttee/s2814.pdf>, accessed 6 December 2006.

———, *Interim Report on East Timor*, Senator J Hogg (Chair), Commonwealth of Australia, Canberra, 1999.

———, *Final Report into the Inquiry into East Timor*, Senator J Hogg (Chair), Commonwealth of Australia, Canberra, 2000.

Hill, Robert, 'Blick Report into DSD and East Timor leak investigations', Minister of Defence Media Release 88/03, 10 July 2003, available at <http://www.minister.defence.gov.au/Hilltpl.cfm?CurrentId=2938>, accessed 28 April 2009.

House of Representatives (Australia), *Votes and Proceedings*, vol. 55, 11 August 1999.

Howard, John, 'Address to the ACT Division of the Liberal Party', 29 September 1999, available at <http://www.pm.gov.au/news/speeches/1999/actliberal2909.htm>, accessed 10 April 2006.

———, 'Statement on East Timor', 23 November 1999, available at <http://www.australianpolitics.com/executive/howard/pre-2002/991123howard-timor.shtml>, accessed 16 April 2006.

Joint Standing Committee on Foreign Affairs, Defence and Trade, *From Phantom to Force: Towards a More Efficient and Effective Army*, Commonwealth of Australia, Canberra, 2000.

Management Advisory Committee, *Connecting Government: Whole of Government Responses to Australia's Priority Challenges*, Commonwealth of Australia, Canberra, 2004.

National Archives of Australia, *Fact Sheet 10: Access to records under the Archives Act*, 2006, available at <http://www.naa.gov.au/about-us/publications/fact-sheets/fs10.aspx>, accessed 17 January 2007.

————, *Fact Sheet 34 Cabinet Records*, August 2006, available at <http://www.naa.gov.au/about-us/publications/fact-sheets/fs34.aspx>, accessed 2 October 2006.

————, *Fact Sheet 128 Cabinet Notebooks*, 2006, available at <http://www.naa.gov.au/about-us/publications/fact-sheets/fs128.aspx>, accessed 2 October 2006.

Royal Australian Navy, *Australian Maritime Doctrine*, Commonwealth of Australia, Canberra, 2000.

Senate Foreign Affairs, Defence and Trade Committee, *Consideration of Additional Estimates (Department of Defence)*, 10 February 1999.

————, *Consideration of Additional Estimates (Department of Foreign Affairs and Trade)*, 11 February 1999.

————, *Consideration of Additional Estimates (Department of Defence)*, 6 December 1999.

————, *Consideration of Additional Estimates (Department of Foreign Affairs and Trade)*, 9 February 2000.

————, *Consideration of Budget Estimates: Supplementary Hearings (Defence Portfolio)*, 2 December 1999, available at <http://www.aph.gov.au/hansard/senate/commttee/s2807.pdf>, accessed 2 December 2007.

Senate Foreign Affairs, Defence and Trade Legislation Committee, *Consideration of Estimates (Department of Foreign Affairs and Trade)*, 11 February 1997.

Collections

Bob Breen, on Australian military deployments

Des Ball, on National Security Structures and East Timor

Newspaper articles and other media

(Note: Factiva is an on-line database of newspaper and magazine articles. Page numbers are not always provided in their versions).

ABC Television (Australia), *The Howard Years* (Episode 2), 24 November 2008, available at <http://www.abc.net.au/news/howardyears/contents/s2422684.htm>, accessed 27 June 2009.

Agence France-Presse, 'Affluent Aussies to fund peacekeeping in East Timor', 23 November 1999 (Factiva version).

————, 'Australia urges Indonesia to tackle irritant of East Timor', 25 May 1998 (Factiva version).

————, 'Malaysian politicians slam "Howard Doctrine"', 24 September 1999 (Factiva version).

————, 'Thailand pans Australian PM over plan to be America's "deputy" in Asia', 24 September 1999 (Factiva version).

Anthony, Shaun, 'Jakarta blocks Canberra's call for armed intervention', *West Australian*, 6 September 1999, p. 6.

Arifin, Zainul, 'Asean should take the lead in East Timor peacekeeping, says PM', *New Straits Times*, 1 October 1999, p. 1 (Factiva version).

Associated Press, 'Asean agrees to support E. Timor peacekeeping force', *Dow Jones International News*, 13 September 1998 (Factiva version).

————, 'US Suspends Military Relations with Indonesia', *Augusta Chronicle*, 10 September 1999, p. A09 (Factiva version).

Associated Press newswires, 'Report: Malaysia ready to send peacekeeping troops to East Timor', 6 September 1999 (Factiva version).

Australian, 'Timorese demand better effort', 2 April 1998, p. 7.

Australian Associated Press, 'Clinton calls on Indonesia to let UN restore peace in East Timor', *St Louis Post-Dispatch*, 12 September 1999, p. A7 (Factiva version).

————, 'Downer denies Aust intelligence wanting', *AAP Information Services Pty Ltd*, 1 November 1998 (Factiva version).

————, 'DSD boss denies spying on Brereton', *Sydney Morning Herald*, 1 May 2003, available at <http://www.smh.com.au/articles/2003/05/01/1051382039622. html> accessed 27 June 2009.

————, 'East Timor committee asks Howard to take stronger stance', 26 January 1999 (Factiva version).

————, 'Moore defends joint military ops with Indonesia', 28 March 1999 (Factiva version).

Aylmer, Sean, 'Timor: Downer Says There's No Rift With US', *Australian Financial Review*, 2 August 1999, p. 7.

Bangkok Post, 'Editorial—Distractions in the Timor issue', 30 September 1999 (Factiva version).

Barker, Geoffrey, 'Australia Bends To People Power', *Financial Review*, 16 May 1998, p. 25.

————, 'Australian foreign minister on possible peacekeeping force', Radio Australia, 4 September 1999.

Birmingham Post, 'Refugee boy crushed by East Timor airdrop', 30 September 1999 (Factiva version).

Bolt, Andrew, 'Don't Expect Praise', *Herald Sun* (Melbourne), 16 September 1999, p. 18 (Factiva version).

Brenchley, Fred, 'The Howard Defence Doctrine', *Bulletin* (Australia), 28 September 1999, pp. 22–24.

Burke, Anthony, 'Labor Could Be Set For A Backflip on East Timor', *Canberra Times*, 22 December 1997 (Factiva version).

Cleary, Paul, 'A policy that's a bit light on detail', *Sydney Morning Herald*, 13 January 1999, p. 6.

Cordeaux, Jeremy, 'Transcript of the Prime Minister, The Hon John Howard MP', Radio 5DN (Adelaide), 18 May 1998, available at <http://www.pm.gov.au/media/Interview/1998/5dn1805.cfm>, accessed 12 February 2006.

Daley, Paul, 'Armed with information, now what?', *Age* (Melbourne), 29 May 1999, p. 4.

————, 'Gunning for the General', *Bulletin* (Australia), 30 June 2004 (Factiva version).

————, 'Rift Denied With US Over Timor', *Age* (Melbourne), 3 August 1999, p. 3.

————, 'Spy effort stepped up in Timor', *Age* (Melbourne), 20 March 1999, p. 5.

————, 'Timor: We Snub Offer To Send In The Marines', *Sunday Age* (Melbourne), 1 August 1999, p. 1.

————, 'Troops Could Go Within Days', *Sunday Age* (Melbourne), 5 September 1999, p. 2.

Datson, Trevor, 'Australian PM popular at home, blasted in Asia', *Reuters News*, 28 September 1999 (Factiva version).

Dodd, Mark; Peter Coleman-Adams and Hamish McDonald, 'Defence report warning of violence', *Sydney Morning Herald*, 24 April 1999, p. 1 and p. 9.

Dunn, James, 'Righting our Past Wrongs', *Sydney Morning Herald*, 13 January 1999, p. 11.

Dupont Alan and Anthony Bergin, 'UN Force Critical to Peace in East Timor', *Australian Financial Review*, 29 March 1999 (Factiva version).

Epstein, Raphael, 'Australians and Indonesian forces clash in East Timor', AM, ABC Radio (Australia), 11 October 1999, available at <http://www.abc.net.au/am/stories/s58222.htm>, accessed 2 January 2008.

Fowler, Andrew, 'Flying Blind', *4 Corners*, ABC Television (Australia), 2007, 29 October 2007.

———, 'Ties that Bind', *4 Corners*, ABC Television (Australia), 14 February 2000.

Garran, Robert, 'The military masses for its biggest march in 30 years', *Australian*, 3 July 1999, p. 7.

Greenlees, Don, 'Habibie rules out Timor referendum', *Australian*, 4 June 1998 (Factiva version).

———, 'Howard reverse on Timor', *Australian*, 12 January 1999 (Factiva version).

———, 'Leak shows no E Timor troop cuts', *Australian*, 30 October 1998, p. 1 (Factiva version).

Head, Jonathon, 'East Timor Breakthrough', *BBC News* (United Kingdom), 28 January 1999, available at <http://news.bbc.co.uk/2/hi/events/indonesia/latest_news/263828.stm>, accessed 20 January 2006.

Holmes, Jonathon, 'East Timor—Balibo: A Special Report', *Foreign Correspondent*, ABC Television (Australia), 20 October 1998, available at <http://www.abc.net.au/foreign/stories/s401582.htm>, accessed 21 January 2006.

Hunt, Greg, 'Timor peace plan more palatable after dinner', *Australian*, 14 January 1999, p. 1.

Hunter, Ian, 'Elite forces scouted island from April', *Sydney Morning Herald*, 11 October 1999, p. 11.

Jemadu, Aleksius, 'Can Australia sever ties with Indonesia?', *Jakarta Post*, 20 September 1999 (Factiva version).

Jones, Sidney, 'East Timor: Stop the Violence', *Human Rights News*, 6 July 1999.

Kelly, Fran, 'John Howard on East Timor', *The Howard Years* (website), ABC Television (Australia), 2008, available at <http://www.abc.net.au/news/howardyears/>, (see Further Recourses Episode 2), accessed 27 June 2009.

Kelly, Fran, 'Alexander Downer on East Timor', *The Howard Years* (website), ABC Television (Australia), 2008, available at <http://www.abc.net.au/news/howardyears/>, (see Further Recourses Episode 2), accessed 27 June 2009.

————, 'John Howard on East Timor', *The Howard Years* (website), ABC Television (Australia), 2008, available at <http://www.abc.net.au/news/howardyears/>, (see Further Recourses Episode 2), accessed 27 June 2009.

Kelly, Paul, 'From the Lips of Prime Ministers: Diplomacy at the Crossroads', *Australian*, 15 September 1999, p. 13 (Factiva version).

Knickmeyer, Ellen, 'Australia: peacekeepers allowed to cross border in hot pursuit', Associated Press Newswires, 30 September 1999.

Kozaryn, Linda, 'U.S., NATO Allies Plan New, Improved Alliance', *American Forces Information Service*, 21 September 1999, available at <http://www.defenselink.mil/news/Sep1999/n09221999_09909223.html>, accessed 21 January 2006.

Lyons, John, 'The Secret East Timor Dossier', *Bulletin* (Australia), 12 October 1999, pp. 25–29.

————, 'The Timor Truth Gap', *Bulletin* (Australia), 30 November 1999, pp. 24–32.

McDonald, Hamish, 'Timor: Fear of "running sore"', *Age* (Melbourne), 29 September 1975, p. 6.

McKenzie, Scott, 'Tough Line on Timor', *Herald-Sun* (Melbourne), 22 November 1997, p. 4.

McKew, Maxine, 'Clinton advisor praises Australian leadership on East Timor', *7.30 Report*, ABC Television (Australia), 13 January 2000.

Mufson, Steven, 'World Bank Chief Warns Indonesia On Militias', *Washington Post*, 12 September 1999 (Factiva version).

Murdoch, Lindsay, 'We're Neutral On Timor: Downer', *Sun Herald* (Melbourne), 1 August 1999, p. 35 (Factiva version).

Nation (Bangkok), 'Editorial—Howard must clarify foreign-policy goals', 29 September 1999 (Factiva version).

Nelson, Jane, 'Australia ready to go to Timor without US', *Reuters News*, 9 September 1999 (Factiva version)

Polgaze, Karen, 'PM's Timor letter "angered Habibie"', *Canberra Times*, 3 November 1999, p. 2.

Reuters News, 'Howard would consider one-off tax for Timor troops', 28 October 1999 (Factiva version).

Riley, Mark, 'UN Backs Downer Plan to Beef Up Timor Force', *Sydney Morning Herald*, 6 August 1999, p.1.

Robinson, Paul, 'Unions Plan Action On Timor Violence', *Age*, 3 May 1999, p. 6.

Rose, Rebecca, 'Howard Urges Habibie To Act On East Timor', *West Australian*, 26 May 1998, p. 4.

Seneviratne, Kalinga, 'Australia casts an eye on Timor's oil', *Straits Times*, 24 September 1999 (Factiva version).

Shannahan, Dennis, 'Muzzling Moore the hottest pursuit—Australia cannot afford to send any more mixed messages', *Australian*, 2 October 1999, p. 10.

Sheridan, Greg, 'Howard error on Timor attacked', *Australian*, 18 September 2000 (Factiva version).

———, 'The Burden is Here to Stay', *Australian*, 17 September 1999, p. 15

Snow, Deborah, and Peter Cole-Adams, 'Army Borrows Uncle Sam's Flak Jackets', *Sydney Morning Herald*, 24 September 1999, p. 1.

Solomon, Jay, 'Habibie Offers East Timor Special Status', *Wall Street Journal Europe*, 10 June 1998, p. 2 (Factiva version).

Sydney Morning Herald, 'What force in East Timor', 11 August 1999, p. 14.

Toohey, Brian, 'PM's Dilemma on Timor Peace Force', *Sun Herald* (Sydney), 1 August 1999, p. 49.

Wilkinson, Marian, 'Why we kept Timor secrets from the US', *Sydney Morning Herald*, 13 August 1999, p. 1.

Wright, Tim and Daley, Paul, 'PM sets up secret unit on Timor', *Age* (Melbourne), 22 October 1999, pp. A1–2.

Web pages and documents

Annan, Kofi, *Annual Report to the UN General Assembly*, 20 September 1999, available at <http://www.un.org/News/ossg/sg/stories/statments_search_full.asp?statID=28>, accessed 5 October 2007.

————, 'Secretary-General urges Indonesia to accept international help to restore order in East Timor at a moment of "great crisis"', *United Nations News*, New York, 10 September 1999, available at <http://www.ess.uwe.ac.uk/Timor/News14.htm>, accessed 3 February 2006.

Brahney, Kathleen J, 'East Timor: Interfet Mission Sparks Continued Debate', United States Information Agency—Foreign Media Reaction, 15 October 1999, available at <http://www.globalsecurity.org/military/library/news/1999/10/wwwh9o15.htm>, accessed 2 January 2008.

Embassy of France in Australia, 'The Noumea Accord', no date, available at <http://www.ambafrance-au.org/article.php3?id_article=1058>, accessed 28 December 2006.

Haas, Richard, 'Kosovo: U.S. Policy at Crossroads', Brookings Institute, Washington DC, 10 December 1998, available at <http://www.brookings.edu/comm/transcripts/19981009.htm>, accessed 25 January 2006.

Hurford, Chris and Margareta Wahlstrom, *OCHA and the East Timor Crisis*, Office for the Coordination of Humanitarian Affairs, November 2001, available at <http://ochaonline.un.org/ToolsServices/EvaluationandStudies/ESSReports/tabid/1325/Default.aspx>, accessed 12 July 2007.

Inbaraj, Sonny, 'East Timor: Disclosure on Troops Mocks Jakarta's Credibility', 3 November 1998, available at <http://www.etan.org/et/1998/november/l-7/03disclos.htm>, accessed 27 June 2009.

Marcus, Bruce, 'There's a leak in my firm', *The Marcus Letter*, (no date), available at <http://www.marcusletter.com/leak.htm>, accessed 16 June 2009.

Murray, William, 'The Situation in Indonesia and the IMF', International Monetary Fund, 16 September 1999, available at <http://www.imf.org/external/np/vc/1999/091699.htm>, accessed 6 February 2006.

Newspoll, 12 September 1999, available at <http://www.newspoll.com.au/image _uploads/cgi-lib.25638.1.0902timor.pdf>, accessed 26 September 2006.

Philips, Lord N., *The BSE Inquiry: The Report, 2000, Chapter 15*, available at <http://www.bseinquiry.gov.uk/report/index.htm>, accessed 20 December 2006.

Roy Morgan Research, 'Labor Stretches Two-Party Preferred Lead As Troops Go In To East Timor', Finding No 3240, 12 October 1999, available at <http://www.roymorgan.com/news/polls/1999/3240/>, accessed 26 August 2006.

————, 'L-NP And ALP Support Steady Despite Clashes Over East Timor Motives', Finding No 3246, 26 October 1999, available at <http://www.roymorgan.com/ news/ polls/1999/3246/>, accessed 26 August 2006.

————, 'L-NP Draws Closer On Primary Vote As ALP Support Eases', Finding No 3228, 28 September 1999, available at <http://www.roymorgan.com/news/polls/1999/3228/>, accessed 26 August 2006.

————, 'The Mood of the People & the Election—Listen Carefully', Finding No 1001, 1 September 1998, available at <http://www.roymorgan.com/news/papers/1998/19981001/>, accessed 14 February 2006.

Tiffen, Rodney, 'Why Political Plumbers Fail – Hypocrisy and Hyperbole in Leak Control', 2005, available at <http://soc.kuleuven.be/io/ethics/paper/Paper%20WS2_pdf/Rodney%20Tiffen.pdf>, accessed 16 June 2009.

United Nations, *Charter of the United Nations*, New York, 1945, available at <http://www.un.org/aboutun/charter/>, accessed 2 February 2006.

————, 'UNTAMET Fact Sheet', August 1999, available at <http://www.un.org/peace/etimor99/Fact_frame.htm>, accessed 24 November 2007.

World Bank, 'Trust Fund for East Timor', no date, available at <http://web.worldbank.org/WBSITE/EXTERNAL/COUNTRIES/EASTASIAPACIFICEXT/TIMORLESTEEXTN/0,,contentMDK:20185391~pagePK:141137~piPK:1411 27~theSitePK:294022,00.html>, accessed 12 July 2007.

Interviews

(This study relied upon the generosity and trust of a number of serving and former officials. A number of interviewees asked for their identities to be protected, while others were happy to be named in the reference list but not quoted in the body. All references to appointments relate to Australian Government positions, unless described otherwise. In general, appointments reflect only their contribution to the events or times covered in this study).

Ayling, Brigadier Steve (Director General INTERFET Branch, Department of Defence, in 1999)

Barratt, Paul (Secretary of the Department of Defence 1998–August 1999. He was an invited official at NSCC and a member of SCNS)

Barrie, Admiral Chris (Chief of the Defence Force 1998–2002. He was an invited official at NSCC and a member of SCNS).

Beazley, The Hon Kim, (Defence Minister from 1984–90, and Opposition Leader in 1999)

Behm, Allan (First Assistant Secretary (FAS) International Policy in 1998 and FAS Strategic Policy and Plans in 1999–2000)

Borgu, Aldo (adviser to Defence Minister John Moore in 1999)

Brabin-Smith, Richard (former Deputy Secretary Strategy and Intelligence in Defence)

Brady, Martin (Director, Defence Signals Directorate in 1999, acting Deputy Secretary Strategy in August–September 1999)

Briggs, Rear Admiral Peter (Head, Strategic Command Division in Defence from early 1997 to May 1999)

Calvert, Dr Ashton (Secretary of DFAT in 1999. He was an invited official at NSCC and a member of SCNS)

Carmody, Shane (former Deputy Secretary Strategy and Intelligence in Defence)

Castellaw, Lieutenant General John (Commander of III Marine Expeditionary Brigade in 1999 and deployed to East Timor)

Clarke, Air Vice-Marshal Kerry (Director General Operations in Strategic Command Division in Defence in 1998–99)

Darvill, Steve (involved in operational planning as part of AusAID's Humanitarian Emergencies section in 1999)

Dahlstrom, Federal Agent Tim (a member of the 'UN and Other Overseas Commitments Coordination' team for AFP in 1999. As part of this team, he was responsible for the detailed planning of AFP's involvement, especially contingent preparation, for UNAMET)

Dawson, Scott (Assistant Director General East Asia Branch in AusAID from June 1999, with responsibility for East Timor. In the post-ballot period, he headed the AusAID Task Force that dealt with the immediate emergency response and then worked on the longer-term program for East Timor)

Fischer, The Hon. Tim (Deputy Prime Minister and NSCC member March 1996–July 1999. He headed the Australian Parliamentary Delegation to East Timor in August 1999)

Hailston, Lieutenant General Earl (lead planner for USPACOM until 31 May 1999. He then moved to Command III Marine Expeditionary Force in June 1999, and was responsible for deploying III Marine Expeditionary Brigade to East Timor)

Hartley, Major General John (Land Commander Australia in 1999)

Hughes, Assistant Commissioner Andrew (Director International and Operations for the AFP in 1999)

Keating, Major General Michael (Head, Strategic Command Division in Defence from May 1999)

Lewincamp, Frank (Director of the Defence Intelligence Organisation from 1998–2005)

Moore, The Hon John (Defence Minister and a member of NSCC in 1999)

Nicholson, Air Vice-Marshal Peter (Head Strategic Policy and Plans mid-1998–June 1999, then Head C4ISREW Division)

Scrafton, Michael (Assistant Secretary Regional Engagement, Policy and Programs at the start of 1999. He became Acting Head International Policy in August 1999, and was appointed to head ETPU in September 1999. He was also Defence's representative on the Taylor Committee)

Skoien, Matthew (Director Indonesia Section in International Policy Division from December 1998 to September 1999)

Taylor, Allan (Director General of the Australian Secret Intelligence Service and the 'Taylor Committee' in 1999)

Titheridge, Air Vice-Marshal Alan (former senior ADF officer)

Treloar, Air Vice-Marshal Bob (Commander Australian Theatre from May 1999)

Varghese, Peter (FAS International Division in DPM&C in 1999)

Whiddett, Commissioner Adrien (Assistant Commissioner responsible for Australian Federal Police Operations in 1999)

White, Hugh (advisor to Prime Minister Hawke and Defence Minister Kim Beazley from 1985–91, Deputy Secretary Strategy in Defence 1995–2000, and acting Secretary of the Defence Department in August–October 1999)

Williams, Colonel Mike (Chief of Staff for the second US contingent in East Timor, 2000)

Williams, The Hon. Daryl (Attorney General and a member for NSCC from 1996–2003)

Protected Identities

005-06 (a former senior ADF officer with knowledge of Strategic Command Division)

007-05 (former senior ADF officer who was closely involved with Defence planning for East Timor, including knowledge of liaison with the United Nations)

009-05 (ministerial adviser and senior Defence official)

010-05 (identity protected)

012-05 (official with direct knowledge of the East Timor ballot)

014-05 (former senior government official with knowledge of the Taylor Committee)

020-05 (former member of DPM&C with direct knowledge of the East Timor case)

021-05 (former senior Defence intelligence official)

024-05 (DFAT official with direct knowledge of the East Timor case)

026-05 (identity protected)

028-05 (DFAT official with direct knowledge of the East Timor case)

030-05 (identity protected)

032-05 (identity protected)

033-05 (identity protected)

035-05 (identity protected)

037-05 (identity protected)

038-05 (ADF officer with knowledge of Strategic Command Division)

046-06 (former senior ADF officer with direct knowledge of the East Timor case)

048-06 (identity protected)

051-06 (former ministerial adviser and senior government official with direct knowledge of the East Timor case)

052-06 (former senior government official with direct knowledge of the East Timor case)

062-07 (ADF officer with knowledge of the East Timor case)

064-07 (former ministerial adviser and government official)

066-07 (Defence official with knowledge of public affairs activities in 1999)

www.ingramcontent.com/pod-product-compliance
Lightning Source LLC
Chambersburg PA
CBHW061240270326
41927CB00035B/3451